SUPPLEMENT

HUMANISTICA LOVANIENSIA

XXIV

SUPPLEMENTA HUMANISTICA LOVANIENSIA

Editors: Prof. Dr Gilbert Tournoy
Dr Godelieve Tournoy-Thoen
Prof. Dr Dirk Sacré

Editorial Correspondence: Seminarium Philologiae Humanisticae
Blijde-Inkomststraat 21 (Box 3316)
B-3000 Leuven (Belgium)

SUPPLEMENTA

HUMANISTICA LOVANIENSIA

XXIV

SPANISH HUMANISM ON THE VERGE OF THE PICARESQUE: JUAN MALDONADO'S *LUDUS CHARTARUM*, *PASTOR BONUS*, AND *BACCHANALIA*

Edited with introduction, translation, and notes by
Warren SMITH & Clark COLAHAN

1425

LEUVEN UNIVERSITY PRESS
2009

This publication was made possible by Pegasus Limited for the promotion of Neo-Latin Studies

© 2009 Universitaire Pers Leuven / Leuven University Press / Presses Universitaires de Louvain, Minderbroedersstraat 4, B-3000 Leuven (Belgium)

ISBN 978 90 5867 708 2
D/2009/1869/15
NUR: 635

CONTENTS

* This edition of Maldonado's *Bacchanalia* is by Clark Colahan, Alfred Rodriguez, and Warren Smith, and reprinted, with corrections, from *Humanistica Lovaniensia*, 48 (1999) 160-233. The readers can consult the introduction there for further information on the *Bacchanalia*.

ILLUSTRATIONS

ACKNOWLEDGEMENTS

* Rick Simmons gratefully acknowledges the inspiration for his illustrations in the characters and compositions of El Greco and Francisco de Goya, two of the masters of classic Spanish art.

** Caleb Smith wishes to thank Simon Wintle, cardseller, of Portsmouth, England (www.wopc.co.uk/Spain/Spanish.html) for permission to model his card pictures on illustrations from his website.

Thanks also are due to Alfred Rodriguez, Professor Emeritus, University of New Mexico, who first suggested the idea of an edition of the *Ludus Chartarum*.

Warren Smith   Clark Colahan
(University of New Mexico)   (Whitman College)

GENERAL INTRODUCTION TO MALDONADO'S
LIFE AND WORKS

Juan Maldonado (c. 1485?-1554) was a Spanish humanist whose studies and career flourished in the progressive years of Cisneros' regency and Carlos V's reign.[1] He was born and raised in a small town in the province of Cuenca, then educated at the University of Salamanca in the years following the hugely successful publication of *The Celestina*. That famous novel in dialogue, as it has often been described, is a brilliant exposé of Renaissance Spanish society, and in capturing the corrupt but classically focused ambience of the university city it left its mark on the enthusiastic student and future writer. Nonetheless, he is most closely associated with the important mercantile center of Burgos in the heart of Castile, where he lived the remainder of his life.

Ordained a priest after his studies in both canon law and classics, he was advanced by a protector, Bishop Juan de Fonseca, to become diocesan examiner in Burgos of the knowledge possessed by candidates to the clergy, and for many years he held that post and other posts in that city as a teacher of Latin language and literature, tutored members of aristocratic families, served as chaplain and administrator of the cathedral, and steadily produced a variety of literary and historiographic writings, apparently all written in Latin. An enthusiastic disciple of Erasmus of Rotterdam for as long as that was politically safe, he corresponded with the famous reformer, reporting to him in the fullest detail that has come down to us on the enthusiastic reception his works were being given by a mass Spanish audience.[2]

He eloquently protested the un-Christian treatment of Spaniards of Jewish descent — as he himself may have been — and like Erasmus and

---

[1] He is not to be confused with the better-known homonomous Jesuit theologian (1534-83), apparently unrelated and a generation younger.

[2] See Erasmus' epistles (Erasmus 1906-1958). As Asensio reports, the letters from Maldonado are in VI, 393-396, number 1742, and VII, 252-254, number 1908. Erasmus' replies are in VII, numbers 1805 and 1971. In addition, Asensio quotes an 18th-century source that describes a book then extant in Valladolid containing numerous other letters between Maldonado and famous writers of the time, including Erasmus, Nebrija and Vives. See Asensio's edition under Maldonado (1980), p. 26, and Allen in Erasmus 1906-1958, VI, 393.

Juan Luis Vives, he advocated more and better education for women, such as his learned friends María de Rojas, Ana Osorio, and Mencía de Mendoza. We shall see that María appears in Maldonado's *Somnium* as his spiritual guide; she was married to a descendant of the famous rabbi, Pablo de Santa María, who converted to Christianity and became bishop of Burgos. Similarly Ana figures as the spokeswoman for the Erasmian cause in Maldonado's *Praxis sive de lectione Erasmi*, 'On the Practice of Reading Erasmus.'

Though little biographical documentation from outside his writings has yet to come to light,[3] autobiographical comments sprinkled throughout his works have made possible a reasonably detailed picture of his life. The most influential examination of him and his work in modern times as an important figure in Renaissance Spanish letters appeared in Marcel Bataillon's monumental history of Erasmus' presence in Spain.[4] The information gathered by the French scholar, together with the end of the conservative and repressive Franco dictatorship in 1975, encouraged Spanish thinkers to explore and celebrate Spain's early sixtenth century, when the country had welcomed new ideas from elsewhere in Europe. Among those fresh intellectual currents was the value of national self-criticism and calls for new and purified customs.

In this spirit Eugenio Asensio wrote a long, important biographical and critical introduction for the publication in 1980 of the text and Spanish translation of Maldonado's *Paraenesis ad politiores literas*, 'Exhortation to Good Literature,' a work in which Maldonado incidentally pays tribute to Erasmus as a luminary of Latin letters. Similar to Asensio's proclamation of Maldonado as an encouragement from out of Spain's past to work for a more enlightened and liberal self-image for the country in the future was a dissertation by Heliodoro García García published at the University of Madrid in 1983: *El pensamiento comunero, erasmista, moral y humanista de Juan Maldonado*, 'The Commoner, Erasmian, Moral and Humanist Thought of Juan Maldonado'. Both Asensio and García brought together and organized practically everything that is

---

[3] Ayala Picón searched with some success for information on Maldonado in the archives of the Burgos cathedral. It was used in his unpublished Master's thesis in theology completed in 1972 at Burgos (see Ayala Picón 1972). His data has been incorporated into Asensio's introduction to the "Paraenesis" (see Maldonado 1980).

[4] It is available in both French and Spanish translation. The original French edition was published in 1937. The most recent revised one is Bataillon-Margolin 1998. The first edition in Spanish was published in 1950. The most recent is Bataillon 2002.

known about Maldonado's life. They also commented on most of his works individually, though with a range of foci from very close to only panoramic.

Although some biographical information in English is available in recent articles by Alfred Rodriguez and the two present authors,[5] a thorough biographical essay on the humanist's life can now be read in Paul Stephen Smith's Master's thesis in history done at the University of British Columbia on Maldonado's colloquy about the revolt of the Castilian towns against the new Hapsburg emperor in the early 1520's.[6] Though his life, which began with high hopes and noble patronage, seems to have failed ultimately to come up to his aspirations — in part due to his democratic sympathies and Erasmian convictions in a progressively reactionary era[7] — still he was a sharp-eyed witness to Spanish society at a time of its transition from acceptance of new intellectual currents to would-be enforcement of Catholic orthodoxy throughout Europe. Maldonado was idealistic and hopeful of reform in his younger years, but the disappointing evolution of the Catholic Monarchs' early efforts for ecclesiastical and social change brought out his literary gift for articulate indignation, keen observation, lively dialogue, and irony. Like other Spanish Erasmians (Vives, the Valdés brothers, and Cervantes, for example) he strikes us as modern in his views and in his calling on readers to think for themselves. Yet many of his works — probably due to their being written in Latin — still have not been published since his lifetime.

While they all come out of the Renaissance tradition associated with Erasmus' Christian Neo-classicism and social criticism, the range of Maldonado's works is still fairly broad, as even a concise overview makes apparent. Taking his works in the chronological order of composition — which has by-and-large been established — the earliest one is a bawdy, humanistic comedy, *Hispaniola*, 'The Spanish Woman,' written in 1519-20. Composed in conjunction with frequent footnotes to explain the more difficult passages in the Latin, it is designed to be taught. Its models are the humorous and satiric plays of amorous intrigue by Roman writers such as Terence and Plautus, and it reflects the university practice in the period of requiring students to stage theatrical works as a pedagogical tool.

---

[5] Among these are Colahan and Rodriguez 1995; Colahan, Rodriguez and Smith 1999; Colahan 2001.

[6] See Paul Stephen Smith 1987.

[7] See Peinador Marín 1991, esp. pp. 42-43.

Already in this first work of his, Maldonado creates dialogue that, although not in his native Castilian, manages to be colloquial and energetic, usually witty, sometimes erudite and always expressive of character. On a deeper level, with no recourse whatsoever to narration, he brings out the resents separating the social classes in a way reminiscent of *The Celestina*. The play enjoyed some success, was once even performed before royalty at the Portuguese court. A modern edition with a Spanish translation has been published by María Angeles Durán Ramas.[8]

At the urging of a protector — Juan de Fonseca, an austerely reformed bishop of Burgos — in the early 1520's Maldonado wrote *Vitae Sanctorum*, 'Lives of the Saints,' a large collection of biographical sketches of the saints worshiped in the Burgos cathedral. It was designed to accompany the breviary used by the clergy there and was popular for a full hundred years, to judge by the dates of its numerous reprintings.[9] There is no modern edition, but the extent to which it was known is pointed to by the presence of some of its most striking images in the picaresque *Lazarillo de Tormes* — though there, as the novel's sarcasm would lead one to expect, their moral connotations are inverted.[10]

About 1524, three years after the conclusion of the so-called Commoners' Revolt against Carlos V, Maldonado wrote a detailed history of the war and the politics surrounding it: *De motu Hispaniae*. Like another historical account of controversial events written by a Spanish disciple of Erasmus, *El diálogo de las cosas ocurridas en Roma* by Alfonso Valdés, it is composed in dialogue form. The literary feel that this formal aspect imparts manifests itself most significantly in the author's adroit placement of arguments in the mouths of the spokesmen for both the imperial cause and for the rebels. While on the surface the arguments in defense of the aristocracy and the emperor carry the day, an ironic undercurrent also reveals Maldonado communicating to perceptive readers his sympathies for the ideals of liberty held by the defeated town leaders. Maldonado kept it unpublished until 1545 — presumably afraid of the possible political consequences. Eventually the lengthy work was the first of his to appear in the vernacular, translated and published in 1840 by José Quevedo, the director of the royal library at the Escorial. In 1975, a

---

[8] For Durán Ramas' edition of *Hispaniola* see Maldonado 1983.

[9] For details on typographical issues in some of the Spanish editions of *Vitae Sanctorum* see Rhodes 1988.

[10] See Colahan 1999.

significant date for the hopes of Spanish democracy as well as for Maldonado scholarship, three different editions of *De motu Hispaniae* came out (one a reprint of Quevado's 1840 translation).[11]

Like the *Pastor Bonus* written the following year, Maldonado's *Paraenesis ad politiores literas*, composed in 1528, takes the form of an open letter. In this case it was directed not to an aristocratic bishop but to that bishop's nephew, a former student who was the young son of the Count of Miranda. In this essay on education and the humanistic reforms he vehemently advocates, Maldonado speaks several times about the stultifying education he himself received. In these years, despite the recent defeat of the ambitious Castilian towns by the nobility, he clearly believed that his talent and innovative ideas would be favorably recognized, perhaps even implemented, by the country's ruling class. In the *Pastor Bonus* there is a similar boldness to the language and to the denunciation of ecclesiastical abuses. To that work we have given a separate introduction, but here it is worth raising the question of whether or not the lack of any previous translation or modern edition is the result of perennial repugnance for the subject matter by the Spanish church.[12]

The works written in the 1530's are generally shorter, but in them Maldonado continues to address controversial issues. *De foelicitate christiana*, 'On Christian Happiness', provides us information on the status in Spain of three religious movements that parallel the rise of Protestantism in northern Europe: Erasmianism, Lutheranism and the *alumbrados*, who sought enlightenment and fulfillment directly from God without the intercession of the church. Though ultimately destined to be extinguished by the

---

[11] Durán Ramas' translation is called *El levantamiento de España* (see Maldonado 1975 a); Quevedo's translation was entitled *El movimiento de España, o sea, Historia de la revolución conocida con el nombre de las Comunidades de Castilla* (Maldonado 1975b). The Fernández Vargas translation is called *La Revolución Comunera* (Maldonado 1975c). Durán Ramas (Maldonado 1983) cites a mention of another work of history by Maldonado, now lost: *Historia Regum Catholicorum Ferdinandi et Elisabetae*. "De este manuscrito tenemos noticias por Nicolás Antonio, que añade: Lo guarda en Burgos D. Diego de Lerma, caballero de aquella ciudad, obra que afirma haber visto Pedro Fernández del Pulgar....".

[12] We know of only two copies of the *Pastor Bonus*, one in the National Library of Madrid, the other in the University Library of Zaragoza (on this see further the headnote of the Latin text, and Asensio's comments in Maldonado 1980, pp. 23-25). This edition is printed after the other works in one of the two versions of the 1549 collection of short works by Maldonado: *Opuscula quaedam docta simul et elegantia...* (Burgos). It is not given a section in the list of errata that corrects the other works, and the decision to include it may have been made at the last minute, even though it was written twenty years earlier.

Counter Reformation, in the first third of the sixteenth century these currents were more widespread in Spain than has frequently been recognized.

Maldonado's *Somnium*, 'The Dream', is a first-person narrative supposedly recounting his fanciful adventures on a night when he stayed up to observe a comet in order to report on it to certain assiduous female students of his. The form of the work recalls Cicero's *Somnium Scipionis*, while the over-all subject matter offers several parallels to Thomas More's *Utopia*. Maldonado tells of a journey guided by his friend María de Rojas, on which they travel around the earth through the upper atmosphere and then up to the uncorrupted society on the moon. It is a work that looks both back to the wise Beatrice in the *Divine Comedy* and forward to the 17th- and 18th-century beginnings of science fiction. The second half gives an account of noble savages in the New World and so voices the humanist reformers' desire to return to a more natural way of life and a religion untouched by Rome, one more closely tied in practice to the morality professed.

In a third work, *Praxis sive de lectione Erasmi*, mentioned above, Maldonado is again a character in his own writings, here discussing with Ana Osorio and another speaker also modeled on a real person — St. Thomas of Villanueva — whether or not reading Erasmus' work is advisable. Like his history in dialogue of the Communers' Revolt, this colloquy seems to take the party line — in this case against Erasmus — while simultaneously questioning it. His *Eremitae*, 'The Hermits', written in 1536, creates a conversation in the countryside among several refugees from a corrupt society, who are trying to decide whether to return to society or remain recluses; after listening to the experiences of others who happen to be passing through the forest and who tell their life stories, they decide to remain in seclusion. The vividly told misadventures of lecherous old men and lovesick fools are very reminiscent of those soon to be described in the picaresque. The *Eremitae* parallels the growing disillusionment found in his other writings from these years. Of these four works from the 1530's only two have Spanish translations and accompanying studies: *Somnium* and *Eremitae*.[13]

---

[13] With the exception of *Eremitae*, these works were all published in 1541 in Burgos, probably by the publisher of one edition of the *Lazarillo*, Juan de Junta (for the full heading see Maldonado 1541). *Somnium* is included in the collection of dream-works translated by Miguel Avilés Fernández (Maldonado 1981, 149-178). The only extant Renaissance edition of the *Eremitae* was published between 1550 and 1554 and is preserved in the Spanish national library, bearing call number R/7935. Recently Peinador Marín has published

The subjects with which Maldonado was engaged in the final decade of his life continued to be grounded in Spain's daily realities and problems in need of correction. His writings are increasingly condensed, briefer and to the point.[14] *Desponsa cauta*, 'The Cautious Fiancée', is a dialogue, expanded and made more sexually explicit from Erasmus'colloquy *Procus et puella*, on the abuse of secret marriages, a problem being addressed at the time by the Council of Trent. Following the example of Vives and Erasmus, he responded to the current mania for games, especially cards and gambling, with two didactic yet lively colloquies in which he again plays fictional roles: *Ludus chartarum triumphus* and *Tridunus*.

A short collection entitled *Paradoxa* contains a dramatically narrated tale about Maldonado's experience in a small town celebrating the defense of a disputed benefice in court, then nearly drowning in swampy land while riding home cross country. With this yarn is an exhortation, drawn from Stoic philosophy, to avoid the mind-numbing effects of ill will, as well as a defense of literary studies as the best path to wisdom and success in one's chosen profession. Nearly identical in subject matter to the latter work is *Oratiuncula*, 'A Little Speech', which is the convocation address that Maldonado delivered at the opening of the academic year on October 18, 1545. *De senectute christiana*, 'On Christian Old Age', is an essay that recasts Cicero's treatise on the subject, blending pagan with Christian thought in a synthesis typical of the early Renaissance.

Of all his later works there is only one that has a modern edition, and it has also been translated into English.[15] *Geniale iudicium sive Baccanalia*, 'A Genial Judgment, or Bacchanalia', is a farcical play written to be performed by his students. Comic allegory and slapstick set at carnival time enliven the story of a legal victory by Self-Control over Glutonny; the latter's disreputable ancestry and deeds are illustrated with a vomiting scene strikingly similar to the episode of the roasted turnip in the first *tratado* of the *Lazarillo*. The Medieval tradition of a battle between Lady Lent and Sir Carnal, most famously illustrated in Juan Ruiz's 14th-century *Libro de buen amor*, 'The Book of Good Love', here lives on. But the flavor is decidedly of the Renaissance. Like Erasmus' *Praise of Folly*,

---

an edition of the Latin text, a Spanish translation and detailed literary contextualization. See Maldonado 1991.

[14] Most of these later writings were published in Burgos by Juan de Junta in the two 1549 printings of the second collection of works by Maldonado.

[15] Colahan, Rodriguez, and Smith 1999.

Juan Luis Vives' Latin dialogue *Ebrietas,* or even more like Rabelais' *Gargantua*, the work allows its author simultaneously to show off his Classical erudition, to reject scholastic metaphysics in favor of a practical morality fully cognizant of the body, and to attack vice with exaggeration and laughter. Those ingredients, with the addition of a biting irony, are also present in the Spanish picaresque, especially at its inception with the *Lazarillo*. A good part of that famous combination of literary attributes is present as well in Maldonado's *Pastor Bonus*, as we will see in the fifth chapter.

LUDUS CHARTARUM TRIUMPHUS,
'THE CARD GAME "TRUMPS"': INTRODUCTION

When in 1541, and again with revisions in 1549, Maldonado published this instructional colloquy demonstrating how to play a well-known game entirely in Latin, playing cards were not much more than a century old in Europe. Nonetheless they had already become a highly popular pastime and there was a wide variety of games, as shown by Gerolamo Cardano's comprehensive and analytic work on the subject. Cardano (1501-1576), an Italian who was about fifteen years younger than Maldonado and became rector of the University of Padua, published over a hundred works. One of them, written in Latin in the 1560's but not published until 1663, long after his death, was entitled *Liber de Ludo Aleae,* 'The Book of Dice Playing.'[1]

The title notwithstanding, the book gives card games extensive treatment, and *triumphus*, or 'trumps,' is included in the third section, which is about various games that depend on both luck and skill. As the classification suggests, Cardano's primary object, unlike Maldonado's, is not to lay out the rules and provide samples of play in Latin for all the games, but instead to characterize the experience of playing them. What he has to say about trumps, however, does shed some light on why Maldonado may have chosen that particular game for a work encouraging his students to play it. Cardano asserts that *triumphus* closely imitates human life and so teaches prudence. Therefore, "it is more fitting for the wise man to play at cards than at dice and at *triumphus* rather than at other games.... Since this is a most ingenious game, I am very much surprised that it has been neglected by so many nations."[2] In fact, it was not to be neglected for much longer, as it gained popularity in Spain as *triunfo* (or *triunfo envidado*) and then *el juego del hombre*, 'the game of man,' and spread from there throughout Europe as a fashionable pastime in the 17th and 18th centuries. Cervantes mentions the game in *Don Quixote* 2.34 when Sancho Panza says that when he becomes a governor he will have no

---

[1] See Cardano 2006 for the Latin text. *Liber de Ludo Aleae* is translated in Ore 1953, pp. 183-241.

[2] See Ore 1953, p. 224.

time for hunting because he plans to amuse himself with playing *triunfo envidado* on feast days, and ninepins on Sundays and holidays. The game is still played in Spain under the name *tresillo*.[3]

Spanish writers of the period also produced works about cards. In the mid-fifteenth century Fernando de la Torre, who like Maldonado lived in Burgos, worked out a detailed description, called simply *Juego de naypes*, 'The Card Game,' of a deck of cards to be used at court.[4] They were to be illustrated by mythological figures and inscribed with corresponding lines in verse, the number of lines matching the face value of the card. Later, as card games became more pervasive in Spanish society, similar — though briefer — allegorical allusions to some of the suits and specific cards appeared in seventeenth-century authors, including the prominent playwright Lope de Vega and the epigrammist Baltasar Gracián.

The fullest treatment of the subject was published in 1603 by Francisco Luque Fajardo with the title: *Fiel desengaño contra la ociosidad y los juegos*, 'Accurate Exposé of Idleness and Games.'[5] Although it presented itself as a manual for those charged with correcting the vices of gambling, the in-depth information provided there on game rules, specialized slang vocabulary and dishonest tricks, betrays a personal knowledge by the author. In that regard it recalls the first-hand experience in low-life matters confessed to/bragged about by the protagonists of picaresque fiction during the period. More typical, however, of Renaissance Spanish books on cards was a diatribe against the evils of gambling written by Diego del Castillo and published in 1528. St. Bernardine of Siena in a 1423 sermon had denounced the tarot figures on the cards then coming into vogue: these are the four suits still used by Maldonado in the game he describes, namely coins, staffs, cups, and swords (on these suits, see further below). Bernardine thought these were perversions of the religious symbols depicted on Christian breviaries, and represented a "mystical evil" (*mysticam malitiam*); he interpreted the suits as follows: "the coins are avarice, the staffs are foolishness or dog-like savagery, the cups are drunkenness and appetite, the swords are hatred and warfare." Diego del Castillo, while discouraging all gambling, sees the suits of cups and swords as symbolic of defensive and offensive warfare, respectively, and addressing himself to the nobility in particular, who would be in charge

---

[3] See J.P. Etienvre 1987 (the citations from Cervantes are on p. 180).
[4] See Torre 1907.
[5] See Luque Fajardo 1603 (apparently never reprinted).

of conducting wars, urges them to follow the superior example of the cups and to avoid the offensive warfare of the inferior suit, the swords.[6]

One of Maldonado's purposes in his own treatise seems to be to establish the intrinsic innocence of card-playing; when Rosarius at one point, for example (p. 25v), seems to suggest that he wants to gamble his money, the others discourage him and say that card-playing should be just for fun; the losers will agree only to pay for wine and fruit at the end, distributed equally. Secondly, Maldonado retains the language of making war which had been prominent in del Castillo's treatise, but diffuses its seriousness by turning it away from the battlefield into the harmless banter of four friends competing against each other. In this positive attitude his literary model was a short dialogue by Juan Luis Vives, which he acknowledges in the work itself. This Spaniard was raised in Valencia by a family of Jewish descent and, like Maldonado, was a classics teacher who wrote in Latin. He is sometimes referred to as the founder of the study of sport and games, and he is often ranked, with Erasmus and Budé, as one of the three greatest humanists of the Renaissance. Among his far-ranging writings there are seminal pages on the importance of recreation for renewal of the mind, body and spirit.

Like Erasmus, Vives wrote individual colloquies on several games, but also elaborated a theory of sports and play, designing five "laws" on how games should be conducted for the benefit of body, mind and spirit. But unlike his famous friend, he penned a colloquy on card playing, which is part of his collection of didactic dialogues set amidst the everyday life of school boys: *Linguae latinae exercitatio.*[7] The date of publication was 1538, just three years prior to the first appearance of Maldonado's corresponding piece, and the title is also similar: *Ludus Chartarum seu Foliorum,* 'The Game of Cards' (both *chartae,* literally "pages," and

---

[6] See Diego del Castillo 1557 [1528]. On St. Bernardine de Siena, see Etienvre 1982, p. 439 n. 8 and p. 442 n. 33. On tarot cards used in Spain see further Etienvre 1987, pp. 291-296.

[7] The standard and complete edition of Vives' works in Latin is still *Joannis Ludovici Vivis Valentini Opera Omnia* (8 volumes, Montfort 1782). The *Ludus Chartarum sive Foliorum* is part of the section entitled *Exercitatio Linguae Latinae* in Volume I, pp. 378-385. Another dialogue by Vives in this section is *Ebrietas,* an account of a drunken revel; this had an influence on Maldonado's *Baccanalia* (edited Colahan, Rodriguez, and Smith 1999) [the 1992 edition of Vives' *Opera Omnia* by Antonio Mestre *(Universitat de Valèn-cia)* is still incomplete in five volumes, of which the first contains essays on Vives, and the remaining four, his commentary on twenty books of Augustine's *City of God*]. The *Exercitatio Linguae Latinae* was translated into Spanish by Cristóbal Coret y Peris under the title *Diálogos* (see Vives 2005).

folia, literally "leaves," were used as Latin equivalents of "cards.") So is the content — an outline of the rules of play, with dramatized examples of basic strategy and identification of the character types (e.g., the poker face) encountered among players — though Maldonado expands the material in all these areas. Both works have a pronounced flavor — which was praised in relation to Vives' work by the Spanish novelist Azorín in the early twentieth century — of daily life in a Renaissance Spanish town.[8] There is a somewhat rougher edge to the game described by Vives, partly due to the fact that while Maldonado has his players competing only for a bowl of wine, in Vives they are explicitly playing for money; this causes tension, and one of the players, Valdaura, accuses another, Castellus, of winning by using marked cards, whereas Castellus retorts that Valdaura actually lost because of his complete ineptitude and ignorance of what cards to play. Vives, anticipating what comes later in Cardano's appraisal of *triumphus*, ends with a poem drawing a comparison between card playing and making one's way in life (compare Rosarius' poem at the end of Maldonado's dialogue) — a poem mocked by the others who suggest that he sings with the voice of a goose, and that his poem has been "squeezed out of a dry sponge" i.e. lacks substance.

Both Maldonado and Vives describe the deck, which is not exactly the same as the one used in French- and English-speaking worlds. Though illustrating the same game as Maldonado, and with the same Spanish rules, Vives lived and taught most of his adult life in the Low Countries and England, so he adapts the local deck to Spanish usage by removing the tens. The other important difference between the two decks — the use in Spain of a 'knight' (also called a 'horse') instead of a 'queen' — is overlooked.

Both decks derive from Italian playing cards, although neither includes the 22 Tarot cards developed in Italy called the *Major Arcana.* The names of the suits are different in France and Spain, as Maldonado's detailed account of a game reminds the reader constantly, though their common origin is descernible: diamonds=*oros*, 'gold coins'; hearts=*copas*, 'cups'; spades=*espadas*, 'swords'; and clubs=*bastos*, 'clubs.' The Spanish names are closer to their Italian source, as is one of the game's oldest and most

---

[8] "Acaso no haya libro en nuestra literatura más íntimo y gustoso. Abridlo: ved cómo pasa la existencia menuda y prosaica de los pueblos en una serie de pequeños cuadros...," 'Perhaps there is no book in our literature that is more intimate and delightful. Open it up: see the little, prosaic details of town life go by in a series of small sketches...' This passage by Azorín is cited in his introduction to Vives 1940, p. 10.

famous rules: the numbered cards, i.e., those that are not face cards, are worth *more* the lower the number shown on the card, though this is applicable only in the two suits of *oros* and *copas*. In the suits of *espadas* and *bastos* the numbered cards are worth more the higher they are, as one would expect. However, the inversion of the values in the first two suits was soon dropped in France and England, though not in Spain.

The parallels between Vives' colloquy and Maldonado's are many and close, and the latter almost immediately refers to the earlier work on the subject of games by both Erasmus and Vives. Many of the shared details show the same pedagogical and edifying purposes. Bad weather forces people indoors for recreation, and cards can be an appropriate alternative to sports. Card games should be of moderate length, so as not to interfere with studying and religious devotions. The stakes should be small, so as not to risk the players' financial security, and the emphasis should be on relaxed pleasure, not on making a profit. It is stressed that intelligent choices and self-discipline give victory, not just luck.

In practical matters, too, many of the details are the same. To avoid interruptions, the friends decide to play in a dining room. There is talk of whether the cards have been marked on the back so that they can used for cheating. There is discussion of whether partners should be chosen by lot or by some personal affinity.

But Maldonado is not simply making an expanded copy. His players are Latin teachers, including himself, not schoolboys, and the point is made that he and his colleagues need to set a good example to their students as regards healthy recreation that also gives practice in Latin usage. Unlike Vives, he states explicitly that one of the rules of the game is that no one may use any non-Latin words, under threat of sanction. He points out that Vives has omitted many card terms necessary to make such an exercise workable, and he takes care that his piece be considerably longer and more thorough than his predecessor's.

Maldonado's treatment of the subject is also more accomplished in literary terms. He develops an extensive analogy between a card game and a war. While what his direct sources here might be is unknown, Diego del Castillo had already drawn the analogy with war in his treatise on gambling, and it is intriguing to compare the metaphor with the origins of the deck rooted in the battle between spring and lent and enacted in late-medieval Italian carnival processions.[9] The greater length also gives

---

[9] See Moakley 1966, chs. 1-2.

Maldonado scope to develop the personalities of the players, including his own. That fleshing out of the characters also goes hand in hand with adding the dramatic, or rather comic, tensions of what becomes a viable theatrical piece.

In general, humor is much more prominent than in the model. A good example is the personality development of Asturianus, 'The Asturian.' He stands out in more than one way. He doesn't come on the scene until the friends are settled at a table in Ferranus' house. It is plausible that he is to be understood as a domestic, though one accorded a certain respect; perhaps he is a butler. To begin with, he acts as referee for the card game instead of playing, a common role for Spanish barkeeps and presumably, in the past, for butlers. He covers the cost of the wine and fruit himself until the game is over, when he will be repaid by the losers. In the Renaissance many Asturians, men and women, emigrated to other regions of the country, often taking work in domestic service — as the soft-hearted but enterprising Maritornes, a maid at an inn, reminds us in *Don Quixote* 1.16.

Asturianus has a well-defined, assertive personality, very different from the indecisive referee in Vives' colloquy who rules that a hand be played over rather than make any decision on an incident. The Asturian is a practical type, more accustomed to managing money than the poor humanists. He makes fun of the players in this regard, and the character Maldonatus authorizes him to spend for them whatever he thinks best. Twice he plays Sancho Panza to the somewhat quixotic type represented by Maldonado, who has his head lost in the mists of classical antiquity. He promises to eat the leftovers, then recommends to the scholars that they eat the apples instead of philosophizing about them.

Finally, it is precisely the wine and the apples that allow Maldonatus an opening for the introduction — very much in character — of classical erudition which is relatively lacking in Vives' dialogue. He explains that the red wine in question is called Toro from its town of origin, not from any connection with bull blood, and gives his own etymology of the name of the typically Spanish variety of apples served. That in turn allows him to propose a link to the apples mentioned by Virgil as being at Numantia (site of a famous heroic battle between Romans and Celtiberians), and so to exalt Spain's classical past.

LUDUS CHARTARUM TRIUMPHUS
THE CARD GAME "TRUMPS"

Sixteenth-century card players (R. Simmons)

Antique Spanish cards: Knight of Coins (C. Smith)

Footsoldier of Cups (C. Smith)

Five of Swords (C. Smith)

Two of Staffs (C. Smith)

LUDUS CHARTARUM TRIUMPHUS: LATIN TEXT[1]

Triumphus. Ioannis Maldonati Triumphus Plenior et castigatior quam antea prodierat.[2]

Collusores: Maldonatus, Ferranus, Rosarius, Padronus, Austurianus Rex.

p.24r   *Maldonatus*: Quid nunc agimus otiosi? Ibimus inambulatum ad Clarae?
Ferranus: Locus est opportunus et amplus, si dies esset profestus. Hodie tamen frequens erit turba cerdonum et opificum omnium; non spatiabimur ex animo.
Rosarius: Bene tu reputas quidem: nam et indulgendum Genio censeo locumque magis aptum *eligendum*.[3]

24v   *Padronus:* Quid igitur uobis aqua, quod aiunt, haeret? Non animaduertitis caelum subnubilum et ab Austro insurgentes nebulas? Tectum et umbram petamus, ubi non deerit, in quo nos oblectemus,[4] unius uel duorum exenterata crumena, praesertim quod, ni multo sole, brumales dies officiunt ualetudini nihilque amoenitatis inambulantibus sub dio conciliant.
Rosarius: Tu quidem, mi Padrone, una opera, ni fallor, cupis tuis faucibus exsiccatis lectione consulere negotiumque simul agere Maldonati, ac etiam, opinor, Ferrani; qui quamuis non pari gradu, ambo prouehuntur aetate proptereaque magis amant focum hibernum et stationem securam, quam inambulationes umentes ac frigidas.

---

[1] We follow the edition of 1549, which was revised by the author, but refer to the first edition (1541) in the critical notes. The orthography has been standardized according to the *Oxford Latin Dictionary*. The punctuation has also been changed to conform more to modern practice.
[2] The title page of the whole book reads: *Ioannis Maldonati Opuscula quaedam docta simul, et elegantia, De Senectute Christiana. Paradoxa. Pastor Bonus. Ludus Chartarum, Tridunus, et alii quidam. Geniale Iudicium siue Bacchanalia.* Burgis Excudebat Ioannes Giunta. Anno 1549.
[3] *eligendum: deligendum* 1541
[4] *unius: uel unius* 1541

THE CARD GAME "TRUMPS": TRANSLATION

Players: Maldonatus, Ferranus, Rosarius, Padronus, Asturianus.[1]

p.24r *Maldonatus:* What shall we do now during our rest period? Shall we go walking to the Claras?[2]

Ferranus: That place is broad enough if it were an ordinary day. But today there will be a multitude of craftsmen and artisans of all kinds.[3] We will not be able to comfortably promenade.

Rosarius: You're right. I think we should satisfy our wish by choosing a more appropriate place.

p.24v *Padronus:* Why then (to cite the adage) does water stick to you?[4] Can't you see leaden skies and rain clouds coming up from the south? Let's find refuge and shade. When one or two of us have emptied their purses, there will not be lacking something to entertain us. Winter days are bad for one's health unless there is a great deal of sun, and they bring no pleasure to those who promenade.

Rosarius: Unless I am mistaken, friend Padronus, I think that you both want to care for your throat, which is dry from so much reading aloud, and for Maldonatus, and, I suppose, for Ferranus, too. Both of them are rather elderly, although not to the same extent, and for that reason prefer a hearth in the winter and a place to sit down to cold and humid walks.

---

[1] The indicated edition adds 'the king' (which we have not transcribed in order to avoid confusion, but whose meaning will become clear in the text) to this last name. We have not translated the speakers' names.

[2] Since the action takes place in Burgos, where Maldonado resided through most of his life, this reference has to be either to the Convent or to the Prados (Meadow) of Santa Clara. See Julián García Sainz de Baranda (1967), I, 236-37. For something on the history and location of the Convent of Santa Clara, see pages 249-50.

[3] We have not been able to determine if before the indicated convent or in the indicated meadow these artisans established outdoor factories or merely sold their wares.

[4] The proverb referred to is: "Aqua tibi haeret", "What detains you?". See Cicero, *Epistolae* 2.62 and other sources cited in Otto 1962, entry 12 under *aqua*.

Ferranus: Quamuis aequo uix animo fero me praepeditum aetate ad munus obeundum quodcumque *putari*,[5] laetari[6] tamen sedentaria quiete ludoque tempestiuo non *utique*[7] negauerim, modo sit ita breuis ac moderatus, ut a Musis non auocet nec omnino loculos exhauriat.

25r *Maldonatus:* Adeamus tuam igitur domum, quae *proximior*[8] est et a gymnasio *paululum*[9] distans. Conuenient Musae immorarique nos ludo non patientur. Breuitas ludum commendat, si qua parte commendabilis est.

Rosarius: Non suae grauitatis existimabunt *utique* Musae ludo *tam*[10] tenui ac plebeio interesse. Ludamus liberaliter ac magnifice, quantum suppeditabunt marsupia.

Ferranus: Abi, malum, cum tua prodigalitate! De leui potiuncula pomisque nobis certandum est. Maiora pignora maioraque certamina ditioribus sed perditis ac deploratis relinquamus.

Maldonatus: Optime censes, mi Ferrane. Nihil hodie magis perdit adolescentiam inconsultamque senectutem quam immodici ludi. Si quem audias iuuenem decoxisse, non quaeras *causam*:[11] ludus et ganea absorpserunt omnia. Si quem uideas senem cum adolescentibus continuo lusoribus diuersantem, non instituendi desiderio, sed colludendi ardore ferri persuadeas tibi. Itaque nos, ne mali simus auctores exempli, ludamus animi causa, non lucri; et ita ludamus breuiter, ut reparasse uires ad studia literaria, non ad superandum et spoliandum sodalem conuenisse uideamur. Plurimum ad instituendam iuuentutem praeceptorum mores *faciunt*[12] et studia. Sed iube tandem *extrui*[13] mensam non ad prandium, sed ad ludum.

---

[5] *putari:* in 1541, this word occurs after *aetate*

[6] *laetari: laetari me* 1541

[7] *utique:* not in 1541

[8] *proximior* (a comparative form found in Seneca and some later authors): *proxima* 1541

[9] *paululum: parum* 1541

[10] *utique…tam:* not in 1541

[11] *Causam: causari* 1541

[12] *faciunt* in 1541 occurs after *plurimum*

[13] *extrui: praeparari* 1541

Ferranus: Although I don't like it to be thought of me that I am impeded by age from doing anything, I can't deny that I'm attracted to the idea of sitting down somewhere peacefully and playing some suitable game, so long as it doesn't last too long and it be moderate, so that it neither distracts me from the Muses nor completely empties my purse.

p.25r *Maldonatus*: Let's go, then, to your house, which is close by and not far from the school. The Muses will be benign, not allowing us to waste too much time gambling. For if gambling has one thing to recommend it, it is its brevity.

Rosarius: The Muses will not in any case deign it worthy of their seriousness to be present at such a trivial and plebian pastime. Let us play lavishly and fully, as much as our purses can supply to us.

Ferranus: Damned be your wastefulness! We shall only gamble some trifling drinks and some fruit. Let's leave the heavier gambling and the stronger bets to those that, being richer, are more sinful and dissolute.

Maldonatus: An excellent idea, friend Ferranus. There is nothing today more destructive among the young, and also among older and senseless persons, than excessive gambling.[5] If you hear that some young man has gone bankrupt, don't bother to look for an explanation. Gambling and bawdy-houses will have eaten up everything. And if you see an old man meeting with young people who gamble incessantly, you can be sure that he's not motivated by the desire to teach them, but rather by the wish to participate in the game.

Let us not be, then, models for a bad example. Let us play only for pleasure and not for profit. And let us play briefly, so that it appear that we have gotten together in order to regain our strength for literary endeavors and not in order to defeat and rob a friend. The character and the customs of teachers contribute greatly to the instruction of the young.[6] But, in any case, Ferranus,[7] give orders to prepare a table, not for eating but for playing.

---

[5] For a broader and more direct criticism by Maldonado of the vice of gambling, see the modern edition and translation of his *The Hermits (Eremitae)* by L. J. Peinador Marin (1991).

[6] For the importance that Maldonado conceded to teachers in the education of youth, see E. Asensio and J. Alcina Rovira (1980).

[7] The dialogue offers no description, naturally, of movement. Here the text indicates (which we clarify by adding the name 'Ferranus,' not given in the text) that they are now in Ferranus' house.

25v   *Ferranus*: Heus pueri, afferte chartas et calculos; parate carchesia poculaque uinaria. Non hic contendemus de regno, ut Caesar et Pompeius apud Lucanum, quem nunc *explicat*[14] Maldonatus, sed de uino: quis hauriat securius ac liberius; quis merum quamuis Samartinium iudicet acetum; quod sit illi pretium persoluendum.

Rosarius: Non placent chartae, nam *color* idem *non*[15] est omnibus a tergo. His nonnullis maculae sunt et uulnera unguibus impacta. Non certabimus aequis condicionibus. Profer, si sunt tersiores.

Padronus: Sine; sufficiunt hae nobis abunde. Non ludus nobis instituitur de toto censu, sed de paucula pecunia. Tu qui soles uel diues uel pauper euadere uno iactu uel una *excursione*,[16] minutias attendis in chartis. Nos in re leuissima fraudem non timemus.

Rosarius: Equidem non ego solus sum in hoc coetu, qui soleam fortunae committere quod est facultatum. Ceterum nemo fert aequo animo fraudem, si potest depellere.

Maldonatus: Tu me quidem petis; et quamuis nobiscum ades, aliam rem agis, aliud agitas negotium. Putas, siue bene siue male cedat *contentio*,[17] certaturum te mox nobiscum non de uino, sed de pecuniis et, si Nemesis fauerit, distenturum[18] crumenam. Pone deuiam spem; locus personaeque refragantur tuis uotis. Qui sit aliis imperaturus, sibi prius imperet oportet. Nos praecipimus adolescentibus, et dabimus eis ansam peccandi?

26r   *Ferranus*: Sane locus non erit apud me ludis eiusmodi. Satis sit ad exhilarandos paulisper animos potiunculam more nostro deponere. Qui lusor et aleator est animo, popinas et loca frequentia ganeonum et perditorum adeat. Nobis sextarius uini sit mensura ludendi.

---

[14] *explicat: enarrat* 1541
[15] *color...non: candor...haud* 1541
[16] *excursione: missione* 1541
[17] *contentio: fors* 1541
[18] *Distenturum: distenturum te* 1541

p.25v *Ferranus*: Say, lads, bring out the playing cards and the counting stones; prepare cups and glasses for the wine! We will not compete here for a kingdom, as Caesar and Pompey in Lucan,[8] whom Maldonatus is now teaching. We will compete about wine: about who can draw it most freely and easily; about who judges unmixed wine to be vinegar even if it be San Martín or Toro,[9] about the price that we must pay for it.

Rosarius: I don't like these cards. They are not all the same color on the back. Some are stained and others have been cut by fingernails.[10] We will not compete on an equal footing. Bring out cleaner cards if there are any.

Padronus: Let it be. These are more than good enough for us. We don't propose to gamble our wealth, but only a small quantity of money. You, who are accustomed to emerge rich or poor from a throw of the dice or from a hand of cards, pay attention to details on the cards. The rest of us don't fear cheating in so moderate a game.

Rosarius: I'm sure I'm not the only one present who is accustomed to put my resources at risk. Besides, no one peacefully accepts being cheated if he can avoid it.

Maldonatus: I know it's me you're referring to. But you, although one of us, while you seem to do one thing are thinking about something very different. You think that, whether you're lucky or not, you'll soon be playing with us not for the wine we have consumed, but for money; and that, if Nemesis favors you, you will fill your purse. Put aside your errant hope. The place and the persons stand against your wishes. If anyone hopes to govern others, let him first govern himself. That is the proper thing. We are teachers of the young, are we to offer them the opportu-

p.26r nity to sin?

Ferranus: Surely, for my part, there will be no opportunity for games of that kind. It is enough that we lighten our spirits for a while and put down some wine as deposit as we usually do. If anyone be an inveterate gambler, let him go to the cookhouses or to places where the dissolute and depraved congregate. As for us, let a pint of wine be the measure of our gambling.

---

[8] The text referred to is Lucan's epic *Pharsalia,* in which the Civil War between Caesar and Pompey is described. Ferranus says that the contest now will not be over a kingdom, as the two generals once fought for power in Rome, but over simple matters such as who has the most facility in drawing wine, who thinks unmixed wine tastes like vinegar, and who knows the prices that must be paid for each kind.

[9] Later, toward the end of the text, it is indicated that Toro wine is so called after the area that produces it. The same is true of San Martín wine.

[10] He suggests that the cards are marked for cheating, an accusation which is also made in Vives' *Ludus Chartarum* 384 (Vives 1782; see footnote 12 below).

Padronus: Extrahimus diem incommode. Sortiamur iam partes et nostri compositionem fortunae permittamus; aut, si sine sortione libet, ego et Rosarius, qui iuniores sumus, uobiscum grandioribus contendemus. Nam pares cum paribus ueteri prouerbio facile congregantur.

Ferranus: Lacessiti sumus, Maldonate; non diffugiamus congressum. Nam si uiribus corporis esset nobis certandum, forte non cederemus omnino; nunc ingenium praestat, et quo quis acutior et memor magis, eo magis strenuus ac fortis. Sedeamus collegae diuersi; media sit mensa, ne iungere ualeamus copias. Unusquisque propriis uiribus expensis aut pugnam ineat aut hosti concedat.

Rosarius: Promulgentur leges ludi, uel potius recitentur a maioribus latae, quas si quis contempserit, depositum perdat.

26v *Maldonatus*: Si iubetis, feram ego leges praeter communes, nostro instituto congruas ac decentes.

Ferranus: Iubemus, ut pro his etiam confirmem.

Maldonatus: Prima igitur lex in hoc ludo sanciatur, ut omnes Latine loquamur neque cuiquam liceat uoculam emittere non Latinam minusque aptam. Qui secus fecerit, censurae[19] subiaceat.

Rosarius: Optima lex haec est et nobis percommoda. Hac lege bene collocabitur ludo tempus impensum.

Padronus: Incidendam aere censeo hanc legem. Nam etsi difficillimum erit nobis ludentibus eam omnino seruare, metus tamen ipse suggeret uoculas si non penitus aptas, certe Latinas. Sunt mihi Viuis Exercitationes, in quibus lusit ille etiam chartis non infeliciter; plurimum me iuuabunt, si non a memoria fuero penitus destitutus.

---

[19] *censurae: regis censurae* 1541

Padronus: We're wasting our time. Let's draw lots to determine the teams for the game, leaving to Fortune the pairings. Or, if we don't want to leave it to chance, Rosarius and I, who are the youngest, will oppose those who are oldest. According to the adage, birds of a feather flock together.[11]

Ferranus: We have been challenged, Maldonatus. Let us not flee the combat. For if we had to fight with the strength of our bodies, perhaps we wouldn't be altogether inferior to the other group; but now intellectual talents prevail. He who is most intelligent and he who possesses the better memory will have greater strength and energy. Let us seat ourselves with partners, opposite one another, and let the table be in between, so that we cannot combine our troops. Let each one, with his own strength, enter the battle or surrender to the enemy.

Rosarius: Let the rules of the game be indicated; or, more to the point, let those already fixed by our ancestors be recited. If anyone should break them, let him lose what he has deposited.

p.26v *Maldonatus*: If you ask it of me, I will propose some rules that go beyond those which are common, fitting and appropriate to our usual custom.

Ferranus: Yes, we ask it of you, if I may speak on behalf of the others.

Maldonatus: The first rule that we must follow in this game, then, is that we all must speak in Latin. And that no one be permitted to utter a syllable that is not Latin and inappropriate. If anyone does anything else, let him be subject to censure.

Rosarius: It's an excellent rule, and it's most agreeable to us. With this rule, we will make better use of the time spent on the game.

Padronus: I think this rule should be engraved in bronze. For although it will be very difficult for us, as we play, to keep it completely, even so, the fear of breaking it will provide us with expressions which are Latin, even if they're not completely appropriate. I have Vives' *Colloquies*,[12] in which he even plays cards felicitously. It will help me a great deal, unless my memory abandons me completely.

---

[11] *Pares cum paribus congregantur*, "equals gather together with equals," an old Latin proverb, see Otto, 1962, s. v. *par*.

[12] The reference is to the *Colloquies* of Juan Luis Vives, which indeed include one, "Ludus Chartarum, Seu Foliorium," involving a game of cards. The Latin version is in the 1782 edition of his *Opera Omnia*, vol. 1 pp. 378-385, and there is a Spanish translation, "El juego de naipes," in J. L. Vives, *Diálogos* (Vives 1959).

27r   *Maldonatus*: Conatus est Viues Latine reddere nonnullas uoces eorum
qui *ludis*[20] chartarum indulgent. Erasmus etiam fuit in ludis quibusdam
ingeniosus et perspicax; multa tamen, quae *ludi chartarum exposcunt*,[21]
reliquerunt intacta; multarum uocum non meminerunt, sine quibus apud
nos *ludi* sunt eiusmodi *manci* uel potius *nulli*.[22] Utere tu quidem uocibus
et figuris dicendi Viuis quae tibi succurrerint; ni tamen habueris paratam
ex multa lectione usu continuo copiam, passim tibi propria uerba rebusque
apta deficient. Confertissimo penu opus est illi, qui non sit haesitaturus
in ludo circa proprietatem et elegantiam; assuescamus tamen et nihil erit
difficile.

Ferranus: Probo maxime legem multis nominibus accommodam. Nam
cum nobis, tum nostro erit exemplo discipulis perutilis, non in ludo quidem, a quo sunt pueri deterrendi, sed in omnibus colloquiis et quotidia-
nis sermonibus. Procede: leges reliquas audiamus.

Maldonatus: Rex ludi sit qui nunc uenit ad nos Asturianus; uinum et
poma iubeat suo arbitrio comparari, quae pendant infeliciores, uel socor-
diores potius. Idem praeterea sedeat iudex et arbiter, ut si quid inciderit
inter nos controuersum, eius *sententia*[23] omnes stemus. Qui distribuerit
chartas, tollat sibique adiudicet designatricem, si humana fuerit imago, uel
monas: abs reliquis abstineat. Nemo uoce aut nutu significet quas habeas
uires; "uolo noloque" sint liberae uoces, ceterae penitus omnes interdic-
tae. Pugnandum est propriis uiribus, et in collega ponendam aliquam
spem, sed non certam,[24] nisi pugnam et ipse lacessat.

---

[20] *ludis*: *ludo* 1541
[21] *ludi chartarum exposcunt*: *ludus exposcit* 1541
[22] *ludi...manci...nulli*: *ludus chartarum...mancus...nullus* 1541
[23] *sententia*: *sententiae* 1541
[24] More logical and grammatically correct would be *ponenda aliqua spes, sed non certa*; possibly a verb of ordering is to be understood, in order to justify the accusatives.

p.27r *Maldonatus*: Vives tried to produce in Latin some of the words used in card games. Erasmus, too, was very efficient and genial with respect to some other games.[13] However, in both cases they failed to touch on many things that the games require. They didn't remember to include many words without which our game of cards is left truncated and impossible. You can use the words and the images that you remember from Vives, but if you don't have a great reservoir of Latin words, gained from extensive reading and constant practice, you'll find yourself, time and again, without words appropriate to the situation. One must have a warehouse filled to bursting with Latin words if one is not to hesitate, regarding elegance and propriety, during the game. Even so, let us practice, and nothing will be too difficult.

Ferranus: I very much approve a rule that is desirable for many situations. It will become very useful, not only for us, but also, from our example, for the students. Not, of course, for gambling, which should be forbidden to children, but in all their conversations and daily talks. Proceed, therefore, and let us hear the rest of the rules.

Maldonatus: Let the king of the game be he who has just arrived, Asturianus.[14] Let him order the wine and the fruit that is to be bought according to his wishes. Let those with the least luck, or, rather, those less active, pay for them. Let him serve, besides, as judge and arbiter, so that if a dispute should arise among us we can all stand behind his judgment. Whoever deals the cards, let him pick and take the card that indicates the trump suit if it is a face card or an ace. If it is not, let him leave it. No player may signal with word or gesture the strength of the hand he holds. Let 'yes' and 'no' be the only words permitted, and all others be completely forbidden. Each player must do battle with the strength he has. One may have some hope in the strength of one's teammate, but not sure hope, unless the latter show his hand.[15]

---

[13] Erasmus, *Colloquia*: "De Lusu," "Pila," "Ludus globorum missilium," and others; but no colloquy on card games. See Erasmus 1997.

[14] The appointing of a *rex cenae*, to set the rules of eating, drinking, and entertainment for the evening, goes back to the ancient Greeks and Romans. See W. Smith 1984. Asturianus does not appear until the others have already walked from the school to Ferranus's house. This avoids having had to choose which four would play, since five cannot. In the version of the game described by Vives, five players begin the game, but the one who receives the first king immediately withdraws from the game to become the referee (*iudex*) in case disputes arise. In Maldonado's version, he himself simply appoints the latecomer Asturianus as both referee and as king of the game, a function which is virtually restricted here to the providing of refreshments.

[15] A player, with enough high trumps in his hand to guarantee winning most of the hands, could merely show them and end the game.

27v   *Rosarius:* Quando ludus hic non minus spectat ad eruditionem quam ad oblectationem et tu, Maldonate, qui superas annis et usu, coepisti, redde Latine nomina chartarum et ordinum, quo modo partiantur, qui sit usus earum, quae superiores, quae sint inferiores et minus ualentes.

Maldonatus: Nihil omittamus igitur, quantum uires *suppetiuerint*.[25] Quatuor sunt ordines, et in unoquoque chartae duodenae, nummi aurei, carchesia, enses, baculi. Praeminet rex in quolibet ordine, post regem eques, deinde pedes. Reliquae chartae numero distinguuntur. Monas in aureis et carchesiis superat omnes sui generis, deinde dyas; ita quod *numerus*[26] minor semper uincit maiorem. In ensibus et baculis contra, maior numerus iugulat minorem. Quod est intelligendum de ludo Triumpho, quem sumus nunc aggressuri; nam in ceteris ludis chartarum, qui sunt propemodum innumeri, diuersae sunt leges et quotidie prodeunt noui legum latores. Sed quia Triumphus fuit (opinor) primus inuentus et eius causa repertae lusoriae chartae, tum nobis magis congruus, in quo minus est fraudis et doli, de eo nunc solum agemus. Triumphus dicitur, quod cum habeat instar pugnae, uidentur Triumphare uictores. Componuntur in eo unus ad unum, uel par ad par. Sed usitatius est et commodius ac etiam

28r   proprius par ad par, ut nos sumus nunc compositi decussate. Duae sunt partes tamquam in proelio, sed quatuor castra *metantur*.[27] Non coniunguntur castra socia, sed ex aduerso se prospectant, hostem habentes ab utroque latere. Duo sunt duces in utraque parte; mensa diuidit omnes, etiam socios.

Rosarius: Quando proelium esse ludum hunc fateris, explica robur exercitus, et in quo militum praestantia consistat.

28v   *Maldonatus*: Bene admones. Quatuor, ut nos nunc, sunt duces; chartae copiae. Distribuuntur primo sorte; deinde qui ad dexteram distributoris sedet distribuit, et ita procedit sors *distribuendi*[28] in circulum a dextera in sinistram, donec uincat omnino pars altera. Distribuuntur chartae singulis nouenae unaque prostat a fronte detecta in meditullio mensae,

---

[25] *suppetiverint: suppeterint* 1541
[26] *numerus: numeris* 1541
[27] *metantur: locantur* 1541
[28] *distribuendi 1541: destribuendi* 1549

p.27v   *Rosarius*: Since this game is as much a matter of instruction as of pleasure, and it was you, Maldonatus, the oldest and most experienced, who
chose it, why don't you translate to Latin the names of the cards and their
order, how they are divided and what is the use of each one, which are
superior and which inferior and with less power.

Maldonatus: Good, let us not omit anything as far as we are able.
There are four suits with twelve cards each: gold coins, cups, swords and
staffs.[16] The king is the highest card in each suit. After the king comes
the knight and then the foot-soldier. The rest of the cards are numerical.
In gold coins and cups, the ace is the highest of the numerical cards, followed by the two, so that the lower number always beats the higher. On
the other hand, in swords and staffs, the higher number beats the lower.
This is so for the game of Trumps which is what we will be playing. In
other card games, which are almost too many to count, the rules are different, and every day there are those who think up new rules. Since the
game of Trumps is, in my opinion, the first that was invented, and card
games became generalized through it, it will go best with us because it
offers little leeway for cheating.

We will speak only of this game. It is called Trumps because it has the
character of a fight, and thus those who win appear to triumph. In it the
players confront each other, one against one, or two against two. But it
p.28r is more usual and appropriate, and even more characteristic, to play two
against two, the way we are now seated, in contraposition. There are two
sides in the game, like in a battle; but four camps should be distinguished.
The two allied camps are not together, but face each other, with an enemy
on each side. There are two generals on each side. The table separates all,
even the allies.

Rosarius: Since you suggest that this game is like a battle, explain the
strength of the army, and what the soldiers' superiority means.

p.28v   *Maldonatus*: Good advice. Just as there are four of us now, there are
four generals. The cards are the troops. The first dealer is determined by
lot, and thereafter the one seated to the right of the last dealer deals. Thus,
then, the obligation to deal proceeds in circular fashion from right to left

---

[16] Spanish card decks today still contain 48 cards; for the modern game *tresillo,* the
eights and nines are removed, resulting in a deck of 40 cards. In Vives' version (Latin text
of 1782, p. 381), it is the tens which are removed.

quae sui generis indicat chartas ea pugna praestare, quique plus habeant
ex eo genere, plus uirium habere, si socordes non sint aut ignaui, qui
nesciant uictoria uti seque timidi dedant.[29] Triumphales dicuntur chartae
dum genus earum praeminet, quoniam qui eis abundant, triumphare plerumque solent. Monas eminet in Triumphalibus et ipsum superat regem,
cum in reliquis numeri seruet, ut diximus, ualorem. Sed tandem quando
mores legesque plerasque aperuimus, ineamus iam ludum, ceteras ludendo
cognoscemus. Rex propinet suo tempore potiunculam, quam eius arbitrio permisimus expendendam.

Asturianus: Misi puerum et ille non longas trahet moras. Si uobis dis-
plicuerit quod affertur, ego reliquias absorbebo. Sed tandem incipite;
cupio iam nosse, qui mihi sint debitores.

Maldonatus: Sortiamur chartarum distributionem. Cui rex primus
obuenerit, ille distribuat.

Padronus: Bene cessit; ego bonis auibus partior primus. Utinam sim
Nicolaus (ut aiunt) qui mihi praestantiora sumam. Habetis, opinor, noue-
nas. Numerate, si uultis. Qui superuacuaneam habuerit *commissa pugna,*
imputet sibi proelioque[30] cedat inutilis. Hanc legem Maldonatus praeter-
misit.

29r   *Rosarius*: Omnibus nota est. Pande triumphalem et insuper adice unam.
Nam ut hoc etiam noritis quod tamquam compertissimum siluit legisla-
tor, duobus et triginta calculis constat *postrema* uictoria, *quae colligit*
spolia et pro trophaeis crateras coronat.[31] Triumphalis charta detecta tribus *calculis penditur;*[32] reliquae superiniectae singulis. Nullus ualet ad

---

[29] *quae...dedant: cum supervacantibus. Quae autem potest aperta facie, indicat sui*
generis chartas ea pugna praestantiores esse, quique plures habeat ex eo genere, plus ui-
rium habere. Si non sit secors aut ignauus qui nesciat Victoria uti seque timidus dedat 1541
[30] *commissa...proelioque: imputet sibi pugnaque* 1541
[31] *postrema...quae...coronat: not in* 1541
[32] *calculis penditur: ualet* 1541

until one side wins the game. Each player is dealt nine cards, and one is placed face-up in the middle of the table to signal that the cards of the suit it represents have a preference in the game.[17] Those who have the greatest number of cards from that suit have the greater strength, if they are not stupid or lazy, or don't know how to seize the advantage and surrender out of timidity.

The cards of the preferred suit are called trumps, since, generally, the player who has the greatest number of them triumphs. In the trump suit the ace is the highest card, beating even the king; but in all the other suits the ace retains only the strength of its number, as already indicated.

Now, having finally revealed the customs and most of the rules, let's start the game. We'll comment on the remaining rules as we play. Let the king of the game, Asturianus, provide at his discretion the wine that we have authorized him to buy.

Asturianus: I have already sent a lad, and he shall not be long. If you don't like what he brings, I'll drink what remains. But start, because I want to know who owes me the money spent.[18]

Maldonatus: Let's determine who will deal first. Let him deal who receives the first king.

Padronus: It came out fine. With good auspices, I am the first dealer. I would like to be Nicholas, as they say,[19] and take the best for myself. I believe you all now have nine cards. Count them, if you wish. If anyone should have more than nine once the battle has started, let him say so and withdraw from the hand without profit.[20] Maldonatus forgot that rule.

p.29r *Rosarius*: Everyone knows that rule. Now, Padronus, reveal what suit is trumps and moreover add one on top. It should be known, too, something that our explainer of the rules omitted, as if everyone knew it, that the final victory, which gives one the booty and allows one to tie a

---

[17] In Vives' game, the players are also dealt nine cards each. The deck has 48 cards; 36 are dealt out to the four players, and one card indicating the trump suit is placed on the table; that card along with eleven additional cards are kept in a heap as replacement cards for the players to try to improve their hands after the initial deal.

[18] Because the losers will be obligated to pay him for the wine.

[19] Padronus as dealer wishes he were the gift-giving St. Nicholas and could "take the best (gifts) for himself" before distributing the cards to others.

[20] The rule given by Vives (*Ludus Chartarum,* p. 382), that the dealer who gives too many cards loses his turn and the hand is dealt by the player whose turn it would be next, is more logical.

unam excursionem praeter unam mittere, ni addiderit aduersarius alteram. Cum indice tamen possunt admisceri duae simul ante primam excursionem, quarum altera irreuocabilis est, de altera consultant aduersarii. *Has omnes, et quae postea fuerint depositae, dinumerant et totidem calculos suis calculis adiungunt, qui uicerint quinquies uelitatione quacunque aut hostes in fugam uerterint, donec numerus duo et triginta constet et omnino expleatur; sed tandem prostet iam index.*[33]

Padronus: Hem, baculi triumphant et indicem ego non aufero.

Rosarius: Feras aequo animo. Numerum auge calculatoriarum chartarum, antequam prouocent hostes. Periclitemur quid ualeant.

Maldonatus: Vide tu satis, Ferrane, quid tibi sit uirium; ego pugnam recuso.

Ferranus: Audeamus paulisper, ne despondisse animum primo statim conflictu uideamur. Numerum insuper augeo calculatoriarum.[34]

Maldonatus: Vide quid agas: nam nec Hercules, ut est in prouerbio, aduersus[35] duos.

---

[33] *Has omnes...iam index:* omitted 1541
[34] *calculatoriarum: calculatoriarum chartarum* 1541
[35] *Auersus* 1541 and 1549

garland around the bowl of wine,[21] consists in accumulating thirty-two counting stones. Each trump is worth three stones, and the rest of the cards only one. No one may, in one round, throw out more than one card, unless his enemy should add another.[22] Nevertheless, with the trump-signaling card can be included two others before the first round. One of these may not be retired. With respect to the other, whether to accept it or not, his enemies will consult.[23] All these cards are counted, along with those played after. The side that wins five plays in a hand or completely routs the enemy doubles the number of counting stones won, until the number thirty-two is reached and is filled up completely. But go ahead, Padronus, and indicate the lucky suit.

Padronus: Okay. Staffs are trumps, and I will not take the card that signals it.[24]

Rosarius: Don't take it too hard. Increase the number of the cards of calculation[25] before our enemies challenge us. Let's see how strong they are.

Maldonatus: Ferranus, measure well your strength. I decline to fight.

Ferranus: Let's remain brave, so that it not seem that we have lost our courage immediately, in the first battle. I increase the number of the cards even more.

Maldonatus: Watch well what you're doing, for, as the proverb says, not even Hercules can fight against two.[26]

---

[21] An epic allusion. In Vergil's *Aeneid,* the heroes crown the wine-bowl with a wreath at the start of the feast (*Aen.* 1.724, 3.525).

[22] In Vives' game, the players are betting real money, but in Maldonado's game the winning of 32 stones exempts the winners from helping buy a bowl of wine which is paid for by the losers. The second part of this rule, that concerning using more than one card in a hand if the enemy does so, never occurs in the game that follows.

[23] Like the previous rule, this possibility never occurs in the game that follows (but see note 44). On what considerations the opponents will consult to accept one of the two cards is not clear.

[24] As dealer, Padronus has the right to exchange the trump-signaling card for one of his own but he declines, indicating that it is neither an ace nor a face card.

[25] The "cards of calculation:" Latin *chartas calculatorias*, sometimes below simply called *calculatorias*. It has been stated above that the cards correspond to a number of stones (*calculi*) which are used as betting tokens, so by playing another round of cards the player increases the value which the hand is worth.

[26] Erasmus 1982, *Adages* 1.5.39: "Ne Hercules quidem adversus duos," a reference to the second labor of Heracles, when the hero fought the many-headed Hydra while being attacked simultaneously by a giant crab.

Rosarius: Non stabit certe per me, quin numerus crescat.

Ferranus: Neque per me quidem.

Maldonatus: Plurimum audes, me praesertim pugnam detrectante.

Ferranus: Decertandum quidem est; de successu uiderit sors.

Maldonatus: Aggredior igitur. En peditem carchesiorum.

Rosarius: En heptadem; non uinco.

Ferranus: Meus collega superat; mihi perit dyas.

Padronus: Quaero mihi regem aut equitem, sed nullus adest. Vincam triade baculorum. Denuo prouoco ensium senione.

Maldonatus: Enneas est mihi.

Rosarius: Penes te maneat victoria. Multiplico calculatorias.[36]

Maldonatus: Haud meo periculo.

Rosarius: Tu quidem non aequus es lusor. Tuus collega responsurus erat prior, qui meam ad dexteram sedet.

Maldonatus: Sine dolo malo praeripui uocem sodali. Veniam peto. Dissuetudine leges minores excesserunt.

Rosarius: Si peccaueris denuo, chartas tuas reddes inutiles.

Maldonatus: Patienter *id quidem*[37] feram. Sed tu, Ferrane, obsecro, tuas uires expende; consultius est in hac pugna suo tempore cedere quam temere pugnare.

Ferranus: Cedamus. Non tam id facio mea sponte, quam ne sim tibi molestus.

Rosarius: Octo calculi aggregantur nobis.

---

[36] *calculatorias: calculatorias chartas* 1541
[37] *id quidem: quidem id* 1541

Rosarius: Let the number go up. I don't oppose it.

Ferranus: Nor do I.

p.29v   *Maldonatus*: You are exceedingly brave, especially since I am declining to fight.

Ferranus: But we have to fight it out. Let Fortune determine success.

Maldonatus: Then I will attack. Here is the footsoldier of cups.

Rosarius: Here is the seven. I lose.[27]

Ferranus: My companion is winning, and my deuce is dead.

Padronus: I would like to have the king or the horse of the suit, but I don't have any cups. The three of staffs will win.[28] Now I attack, with the six of swords.[29]

Maldonatus: I have the nine.

Rosarius: May victory be on your side! I increase the cards of calculation.[30]

Maldonatus: That is no risk to me.

Rosarius: You are not following the rules of the game. Your companion, who is seated to my right,[31] had to answer.

Maldonatus: Without any devious intention I stole my companion's turn. I beg forgiveness. For lack of practice, we have forgotten some of the minor rules.

Rosarius: If you break the rules again you will be disqualified.

Maldonatus: I would resignedly accept it. But I beg you, Ferranus, to consider carefully your strength. It is more prudent, in this hand, to surrender in timely fashion than to fight imprudently.

Ferranus: Let us surrender.[32] But I do so not so much because I want to as because I do not want to be bothersome to you, Maldonatus.

Rosarius: Count out eight stones for us.[33]

---

[27] Rosarius plays the seven of cups, because it is a not mentioned rule of the game — as indicated by all the plays that follow — that the players are obligated to follow the suit initiated. Only if they lack cards in that suit can they use trumps or other suits.

[28] The dealer always closes the first hand. Padronus wins because clubs are trumps.

[29] The winner of a hand begins the next.

[30] Again, the player whose turn it is raises the stakes.

[31] Only the player to the right of the raiser can accept or reject the raised stakes.

[32] When the hand is conceded there is no need to play the remaining cards, and the cards are dealt for a new hand.

[33] Since the amounts of the bets are not indicated concretely, it is difficult to confirm this number.

Maldonatus: Nihil refert; *arridet fortuna primo, ut postremo destituat.*

Rosarius: Praecedere utcumque uolo; *uos aniles fabellae solentur.*

30r   *Maldonatus: Iocaris*; *sed uultum indues forte diuersum ante horam.*[38]
Mea nunc est distributio. Utinam mecum auferam indicem! Numeret sibi
quisque aut suo periculo ludat. O bona sors! Monadem carchesiorum ape-
rui; tam mea est quam si protulissem imaginem, et haec iugulat regem,
cum est triumphalis, suaeque parti uendicat *calculos tres*[39]: appone, Ferrane.

     Ferranus: Pone[40] curam calculorum: nihil tibi peribit me calculatore.

     Rosarius: Gaudes tu, Maldonate, sed ego non cedo. Immo faueo nume-
ris.

     Ferranus: Consule uires tuas, Maldonate; ego non pugno.

     Maldonatus: Consiste gnauiter; ego uel solus pugnabo. Profer, Rosari,
chartam auspicatoriam.

     Rosarius: Accipite senionem ensium.

     Ferranus: Enneas est mihi; non uincitur sine imagine.

     Padronus: Ensifera non est mihi charta: Ogdeas carchesiorum urget
satis.

     Maldonatus: Male tu quidem, Ferrane; debuisses triumphalem obicere.

     Ferranus: Et tu quidem in quercu nuces quaeris.

---

[38] *Rosarius: Octo…ante horam:* not in 1541
[39] *calculos tres: tres calculos* 1541
[40] *Pone: Tu pone* 1541

Maldonatus: It doesn't matter. Luck may smile at first; later it looks in another direction.

Rosarius: I want to go on in any case. You may comfort yourself with old wives' tales.

p.30r   *Maldonatus*: You joke, but you may show a different face in another hour. Now it's my deal.[34] I'd like to take the trump-signaling card. Let each one count his cards or play at his own risk.[35] What good luck! The ace of cups signals trump, and it is as mine as if it were a face card. It is a trump and beats even the king. Its power is worth three counting stones.[36] Mark them up, Ferranus.

Ferranus: Don't worry about the score. You will lose nothing with me keeping it.

Rosarius: You're very happy, Maldonatus; but I don't surrender. On the contrary, I like the numbers.[37]

Ferranus: Calculate your strength, Maldonatus. I can't compete.

Maldonatus: Keep up your spirits; I will fight, even if it be alone. Throw out an auspicious card, Rosarius.[38]

Rosarius: Take the six of swords.

Ferranus: I have the nine. Only a face card can beat it.

Padronus: I have no swords. The eight of cups is enough.[39]

Maldonatus: Poorly done, Ferranus! You should have countered with a trump.[40]

Ferranus: You're asking nuts of an oak tree.[41]

---

[34] Maldonatus is seated to the right of the first dealer, Padronus, and it is, thus, his turn to deal.

[35] The risk referred to is to be disqualified for having too many cards.

[36] The ace of the trump suit is invincible and thus guarantees three points.

[37] At the start of the game (p. 25r) Rosarius had said he wanted to make bets lavishly and fully; now he welcomes the fact that Maldonatus has raised the stakes of the hand by playing a card that is worth three counting-stones.

[38] Maldonatus apparently wishes that his enemy, Rosarius, should play a card that he can beat. But it is not certain what is meant here by the unusual form *auspicatoriam*.

[39] Remember that cups are trumps.

[40] What Maldonatus suggests, since Ferranus has the nine of swords in his hand, would contravene the game rule of having to follow suit.

[41] This proverb is clearly in the same class as *aquam e pumice postulas*, "you are asking for water out of a pumic stone," (Otto 1988, 290), *humi hauris*, "you draw water from dry ground," Erasmus *Adages* I.iv.75, II.x.87, and *nodum in scirpo quaeris* "you are looking for a knot in a bulrush" (*Oxford Latin Dictionary* under *scirpus* 1.B).

Rosarius: Peccastis uos in leges ludi; tu maxime, qui triumphalem habere negasti. Depone chartas cedeque protinus ludo.

Asturianus[41]: Non indebita poscit. Seruentur leges. Dices tu libere uelle uel nolle pugnare; de copiis quas habeas uel non habeas, silebis omnino.

30v *Maldonatus*: *Regia sane sententia.*[42] Cedo etiam ego: quoniam solus non sufficio. Distribue, Rosari.

Rosarius: Prius rationem subducam calculorum; tredecim sunt nobis; uobis tres.

Ferranus: Si fauerit Nemesis, non diu praeibitis.

Rosarius: Viderit *ipsa.*[43] Distribuo.

Padronus: Non tollis indicem; lusor infelix es.

Rosarius: Quid uis faciam? Fortuna non cogitur. Cedat *tamen illa*[44] utcumque, quinque calculorum erit prima missio. Trias aureorum est index.

Padronus: Vide quid agas, obsecro.

Rosarius: Factum est; *quamuis ludi huius periti censent imperitiam, duas in distribuendo cum indice coniungere chartas, stomachus tamen raro non rationi repugnat.*[45]

Ferranvs: Ego pugnarem, quamuis *his*[46] augeat numeros, si tu non refugeres omnino.

Maldonatus: Experiamur quid possint prouocatores; inito possumus proelio receptui canere.

Ferranus: Triadem carchesiorum mitto.

Padronus: Peditem ego.

Maldonatus: Rex adest.

---

[41] *Asturianus: Maldonatus* 1541
[42] *Maldonatus: Regia sane sententia:* not in 1541
[43] *ipsa: sors* 1541
[44] *Tamen* added 1541
[45] *quamvis...repugnat:* not in 1541
[46] *his: hic* 1541

Rosarius: Both of you have broken the rules of the game. Above all, you, by saying that you have no trumps. Drop your cards and abandon the hand immediately.

Asturianus: What he asks is just. Let the rules be maintained. One may freely say whether one accepts a bet or not, but one has to keep absolutely silent about the strength that one may or may not have.

p.30v *Maldonatu*s: A truly royal decision. I, too, abandon the hand, since I cannot compete by myself. You deal, Rosarius.

Rosarius: First I will add up the counting stones. We have thirteen; you have three.[42]

Ferranus If Nemesis favors us,[43] you won't be ahead for very long.

Rosarius: Let her see to it. I deal.

Padronus: You don't get the trump-signaling card. You're an unlucky player.

Rosarius: What can I do? You can't force luck. Nevertheless, let it bend to one side or the other. I bet five stones. The three of gold coins signals the trump suit.

Padronus: Watch what you're doing. I beg of you!

Rosarius: It's already done.[44]

Ferranus: I would do battle, even if he's raising the bet, if you, Maldonatus, were not giving up completely.

Maldonatus: Let's see what strength our enemies have. We can sound the retreat once the battle has started.

Ferranus: I play the three of cups.

Padronus: And I the foot-soldier.

Maldonatus: Here is the king.

---

[42] Although they have won no hand, conceding before doing so, the possession of the ace of trumps gives them three points.

[43] It is the norm of Nemesis, Justice, to lower what has been raised too high.

Maldonatus may be making a learned allusion here to Catullus 50, where the poet describes a delightful day with his friend Licinius playing (i.e. composing light verse) on their tablets, and says that unless Licinius answers his request for another meeting, Nemesis may bring revenge on him.

[44] The augmented and corrected edition of the dialogue adds here: "Although those who play well think that it is ineffective to add two cards to that signaling the trump suit when dealing, it's normal for intuition to struggle against reason."The reference appears to be to the rule commented on in note 23, and, by what follows in the text, the player decides against doing it. We believe, therefore, that this addition to the text would only be confusing.

Rosarius: Enneas aureorum iugulat tuum regem.

Maldonatus: Indignum regem ab infimo trucidari milite.

Rosarius: Sic ludus est: equitem baculorum mitto.

Ferranus: Enneadem ego.

Padronus: Accipe quaternionem, nam penes collegam est adhuc uictoria.

Maldonatus: Ogdoas aureorum conficit uestrum equitem. Ensiferum
regem denuo mitto.

Rosarius: Enneadem ecce.

31r   *Ferranus:* Regem supera. Dyas mihi perit.

Padronus: Aureorum quaternio mihi, sed uinco. Cedo tamen pugna;
instant aduersarii et augent calculatorias.[47]

Rosarius: Ego insuper augeo; ne despondeas animum.

Maldonatus: Timeo pugnam; nolo certare.

Ferranus: Contendamus quocumque periculo. Multiplico numeros.

Padronus: Hem, noli certare, obsecro. Melius est experiri denuo fortunam, quam nunc uiribus imparibus aperte uictoriam hostibus tradere.

Rosarius: Inuitus facio: tres mihi sunt triumphales quamuis debiles,
cedamus tamen.[48] Nolo, te inuito, manu debili pugnare.

Maldonatus: *Decem*[49] calculi sunt nobis, pugnemus gnauiter; penes
nos erit uictoria.

Ferranus: Ego distribuo; copias fortes opto et indicem sublatum.
Longe mea sors abhorret a rapinis. Dyadem ensium protuli. Monadem
iam cupio, et adest quidem. Appono tres calculos, tredecim habemus, ut
uos.

Padronus: Augeo *calcula<to>rias.*[50] Praestat fortiter pugnando perire,
quam toties de uictoria segniter dubitare.

Rosarius: Vide quid tentes; magis ego sum pronus ad fugam quam ad
pugnam.

---

[47] *calculatorias: calculatorias chartas* 1541
[48] *cedamus tamen: sed cedamus* 154
[49] *decem: duodecim* 1541
[50] *tredecim habemus ut uos. Padronus. Augeo cabulterias. Quindecim habemus.*
Padronus. Augeo calcularias 1541

Rosarius: The nine of gold coins strangles your king.[45]

Maldonatus: It's not proper that a king should be killed by a mere soldier.

Rosarius: Such is the game. I play the knight of staffs.

Ferranus: And I the nine.

Padronus: Here is the four, because victory is still in the hands of my companion.

Maldonatus: The eight of gold coins does in your horse. I play the king of swords again.

Rosarius: Here is the nine.

p.31r   *Ferranus*: The king has to be beaten. My deuce is dead.

Padronus: For me the four of gold coins, but I win. Still, I withdraw from the fight, because the enemy is pushing hard and accumulating many stones.

Rosarius: I will raise even more. Don't lose hope.

Maldonatus: I fear to go on fighting. I prefer not to compete.

Ferranus: Let's do compete, no matter what the risk. I raise the bet.

Padronus: Say, don't compete, I beg of you, Rosarius. Better to try our fortune on another occasion than, with unequal forces, blatantly hand victory now to the enemy.

Rosarius: I surrender against my will. I have three trumps, although weak ones. Let's surrender, nevertheless. I don't want to fight, with a weak hand, against your will.

Maldonatus: We have twelve stones. Let's fight hard. Victory is in our hands.

Ferranus: I deal. I wish for good troops and to take the trump-signaling card. My luck, however, refuses to allow me to despoil my enemies. Before I produced the two of swords.[46] Now I want the ace. And here it is! I add three stones and we have thirteen, like you.

Padronus: I increase the cards. It's better to die fighting than always to be lazily doubting about victory.

Rosarius: Watch what you're doing. I'm more disposed to flight than to fight.

---

[45] Remember that gold coins are trumps.
[46] He is referring to the previous hand.

31v   *Padronus*: Equidem *ego uel solus pugnabo forteque simul etiam expugnabo*:[51] uos si admittitis augmentum, dispicite.

Maldonatus: Admittimus quidem *et confidimus te debellandum*.[52] Quid tu, Ferrane: placet?

Ferranus: Non omnino plane; sed tua me recreat audacia.

Padronus: Baculorum mitto triadem.

Maldonatus: Conficitur ab enneade.

Rosarius: Eques superat.

Ferranus: O fortuna! Deteguntur meae uires; triumphali monade uincendum est.

Maldonatus: Potuisses in aliam difficiliorem excursionem seruare, sed praemonuisti me parum tuis copiis fidendum; excurre tandem denuo.

Ferranus: Regem carchesiorum mitto; sine triumphali non uincitur.

Padronus: Triadem ego.

Maldonatus: Heptadem uide.

Rosarius: Ensiferum peditem non omnino perdam.

Padronus: Bene habet. Mitte denuo.

Rosarius: Equitem carchesiorum mitto, chartam inuincibilem, si desit triumphalis.

Ferranus: Enneadem accipe.

Padronus. En ogdoadem.

Maldonatus: Penes pentadem ensium erit hac excursione uictoria.

Ferranus: Multiplico numeros.[53]

Padronus: Intelligo; petis ut collega triumphali prouocet. Quid tu, Rosari?

Rosarius: Non equidem admitto.

Padronus: Ego quidem non cedam. Augeo insuper.

Ferranus: Ego plane cedo.

---

[51] *ego vel solus...expugnabo: nullam excursionem omittam, quin augeam calcularias* 1541

[52] *Quid tu: quid ais* 1541

[53] *Multiplico numeros: augeo calcularias* 1541

p.31v   *Padronus*: I certainly am going to compete, even if I'm alone; and maybe I'll win. If you two are going to accept the raise, think about it carefully.

Maldonatus: Yes, we accept the challenge, and we are confident that you shall be defeated. And you, Ferranus, what do you say? Do you agree?

Ferranus: Not completely by any means, but your boldness inspires me.

Padronus: I play the three of staffs.

Maldonatus: The nine destroys it.

Rosarius: The knight wins.

Ferranus: What bad luck! My strength is exposed. I have to win with the ace of trumps.[47]

Maldonatus: You should have held it for a more difficult attack. But you had already advised me not to confide too much in your strength. Come, attack again.

Ferranus: I play the king of cups. It cannot be beaten without a trump.

Padronus: I play the three.

Maldonatus: Here you see the seven.

Rosarius: I shall not completely waste my foot-soldier of swords.[48]

Padronus: That's good. Play again.

Rosarius: I play the knight of cups. It's an invincible card, unless there is a trump.[49]

Ferranus: Take the nine.

Padronus: And here is the eight.

Maldonatus: The victory in this hand goes to the five of swords.

Ferranus: I raise the stakes.[50]

Padronus: I understand. You want your companion to play a trump.[51] What do you say, Rosarius?

Rosarius: Indeed, I don't allow it.

Padronus: Well I'm not giving up. I raise the stakes even more.

Ferranus: It's clear that I surrender.

---

[47] Since he could have won with any trump card, his use of the ace suggests that he has no other trumps.

[48] Remember that swords are trumps.

[49] The king of cups has already been played.

[50] Ferranus "increases the number of calculating cards," i.e. raises the stakes by forcing those who still wish to compete to play another round of cards, thus adding to the value of the pot.

[51] To lead with a trump card, thus forcing the other players to use their trumps.

Maldonatus: Persiste tandem. Ensiferus rex percurrat nunc campum.

Rosarius: Perit mihi enneas!

Ferranus: Mihi nihil.

32r   *Padronus*: Pereat mihi senio; nihil ad rem.[54]

Maldonatus: Ensium ogdoas quid habeas uirium explicabit.

Rosarius: Nihil a me auferes *triumphale: heptadem cape aureorum.*[55]

Ferranus: Monadem baculorum proicio libenter.

Padronus: Ensiferus eques ogdoadem tuam *conficiat*; augeo *calcula-torias.*[56]

Maldonatus: Durae ceruicis hic homo est! Vincimur, opinor.

Ferranus: Diuinabam ego multiplicationem huius calculariam non esse temerariam. Raro sic audet, quin certam habeat et exploratam uictoriam.

Maldonatus: Quid facias? Supersunt triumphales mihi duae. Quis cede-ret copiis eiusmodi? Non tamen temere contendamus. Conturbo chartas. Tu, Padrone, distribue.

Padronus: Vicimus *septem;*[57] habemus uiginti. Miscebo[58] diligenter, si forte similem manum possem nancisci. Enses iterum dominantur. Male sit quaternioni! Si protulissem imaginem, actum erat de uobis. Utcumque tamen quinque calculorum erit prima missio, si uos admittitis.

Ferranus: Admittimus quidem, ut pro me libere respondeam.

Maldonatus: Auge tandem igitur, si audes.[59] Non adeo magni refert uincere seu uinci, ut euentum pugnae sic formidemus.

32v   *Rosarius:* Non bene sentit meus in hoc ludo collega, qui uoluit quinque ualere primam missionem, cum haberemus uiginti iusque monadis de tribus calculis *post uiginti et quinque nullum sit.*[60]

Padronus: Non aduerti satis; feras patienter et uide quid possis.

Rosarius: Dispersus est mihi ludus ac uarius. Vix uere dicam quid potius optem, fugere an firmo pede pugnare.

---

54 *ad rem*: ad rem. *Augeo calcularias.* Mal. *Admitto* 1541
55 *triumphale: heptadem cape aureorum: aureorum Heptadem cape* 1541
56 *conficiat...calculatorias: conficit...calcularias* 1541
57 *septem: decem calculis* 1541
58 *Miscebo: miscebo nunc* 1541
59 *Si audes*: si audes; *fessus sum iam sedendo* 1541
60 *post uiginti et quinque nullum sit: amittant post uiginti quinque* 1541

Maldonatus: No, wait! Let the king of swords now dominate the field.

Rosarius: My nine is dead.

Ferranus: I don't have any trump cards.[52]

p.32r   *Padronus*: To hell with my six. It's worthless. [*I raise the stakes.*

Maldonatus:[53] *I accept (omitted 1549)*]. The eight of swords will soon declare your strength.

Rosarius: You're not getting any trump cards from me. Take the seven of gold coins.[54]

Ferranus: I happily throw down the ace of staffs.

Padronus: May the knight of swords destroy your eight. I raise the bet.

Maldonatus: What a stiff-necked fellow he is! I think we are lost.

Ferranus: I imagined so. He had his motive in raising the bet. He is rarely so bold unless his victory is safe and sure.

Maldonatus: What can we do? I still have two trump cards. Who would surrender with such strength? But let us not fight impetuously. I'll mix the cards. You deal, Padronus.

Padronus: We are winning by seven stones. We have twenty. Now I'll mix the cards carefully and see if I get another good hand. Swords are trump again. Damn the four! If it had been a face card, you would have lost the game. In any case, the first play will be for five stones, if you accept.

Ferranus: Yes, we accept, if I may speak for myself.

Maldonatus: Okay, raise if you dare. [*I'm tired of sitting. (Omitted 1549)]* Winning or losing is not so important that we should fear the result of the game.

p.32v   *Rosarius*: My companion shows no common sense in this game. He has bet five stones on the first play when we'd already accumulated twenty points. But the rule that the ace[55] is worth three stones should not apply after twenty-five points are accumulated.

Padronus: I wasn't all that attentive to the game. Take it with resignation, Rosarius, and let's see what you can do.

Rosarius: My hand is too diverse and mixed.[56] I can't say whether I prefer to retire or to stay and fight.

---

[52] He doesn't indicate what card he plays.
[53] A new hand begins.
[54] He has no trump cards, nor does Ferranus, who follows.
[55] The ace of trumps, of course.
[56] He indicates that he has many suits and, therefore, few trumps.

Padronus: Satis mihi est te dubitare. Singulari certamine nullum ego fugerem. Audeamus *bono animo.*[61] Augeo calculatórias.

Ferranus: Enimuero uiderit sors, retrocedendum non est.

Maldonatus: Miscebo calculatorias *cum fasciculo,*[62] si iubetis. Haec pugna decernat, qui *sint regi debitores ac obnoxii.*[63]

Padronus: Ita uolumus: quamuis superamus calculis, misce. Sed tu, uinarie rex, uide munus tuum obeas diligenter; sit uinum et poma rege digna.

Asturianus. Erunt quidem; proptereaque cupio uinci ditiores, quo benignius soluant et maturius. Nam cum a grammaticis difficile corradantur pecuniae, et quo grandiores, eo tenaciores, malo tamen pumicem scalpere quam marmor; aut si sunt tanquam spongia comprimendi, malo udam quam penitus aridam comprimere.

33r   *Rosarius:* Heus[64], inauspicate rex, age tu quod tuum est, nostram fortunam noli uellicare. Ponas anxietatem; quicunque uicerint, uincant; tuae tibi pecuniolae non deperibunt.

Maldonatus: Sinite uos regem regnare, cuius proprium est libere loqui quodque uelit efficere. Mitte tu, Ferrane, qui praeis.

Ferranus: Tu quidem praeis; Padronus distribuit.

Maldonatus: Quis profert monadem?

Padronus: Eccam! Sed non adicio tres calculos, quod ultima manus haec est ex utrorumque decreto.

Ferranus: Hac utique pugna debellantur alterutri.

Maldonatus: Mitto dyadem triumphalem, ut pertentem uires.

Ferranus: Hem, quid agis?

Maldonatus: Excutiam forte monadem.

Rosarius: Enneas mihi rapitur.

Ferranus: Eques mihi, si non uinco.

---

[61] *bono animo: bonis auibus* 1541
[62] *cum fasciculo* not in 1541
[63] *sint regi debitores ac obnoxii: regi sint obnoxii ac debitores* 1541
[64] *Heus: Heus tu* 1541

Padronus: That you should merely have doubts is good enough for me. I, in a hand to hand battle, would flee from no one.[57] Let's be brave, with courage. I raise the stakes.

Ferranus: Very well. Let Fortune decide. We shall not retreat.

Maldonatus: I'll mix our stones with the packet, if you wish, and let this hand alone determine who are the debtors and subject to the king.[58]

Padronus: Let it be so. Although we are winning in stones, mix them. And as to you, king of the wine, make sure to fulfill your duties well. Let the wine and the fruit be worthy of a king.

Asturianus: And they will be. Moreover, I wish that the rich will be defeated so that they will pay me more quickly and generously. For although grammar teachers save money with great difficulty, and the more important they are the more avaricious they tend to be, even so, I prefer working pumice stone to marble. Or, if they are to be squeezed like sponges, I prefer squeezing a wet sponge than a completely dry one.[59]

p.33r *Rosarius*: Say there, king of bad omens! Look to your own business and don't taunt us for our own good. Forget your anxiety. Whoever wins, let them win; your paltry money will not disappear.

Maldonatus: Come on, let the king be king. He has the right to speak freely and to do whatever he pleases. You, Ferranus, who go first, play a card.

Ferranus: No, you go first. Padronus dealt.

Maldonatus: Who produces the ace?[60]

Padronus: Here it is.[61] But I'm not going to add the three stones it's worth because we've decided that this will be the last and decisive hand.

Ferranus: In this hand, to be sure, one side or the other will be defeated.

Maldonatus: I play the deuce of trumps in order to test my strength.

Ferranus: Hey, what are you doing?

Maldonatus: Maybe this way I'll force him to use his ace.

Rosarius: You've managed to get my nine out.

Ferranus: And my knight, unless I win.[62]

---

[57] He suggests that he has a very good hand.

[58] Maldonatus proposes that they disregard the score up to that point and that a final hand decide the victors.

[59] A dry sponge is, of course, unlikely to produce anything. There is a similar joke at the ending of Vives' *Ludus Chartarum*, and see A. Otto 1988 entry under *spongia*.

[60] Maldonatus asks, but without yet playing.

[61] Padronus admits he has the ace of trumps before the hand begins.

[62] Ferranus should know that he cannot win, since Padronus, who follows, has the ace.

Padronus: Semel uictura erat monas et nunc equitem perdit. Mitto denuo carchesiorum ogdoadem.

Maldonatus: Dyas uincit.

Rosarius: Superat eques.

Ferranus: Trias ensium iugulat tuum equitem. Mitto baculorum peditem.

Padronus: Eques tibi praesto adest.

Maldonatus: Quid immoramur? Vincamus quomodocumque; ogdoadem ensium non amplius mihi seruabo.

Rosarius: Per me quidem tibi licet uincere.

Maldonatus: Mitto regem aureorum.

Rosarius: Monadem ego.

33v *Ferranus*: Huius generis non est mihi charta. Vince tu regem.

Padronus: Pentas ensium mihi uictoriam ascribet. Sed tandem ne longius immoremur, ensiferus rex percurrat nunc campum et uerrat quicquid est usquam triumphalium.

Maldonatus: Hem, perimus: rapitur mihi pedes.

Ferranus: Mihi heptas.

Rosarius: Perdo senionem. Male tu quidem triumphali prouocasti.

Padronus: O perdite lusor! Cur ex transuerso priori uelitatione non proiecisti?

Rosarius: Non mihi placuit opportunitas. Nec omnino male cessit; uictores plane sumus.

Maldonatus: Iam certe contentione non opus; nullae nobis uires supersunt.

Ferranus: Ad triarios, credo, uentum est; triumphales perierunt omnes.

Maldonatus: Sed *triarii nostri*[65] debiles *omnino,*[66] ac ignaui sunt; herbam demus.

---

[65] *triarii nostri: nostri triarii* 1541
[66] *omnino: penitus* 1541

Padronus: The ace was destined to win and now destroys the knight. I play the eight of cups.

Maldonatus: The deuce beats it.[63]

Rosarius: The knight prevails.

Ferranus: The three of swords cuts your knight's throat. I play the foot-soldier.[64]

Padronus: Here is the knight waiting for you.

Maldonatus: What are you waiting for? Let's win one way or another. I will no longer keep my eight of swords.

Rosarius: As far as I'm concerned, you win.

Maldonatus: I play the king of gold coins.

Rosarius: And I the ace.[65]

p.33v *Ferranus*: I have no gold coins. You, Padronus, beat the king if you can.

Padronus: The five of swords will make me victorious. And finally, and so that we don't waste any more time, let the king of swords command the entire field and gather up what trumps are left.[66]

Maldonatus: There, we've lost! My foot-soldier is lost.

Ferranus: And my seven.

Rosarius: I lose the six. Damn you for leading with trumps!

Padronus: What a poor player you are! Why didn't you use that card unexpectedly in the previous play?[67]

Rosarius: I didn't think it opportune. In any case, it hasn't come out all bad. It's clear that we are the winners.

Maldonatus: It's true that we no longer need continue playing. We have no strength remaining.

Ferranus: I think we've come down to third-rate soldiers. We have no trumps remaining.

Maldonatus: And our third-rate soldiers are, besides, weak and lazy. Let us concede the game.

---

[63] Remember that in two suits, gold coins and cups, the number value is reversed.

[64] Either of gold coins or staffs.

[65] In all but the trump suit the king beats the ace.

[66] The ace of trumps has already been played.

[67] Padronus does not refer to the previous hand, in which Rosarius, following suit, had to play his ace of gold coins, but to an earlier hand in which Rosarius played the nine of trumps, instead of the six, in order to beat a deuce.

Rosarius: Potestis manus dare; mihi sunt imagines inuincibiles, et meo collegae supersunt adhuc triumphales.

Maldonatus: Proferat et frustra non contendemus.

Padronus: Ecce.

Ferranus: Victi plane sumus; mea tamen an collegae socordia, deuiaue sorte, non affirmauerim.

Rosarius: Postea diiudicabitis; nunc uinum et poma inferantur.

Asturianus: Adsunt poma.

34r   *Rosarius*: Pulchra quidem. Aueo maxime scire quo modo sint haec priscis appellata Latinis.

Ferranus: Difficilimum id esset, quod Hispania caruit scriptoribus et sunt poma nunc, quae olim non fuerunt.

Padronus: Tam insignia sunt haec ut non dubitem maioribus fuisse *percognita*[67]; quo tamen nomine diuinet Maldonatus.

Maldonatus: Nos appellamus camuessa; sed cum a Latinis et Graecis traxerimus uoces plerasque, non dubitauerim *olim dicta comessa*,[68] quod in comessationibus adhiberentur praeclara bellaria, temporisque longinquitate mutasse multiplicasseque literas. Plinius commemorat multa genera pomorum nobilium quae a locis natalibus compellabantur et in iis Numantina recenset. Non *est dubium*[69] haec poma propria huius esse regionis Burgensis. Nam si in aliis Hispaniae *prouinciis*[70] quibusdam proueniunt, peregrina sunt et non plane respondent ubique seminibus. Hic uigent, hinc deuecta habentur in pretio. Numantia non admodum distabat ab hac regione Burgensi et quicquid est interiectum soli, eiusdem est naturae: frigidum, siluestre, montibus inaequale. Cumque Numantia erat, Burgi non erant. Numantiam igitur, regionis caput, uelut frequentissimam ciuitatem quicquid erat optimum cuiusque generis deportabatur, quo uendibilius esset. Quare nil mirum, si Romani, qui cum Numantinis bella continua quatuordecim annos gesserunt, poma praecipua huius regionis appellarunt Numantina, quod Numantiae primum uisa cognitaque illis fuerunt, et inde Romam deuecta, surcis[71] fuere commissa. Non equidem

---

[67] *percognita: cognita* 1541
[68] *olim dicta comessa: dictas olim comessas* 1541
[69] *est dubium: dubium est* 1541
[70] *provinciis: regionibus* 1541
[71] *surcis*: probably intended for *sulcis*

Rosarius: You do well to surrender. I have face cards that are invincible and my companion still has trump cards.

Maldonatus: Let him show them and we won't go on playing needlessly.

Padronus: Look.

Ferranus: It's clear that we've lost, but I couldn't say if because of my mistakes or my partner's or if fate was against us.

Rosarius: You can argue over that later. Now, let the wine and the fruit be served.

Asturianus: Here is the fruit.

p.34r *Rosarius*: It is certainly beautiful. I'd like to know what the ancient Romans called these fruits.

Ferranus: That would be difficult to know because Spain had no writers and there are now fruits that didn't exist before.

Padronus: These are so large that I do not doubt they were well known to our ancestors. Nevertheless, let Maldonatus speculate about what they called them.

Maldonatus: We call them 'camuesas', but, since we've taken most of our words from Romans and Greeks, I don't doubt that they were at one time called 'comesas,' because the best desserts were served at banquets, 'comessationes,' and across a long period of time the letters have been changed and added to. Pliny indicates that there are many types of noble fruits that were named for the regions in which they were found. Among these he includes 'Numantina.'[68]

There is no doubt that these fruits are peculiar to this Burgalese region. For if they appear in some other regions of Spain they are foreign imports. It's clear that they don't grow from seeds just any place. Here they flourish, and they are much esteemed when taken elsewhere. Numantia was not far from this Burgalese region, and the terrain that separates them is very similar: cold, mountainous, and rugged with forests. When Numantia existed Burgos did not exist. Therefore, all excellent products, whatever they were, were taken, in order to facilitate their sale, to Numantia, a principal place and the most populous city of the region. It is not at all

---

[68] Pliny, *Natural History,* 15.55. Maldonado's speculation about the etymology of *camuessa* is dubious; the *Vox diccionario actual de la Lengua Española* speculates that the word derives from an earlier form *camosia, but the *Diccionario de uso del Español* simply says: *De origen incierto.*

dubitauerim de his Virgilium sensisse, cum dixit "Sunt nobis mitia poma castaneaeque molles". Quid his pomis dulcius? Quid mitius? Quid elegantius?

34v   *Asturianus:* Mitte concertationem de nomine; sapori indulgeamus. Duo sibi quisque sumat et inter diribitores reliqua distribuantur.

    Rosarius: Color, sapor et magnitudo placent. Propina uinum, ut de eius nobilitate disseramus.

    Maldonatus: Amineum attulisti? Malim rubrum.

    Rosarius: Samartinium est.

    Maldonatus: Malim taurinum.

    Ferranus: Falleris, opinor. Multis quidem rebus superat Hispania plerasque nationes, sed nulla magis quam uini nobilitate. Sunt in Hispania uina nobilia, sed gentium consensu Samartinia tenent primas. Celebrantur etiam Taurina cis montes: *sed transmontana etiam rubella maiorem uim habent citiusque pedes et linguam praepediunt.*[72]

35r   *Padronus:* Cum audiunt externi taurina uina, putant propterea dicta, quod referant colore Taurinum sanguinem, cum uere lucida sint et clara, *quamuis rubra,*[73] traxerintque nomen ab oppido Hispaniae sane celebri, sicuti cetera uina a locis natalibus.

---

[72] *sed...praepediunt* not in 1541
[73] *quamuis rubra* not in 1541

surprising, then, that the Romans, who fought the Numantines for four-teen years, [69]should have called the principal fruits of the region 'Numan-tine', because they were first seen and known by them in Numantia. From there they were taken to Rome, together with cuttings for their cultiva-tion. I would not even doubt that Virgil was thinking about them when he wrote "we have soft fruits and juicy chestnuts".[70] What is sweeter than these fruits? What is softer? What is more elegant?

p.34v   *Asturianus*: Let's cease discussing the names and enjoy the taste. Let each of us take two and the rest can be distributed among the servants.

Rosarius: What an agreeable color and taste and size. Give us wine to drink, so that we may discuss its nobility.

Maldonatus: You've brought Aminean wine?[71] I would have preferred red.

Rosarius: It's from San Martín.

Maldonatus: I prefer the wine from Toro.

Ferranus: I think you're wrong. Spain surely outdoes most nations in many things, but in nothing so much as in the nobility of its wines. There are many noble wines in Spain, but the general opinion of the people is that the wine from San Martin is the best. The wine from Toro is also famous from here to the mountains, but the red wine from the other side of the mountains is stronger and more quickly makes one's tongue and legs wobble.

35r   *Padronus*: When foreigners hear talk about the wine from[72] Toro they think that it is so called because its color is like the blood of a bull. In reality, it is clear and pure, although red, and they call it so after the famous town in Spain, like many other wines that take their name from the region that produces them.

---

[69] The bloody Spanish Wars against the Romans lasted from 154-133 B.C; in the lat-ter year under Scipio Aemilianus, the city of Numantia in Nearer Spain was conquered and razed. Apparently Maldonado arrives at the figure of 14 years by beginning his count with the revolt against Rome in 147 B.C. of the guerilla leader Viriathus of Lusitania, who won a series of victories over the Romans.

[70] Virgil, *Ecl.* 1.80-81.

[71] Wine from the Italian region of Aminea. Celsus, 4.5.4, calls Aminean wine 'austerum', dry. The wine is further discussed by Columella *De Re Rustica* chapter 3.2 and chapter 9, and by Isidore of Seville *Origines* xvii.5.18 who argues that its name "Aminean" means that it is "without red" (*minium*), in other words, it is a white wine.

[72] As early as the beginning of the Middle Ages, the full-bodied wines of Toro were famous and widely appreciated. In 1208, Alfonso IV, King of Léon, gave large tracts of vineyard-suitable land around Toro as a gift to the cathedral in Santiago de Compostela, to cover the needs of the clergy. At one time Toro wines were the benchmark of Spanish red wine.

Maldonatus: Delassatus sum sedendo. Depositas tu, rex, cape pecunias, teque protinus abdica regno, quo liberi nos discedamus.

Asturianus: Abdico quidem me uosque liberos esse iubeo.

PETRI ROSARII[74]
In ludi Triumphi commendationem tumultuarium Carmen

Ludere quisquis amat Latio sermone triumpho
 Hispano et Musis inuigilare simul,
Hic hoc imprimis paruus summa arte libellus
 Et proprie, et multa non sine fruge docet.
Cum Musis facili sunt istud Apolline multi
 Experti, et uires exeruere suas:
Albis ascendit uerum Capitolia solus
35v *Maldonatus equis, cetera turba pedes.*

IOAN. MALD.
Eiusdem Aliud

Lucidus aspectu quod praestat Lucifer astris,
 Quod satyro cantu Phoebus Apollo suo,
Hoc quocunque alios superat uel iudice comptus
 Partibus hic multis utilitate liber.
Ingens auctori debetur gratia, cuius
 Ludendo Musis Musa merere facit.

FINIS

---

[74] The closing two poems in elegiac couplets are omitted in the 1541 edition.

Maldonatus. I'm tired of sitting. You, king, take the money that was deposited and abdicate the throne immediately so that the rest of us may go off freely.

Asturianus. I certainly do abdicate and declare all of you free.

Improvised Poem by Peter Rosarius[73]
Written to Commend the Game of Trumps

Whoever wants to play Spanish trumps in the Latin language,
And at the same time devote himself to the Muses,
Here is an outstanding little book of great skill.
It teaches much in its own way, and is not without merit.
Many have already experienced this, with the Muses and
An easy Apollo, and have tried out their strength.
But with white horses Maldonatus alone climbs up the
Capitoline hill; the rest of the crowd is on foot.

p.35v To Juan Maldonado; another poem by the same author

How far does Lucifer, bright in appearance, outshine the other stars?
How much does Phoebus Apollo outdo a satyr in singing?
That is how far this book outdoes others, elegant in everyone's judgment
And useful in many ways.
Huge gratitude is owed to its author. By his playing
The Muse adds value to the Muses.

THE END

---

[73] We have no independent information about him, but he is evidently the same as the speaker of the dialogue, Maldonado's fellow teacher at Burgos.

INTRODUCTION TO THE PASTOR BONUS

Writing reform for Spanish bishops: an overview[1]

Maldonado's *Pastor Bonus* offers urgent advice for church and social reform in late 1529. It takes the form of an open letter to the recently appointed bishop of Burgos, Don Iñigo López de Mendoza. In response to the work's abundant anecdotes illustrating widespread corruption, both Marcel Bataillon and Heliodoro García García have stressed its picaresque tone. Bataillon points out in Maldonado's grim portrait of Spanish society "la influencia de la *Moria*, de la diatriba moral en que se pasan en revista todas las categorías de hombres. En él se presiente, por otra parte, la amarga elocuencia del Guzmán de Alfarache. Y, sin embargo, abundan los rasgos precisos que hacen vivir ante nosotros la gran ciudad mercantil que es Burgos, con toda la porción de España que la rodea: desde los magnates del negocio internacional hasta los campesinos oprimidos y hasta los artesanos reducidos, por la decadencia de sus oficios, a la mendicidad o al suicidio."[2] Similarly, García García writes, "Ningún ejemplar del siglo XVI nos ofrece, como el *Pastor Bonus*, un cuadro social de un obispado español con tanto realismo, con pinceladas tan vivas, con matices tan concretos, con un estilo tan directo y con un nivel tan alto de psicología social."[3]

Anne Cruz's recent neo-historicist study, *Discourses of Poverty: Social Reform and the Picaresque Novel in Early Modern Spain*,[4] makes a similar and illuminating connection between the canonical picaresque novels and works not usually seen as germane to the genre. Throwing her net wide, she has included "religious writings, reformist treatises, and state documents."[5] The present effort to place Maldonado's *Pastor Bonus* in both its historical and literary context similarly goes out of bounds generically on many occasions. But it is also different from *Discourses*

---

[1] In gathering data on Spain in 1530, as well as in analyzing the *Libro de instrucción para los perlados* by Juan Díaz de Luco, we were skillfully assisted by Kara Lashley, at the time a double major in Spanish and English literatures at Whitman College.

[2] Bataillon 2002, p. 353.

[3] García García 1983, p. 266.

[4] Cruz 1999.

[5] Cruz 1999, p.xiii.

of Poverty in two ways. First, it focuses on the years immediately prior
to those studied by Cruz, and not only in response to the date of Maldonado's open letter. We have worked from the hypothesis that the anonymous but clearly embittered author of the first picaresque novel, *Lazarillo
de Tormes*, did not write in the first flush of a youthful indignation. In
other words, it seems likely that this darkly satirical and pessimistic survey of Spanish church and society shortly after 1550 can reasonably be
thought of as the expression of disillusionment by someone who once
believed in the possibility of change but has seen it fade into bitterness.
Such writers would plausibly have been born and educated around the
turn of the sixteenth century, and that, it turns out, is the moment in Spanish history when the class of writings represented by the *Pastor Bonus*
began its development. The betrayal of the ideals of that time, perhaps
even more than those of the years surrounding the appearance of the
novel, might well be what is protested in the work.

The second difference from the preceding study in this area is one of
purpose. Whereas Cruz writes that she has striven to "foreground the
pressing questions of poverty, delinquency, vagrancy, and prostitution
embedded in the novels,"[6] what we have attempted centers more on literary history. In comparing Maldonado's open letter with works like it
we have found that they can take the form of a dramatized, first-person
and sometimes even epistolary narrative that expresses outrage and a
call for social reform — all of which together foreshadows what will
appear twenty years later in the *Lazarillo*. In addition, it is clear that this
was a permeable proto-literary form well suited to incorporating the
classical genres that Erasmus and other humanists had recently revived,
often with similar reforming purposes. In short, it appears to have been
a malleable sub-genre whose evolution could plausibly have contributed
to the invention of the picaresque. And finally, the discovery of historical roots for the famously sardonic literary genre in writings that focus
on failures by bishops to meet their responsibilities — responsibilities
which Spanish reformers defined as caring for the material suffering of
the poor while simultaneously improving their moral character — provides an unexpected origin for the author's markedly ambiguous
attitude toward the novel's protagonist, his tone that melds pity with
condemnation.

[6] *Ibid.*

From Pastoral Ideal to Ironic Denunciation

Many sorts of writing have been considered as possible raw materials for the first picaresque novel,[7] and most recently David Gitliz has shown the relevance of letters of self-justification written by those under investigation by the Inquisition.[8] The related but little studied writings addressed to Spanish bishops naturally share some of the self-serving character of those letters to the Inquisition when written by subordinates in the ecclesiastical hierarchy. Just as logically they feature a sweeping analysis of church and social problems, which is fundamental to the *Lazarillo* and its literary descendants.[9] Maldonado was only one of many sixteenth-century Spanish authors who dedicated treatises, or parts of larger works, to describing qualities necessary in good bishops and the current forms of corruption they were called to confront. Certain writings by Erasmus criticizing the church were also, of course, influential in Spain in the first half of the sixteenth century, but we shall see that the channeling of reform efforts through bishops was a specifically Spanish ideal tied to the strategies of national consolidation during the reign of Ferdinand and Isabel.

Francisco de Vitoria, Santo Tomás de Villanueva, Juan Bernal Díaz de Luco, Luis de Granada and others contributed to this body of literature in Spain — not unrelated to Santa Teresa de Avila's austerity reforms among Carmelite nuns. In all of these there is, to one extent or another, a shift from stressing utopian planning to emphasizing the ethical abuses the new program urgently needed to address. As a result the *Pastor Bonus* — and its points of contact with the picaresque — are best read in this context. As the 1991 edition of Bataillon's *Erasme et l'Espagne* puts it, "Pour apprécier l'idéal qu'il lui propose, le replacer dans l'ensemble étudié par José Ignacio Tellechea."[10] Tellechea's work, the only one that provides a detailed comparison of several writers on the subject, is certainly the starting point, but it suffers from the limitations one would

---

[7] See Dunn 1988, and Lázaro Carreter 1972.

[8] Gitlitz 2000.

[9] This element in Spanish literary works did not, of course, begin with the invention of the picaresque, or even with the great popularity of Erasmus' works there beginning in the 1520's. In reference to Juan de Lucena's 1483 work entitled *Vita beata*, when the Spanish church had already begun to attempt self-reform, Bataillon describes it as an example of a pronounced Spanish taste for more-or-less satiric parades of the various human conditions, a genre that would flourish in the sixteenth century. Clearly it was a tendency in Erasmus' work that Spaniards found congenial. See Bataillon 2002, p. 50.

[10] Bataillon 1991, p. 113.

expect from its publication at Rome by the Spanish National Church in 1963. And it approaches this body of writings not for its literary value, but primarily as moral teachings that show the Spanish church's capacity for self-improvement. Fortunately we can also draw on a post-Franco study that is much broader in its perspective and firmly based on the findings of economic, political and demographic history. It is Tarsicio de Azcona's "La Elección y reforma del episcopado español en tiempo de los Reyes Católicos y de Carlos V (1475-1558)," published in 1980.[11] While not hostile to the Spanish church, it is nuanced and forthright in its analysis of the causes and extent of the problems of the time, as well as of the efforts made to correct them.

In selecting a few representative writers to be characterized briefly here, we have modified Tellechea's survey, omitting works from the second half of the sixteenth century, and adding others closely tied in subject matter but cast in a more literary mold. In attempting an evaluation of possible links to the picaresque tradition we have limited ourselves to the *Lazarillo*. It is the novel in that genre closest in time to the *Pastor Bonus,* it establishes the fundamentals for the works that follow it a half-century later, and we perceive it as the closest in form and content. For these reasons we have chosen to delineate parallels between the scoundrels Maldonado and his contemporary reformers bring to life and the proto-*pícaros* themselves, Lázaro de Tormes and his masters.

While the Protestant and Erasmian criticisms of the pursuit of power and pleasure among Renaissance prelates are well known, the Spanish church was especially prone to involvement in politics as a result of the powers bestowed upon it throughout the Middle Ages by Spanish monarchs. Apart from the military-religious orders, which had powerful feudal holdings in Spain as elsewhere in Europe, it played a Christianizing and administrative role in the lands that were gradually reconquered. It became not only rich and powerful, but a competing system of legal jurisdiction. The list of resources controlled by many Spanish bishops is impressive: territorial possessions, including cities, towns, and fortresses, as well as the people who lived in them and their agricultural produce; taxes, custom duties and tithes, payable in both kind and money; and legal proceeds, including fines and the concession of positions as judges, notaries, constables and others. Spanish bishops were often feudal lords. The richest bishopric was Toledo, the seat of the national church. Next

---

[11] Azcona 1980.

stood Santiago de Compostela. Far behind these came others in Galicia and Castile, including Burgos.[12]

Naturally Fernando and Isabel, intent on establishing a centralist administration, wanted to recover this power and this source of income vested in ecclesiastical hands. Just as the French crown sought during much of the sixteenth century to control the appointment of bishops in their territory, the Catholic Monarchs entered into a diplomatic campaign against the Vatican to secure the right to appoint all new Spanish bishops, with the idea that the latter would be loyal to them instead of Rome. In the years following their death it was a cause whose importance Carlos V fully grasped and vigorously pursued. His persistence and imperial power were rewarded in 1523 with a bull from Pope Adrian VI conceding to the kings of Spain the right to name the heads of metropolitan churches, cathedrals and consistorial monasteries.[13] This victory, which had been sought to assure loyalty to the crown and increase revenues from within each bishopric, was increasingly effective with time and became a major political tool of the emperor.

Such a move limiting the traditional prerogatives of the church did not, of course, remain unopposed. It needed ideological bolstering, but almost all potential theorists were found within the church itself. Fortunately for the crown, there was in the country a group of ecclesiastical writers who were dissatisfied with Rome's pursuit of material splendour based on entrenched privilege — austere reformers like the Salamancan professor, writer and preacher Alfonso de Madrigal, or the royal advisor Fernando de Talavera. Such clergymen were not as rare as has sometimes been supposed, and the changes they wanted were repeatedly endorsed by church councils in Spain, notably at Aranda del Duero in 1473 and Seville in 1482.[14] These reformers saw the opportunity to increase the clergy's commitment to spirituality — and through the clergy that of all the faithful — by forming an alliance with the monarchs. Isabel, of course, was sympathetic to them by religious temperament as well as for reasons of state.

These advisors then urged the crown to use their new power of appointment to name only reformist candidates to the episcopate, and early in the reign four basic requirements were laid down. Bishops had to be natives

---

[12] Azcona 1980, p. 121.
[13] Azcona 1980, p. 138.
[14] Azcona 1980, p. 169.

of the kingdom where their diocese was, demonstrate good moral character, come from the middle class, and have studied at a university.[15] Several benefits to society were thereby to be obtained. Being from the region, bishops could more easily be required to live in the diocese and so promote reform. Coming from the middle class, they would be inclined to support the power of the crown as they were bound by no aristocratic loyalties, although Carlos V often broke this rule in order to win nobles to his side. The requirement that bishops should have attended a university reflected the Renaissance confidence in study in recuperation of the biblical text and message, evidenced in the founding of the university at Alcalá de Henares and the preparation there of the magnificent Polyglot Bible by Diego López de Zúñiga (Stunica) and others, under the direction of the cardinal primate of Spain, Francisco Ximenes de Cisneros.[16] Better educated bishops would in turn choose a clergy better prepared to teach a purified Christianty, one closer to the Gospel message.

But the central requirement for being a bishop, of course, was a good moral character. This was felt to be the surest hope for the future since the head of each diocese would hold up to others a new moral paradigm. Azcona stresses this repeatedly: "En la mente de los Reyes Católicos, este criterio transcendía, con mucho, a la simple moralidad y a la observancia del celibato. Lo habían situado en los cimientos de la reforma vivificante del episcopado por un imperativo de ejemplaridad para el pueblo cristiano."[17] The prominence of the idea is confirmed by the crown laying down the same four standards for all priests who would be ordained.[18]

To this central idea another was added when treatises elaborated on the thinking behind these requirements. In light of the foundational role the reformers of the time gave to the biblical text, it was naturally from there that the rhetorical image used to represent all the desired changes — as though consensed within a single emblem — should come. Although literary critics have not taken into account this branch of church literature in studies of *libros de pastores*,[19] invariably the treatise writers centered on Jesus' words to Peter, the original bishop, commanding him to feed

---

[15] Azcona 1980, pp. 153-159.
[16] On this Polyglot Bible, printed in 1514 (ahead of Erasmus' ground-breaking 1516 edition of the New Testament) but not distributed (i.e. published) until 1522, see Metzger-Ehrman 2005, pp. 138-142.
[17] Azcona 1980, p. 155.
[18] Azcona 1980, pp. 170-175.
[19] López Estrada 1974, p. 13.

his sheep if he loves him.[20] That metaphor soon became axiomatic, and each writer deduced from his own perspective the ethical consequences for Christian leaders. All speak in terms of adherence to moral principles and the accountability of bishops before God for their success or failure in helping and improving the Christians given into their charge. Most, though, go into practical detail about the specific episcopal duties and problems prominent in the sixteenth century.

So that bishops might be convinced to use their authority to bring about real change, evidence of the nature and extent of abuses had to be convincingly presented. Vivid examples naturally flowed from the author's own experiences, especially since the writers, as members of the church, would have seen at first hand many of the abuses addressed. In this way a first-person perspective within what began as an exposition of general precepts evolved. In addition, the writers' position as insiders tended to create the self-serving quality apparent in Lazarillo's portrait of the church and his relationship to it. Any clergyman exposing corruption in the church would — whether to protect himself or out of a genuine sense of moral superiority — be strongly inclined to make himself look better than those around him, as well as to put the blame for any of his own shortcomings on the pressures inherent in a bad system.

Thus a vivid, first-person and epistolary literature of social reporting, but with the characteristic picaresque emphasis on all that is wrong with everyone else, could develop among indignant inside observers. The next step toward the picaresque — plausible if a need to vent pent-up outrage is postulated — would have taken place when a writer felt relatively powerless in the face of vested interests and ossified institutional habits. From a position within a hierarchy weighing down upon him, unable to speak out directly without danger of punishment, he might well abandon the hope of effecting change and so resort to ironic, veiled expressions of dissent.

Such may have been — as we shall see — the inner history, the evolution, of this group of writings toward a shape like that of the picaresque novel. But there were also extrinsic factors that came into play. Just as the political circumstances surrounding the unification of the nation

---

[20] John 21:15-17. Due to the metaphor's prominence in the Gospel, it had also been used at times by Spanish writers in the Middle Ages and early Renaissance. Juan de Mena, for example, wrote against the church abandoning the sheep in order to enjoy a luxurious style of life. See Azcona 1980, p. 168.

created this typically Spanish branch of ecclesiastical and social theory, so the social consequences set in motion by Fernando and Isabel would turn it toward imaginative literature and irony. In essence, the promising commitment to reform was thwarted by emerging interests in the Spanish church and crown. As the century advances one finds examples of writings that, indeed, contain recommendations for bishops, but now combined with a tone that waffles between outrage and despair. The prime example, as mentioned above, is the *Pastor Bonus*, but another is Díaz de Luco's *Instrucción para perlados*, written the same year. We shall look at it more closely below.

Their date is significant. In late 1529 and in 1530, the first generation of reformers, though they had cause for some disillusionment, had not yet become thoroughly embittered. True, two of the three decisive victories for reactionaries in the early years of the 16th century, all of which had been criticized in writing by Maldonado, had already taken place. Following the expulsion of the Jews in 1492 a systematic and far-reaching discrimination against *conversos* had firmly entrenched itself, often even denying entrance to the priesthood to those of known Jewish descent, while the Commoners' Revolution by the mercantile cities of Castile against the emperor had been put down with bloody repression.[21]

The third defeat for reformers was the end of high-ranking support for the ideas of Erasmus. In the mid-1520's, as Bataillon has reiterated, "comienzan a agruparse en torno al nombre de Erasmo todas las fuerzas locales de renovación intelectual y religiosa....Esa influencia de Erasmo había de sumarse a otras corrientes de erasmismo brotadas de manera más oscura de los centros de la vida eclesiástica e intelectual.... El evangelismo español..., en la medida en que depende de fuentes extranjeras, toma su alimento casi exclusivamente de Erasmo. En todo caso, lo adopta como guía, como si su mezcla de osadía y de prudencia, de ironía y de fervor, le cuadrase perfectamente."[22] After such a hopeful turn of events, the wave of official condemnation of Erasmian ideas that took place in the 1530's made almost inevitable an atmosphere of growing frustration

---

[21] The victory over the local interests of the mercantile class by an aristocracy allied with a northern European emperor was in some ways a step toward a more international, less xenophobic Spanish worldview, especially as Erasmus was highly respected at court and an official advisor to Charles V. However, that was not the position taken by most of the country's humanists, as shown by the strong support for the rebels among the faculty at the new university at Alcalá de Henares. See Bataillon 2002, pp. 155-157.

[22] Bataillon 2002, pp. 155, 158, 162.

and a retreat into silence or irony, at least among reformers targeted for hostility by their connection to the social groups affected.[23]

From such disillusioned writers one would also expect an appeal to a different audience. Writing from a position of alienation from the church, the author's appeal for justice would logically turn from the ecclesiastical hierarchy to a broader group of readers less compromised by their vested interests. To reach that audience the vernacular might logically have been used, enhanced by the emotional force of imaginative literature, just as the Erasmians had done. Under this latter influence, models from Classical literature could easily have been adopted (e.g., Apuleius's *The Golden Ass*), models which offered the ingredients of social critique and first-person narrative that also characterize the tradition of reform proposals for bishops. Indeed, such a hypothesis regarding the sort of literary outlet available at the time for the feelings of disaffected humanists concerned with church reform is lent support by the fact that just prior to the conclusive defeat of Spanish Erasmianism at the end of the 1550's, and the stepped-up censorship that went with it, we find the publication in Spanish of two satiric works — *Lazarillo de Tormes* and *Las cortes de la muerte* — that both show the typically Spanish stress on the great moral responsibility of the clergy at all levels and a sweeping analysis of church and social problems.

It is precisely here that the origin of writings for and about bishops illuminates the tension in the author's attitude toward his protagonist. While Erasmus rebuked the church for its failure to carry out the apostolic ideal as it appears in the Bible, we have seen that in Spain a national ideal had foregrounded the things to be accomplished by Spanish bishops and priests for the material and spiritual benefit of lay men and women. In articulating the similarities and differences between the two movements Azcona writes, "fue en la línea de escritores nativos donde fue mandando una encrestada teoría sobre la figura y el quehacer episcopal."[24] Since the time of the Catholic Monarchs all who cared about moral

---

[23] Naturally there were some reformers who did not lose hope or fall into irony, keeping alive the debate about what should be done regarding the increasing numbers of the destitute and homeless. In the 1540's Domingo de Soto and Juan de Robles argued about the extent to which collection of alms for the poor should be secularized, and the earlier theme of "Feed my Sheep" as the church's mission was still alive with some writers. Francisco de Osuna, for example, urged the council of the Franciscan order to divide its monies among the poor and to view charity as its major expense. See Cruz 1999, p. 28.

[24] See Azcona 1980, p. 162.

reform had looked to the church hierarchy, and to bishops, to work for
the two goals mentioned above — to feed and care for the poor, and to
teach moral improvement through personal example. The seeming split
in the *Lazarillo* comes from it being the story of the church establishment
failing to live up to those two specific ideals. Reduced to its core, the
novel recounts how the young protagonist suffers starvation and corruption.

True, the vices that Lázaro has absorbed from his masters condemn
both the shepherds and the sheep. From the theological perspective of
the time, the boy, and later the young man, has failed to exercise his free
will to resist evil and so assumes part of the responsibility for his situation, though he attempts to conceal that in his narrative. For these shortcomings the author establishes parallels between Lázaro and the hypocritical stoics whom Lorenzo Valla and Erasmus had portrayed in colloquies
as being self-indulgent and self-excusing pleasure-seekers in disguise.[25]

Other suggestions, from the realm of social psychology, about why the
author and the original audience of the novel would have felt a measure
of hostility to the protagonist have been proposed by Cruz.[26] In essence,
he could have been perceived as part of the growing and menacing masses
of the poor, who had become linked in the popular mind with the period's
rise in crime. Cruz also sees a pragmatic duplicity on the part of the
authors of picaresque literature in that they both criticize society's faults
but cater to the prejudices of the establishment by using an ironic discourse that permits placing the blame on the poor themselves.[27] While this
seems true in the later novels, the earlier ideological context surrounding
the responsibilities of bishops softens this charge against the author of the
Lazarillo. From the perspective of the Spanish church's well publicized
mission-statement in the first half of the sixteenth century, a condemnation of the poor is primarily a condemnation of inauthentic priests who
have allowed the poor to become corrupt through the hardships they
endure and the poor examples they are given.

But in spite of the ambiguity toward Lazarillo by his creator, the spread
of hypocrisy and greed to the young clearly expresses a terrible disillusionment. The generation of moralists into which the author of the
Lazarillo was probably born, enouraged by a parallel call for change from

---

[25] See Colahan 2001, pp. 556-557.
[26] See Cruz 1999, pp. xiii-xv, 5-10.
[27] See Cruz 1999, p. 15.

reformers across Europe, must have felt with exceptional intensity that it had seen the collapse of the moral ideals of its formative years. Such are the historical roots that confirm Lázaro Carreter's insight that the author of the *Lazarillo*, having given up hope of reform, hands himself over to writing sarcasm.[28] We can add that they also shed light on why the particular form of sarcasm that defines the picaresque was invented in Spain.

Vitoria

Within a group of writings, then, which originally consisted of optimistically reasoned social criticism, there is a didactic pole and another more characterized by protest and the urgency of reform. We shall begin with the former. Tellechea, eager to show that the abuses of the sixteenth-century Spanish church were not ignored by perceptive and responsible ecclesiastics, presents Vitoria (1486-1546) as a reformer embued with ideas received not only in France, but also in the heart of Castille: "Vitoria se crió en el fervor reformista del París de los Colegios de Santiago y Montaigu, vivió el espíritu de sus conventos de Burgos y Valladolid, y sobre todo se alimentó del fervor extraordinario del convento de San Esteban de Salamanca."[29] Although the theorist includes a section on the status of bishops ("De his quae pertinent ad statum episcoporum"),[30] his comments are structured not as narrative but as tightly reasoned, prescriptive observations on abstract topics, such as the virtues and the vices.

Vitoria's advice to bishops principally comes in the form of positive duties, as can be seen in the list of fundamental episcopal responsibilities Tellechea has culled from the work's more general ethical concerns: "Orare et docere," 'To pray and to teach;' "Et incumbit ex officio praedicare," 'And he is obligated by his office to preach;' "Animam ponere pro ouibus... [et] ponere bona temporalia;" 'To lay down his life for the sheep... [and] give his worldly goods;' "Ipse pascere per se," 'He himself should feed the sheep personally;' "Oportet quod pastor cognoscat oues suas," 'It is important that the shepherd know his sheep;' "Officium episcopi exigit multa et doctrinam et administrationem sacramentorum et sacramentalium et consecrare ecclesiam, et ordinare," 'The office of

---

[28] See Lázaro Carreter 1972, p. 130.
[29] Tellechea Idigoras 1963, p. 71.
[30] Vitoria 1932-1952.

bishop demands many things: the knowledge of doctrine and the administration of the sacraments and sacramental things, the consecration of
churches and ordination (of clergy);' "Praesit in sollicitudine... consolari... sanare, alligare... redimere... custodire... reducere... promouere,"
'He should take the lead in showing concern, comforting, healing, bind-
ing up wounds, ransoming, protecting, leading sheep back into the flock
and advancing it.'[31]

The underlying, albeit inverted, logic linking the whole subject with the
beginnings of the picaresque can be seen in Vitoria's stress on the duty
of bishops to give everything for their flock, as it is the exact opposite
behavior that defines the clerics in the *Lazarillo*. Joseph Ricapito points
out the same idealization of the clergy in contrast to picaresque realism
in the work of the humanist pedagogue Juan Luis Vives (1492-1540). As
Ricapito writes, "Rather than noting the real aspects of the clergy, Vives
regards them in an ideal role... His desire to project an ideal role for the
clergy derives from their less-than-ideal conduct."[32] Similarly Vitoria
brings out the responsibility for appointing worthy candidates to ecclesiastical positions,[33] an idea found in all these treatises and that bulks large
in the novel by the marked presence of its opposite.

The negative examples that would take the reader from preaching to
picaresque are relatively sparse, in spite of Tellechea's description of
Vitoria's tone in terms of "[el] calor de lo concreto y existencial [que]
anima sus lecciones, así como el tono casi picaresco de sus ejemplos en
castellano que van salpicando sus explicaciones latinas."[34] Still, the brief
interpolations in Spanish are windows onto contemporary social practices. For example, in the section on simony, Vitoria writes that priests
may not accept payment directly for administering the sacraments, but
they may be reimbursed for their travel expenses: "A mí por camino de
un día, aunque no fuese a veros, sino por vuestro placer, y no a confe-
saros o administraros otro sacramento, me daríais, pongo por caso, el
gasto de tres o cuatro reales."[35] Furthermore, priests should not charge
significant fees for reading to others: "Et sic parum deberent dare por leer
una hora, quia ipse labor in se nihil valet; et tamen danle por una hora

---

[31] Tellechea 1963, p. 80. All translations are ours unless otherwise indicated.
[32] J. Ricapito 1997, 24-40, p. 29.
[33] Tellechea 1963, p. 96.
[34] Tellechea 1963, p. 70.
[35] Vitoria 1932-1952, vol. 5, p. 122.

que lee dos ducados, y tres ducados."[36] Vitoria also writes, "Ego uolo, v.g., commutare canonicatum ualentem quatuor millia ducatorum pro curato ualente duo millia ducatorum. An liceat dare aliquid temporale, scilicet mille ducatos in tali commutatione pro recompensa, por lo que vale más el canonicato que el curado."[37] Similarly, "Possum ego facere istam donationem: yo dejo a los canónigos de la iglesia mayor diez mil maravedís cada un año para que me digan una missa cantada cada año."[38] While the pieces of text in Spanish are usually less than a complete sentence, they point to the popular flavor, and the possibilities for abuse, that later blossom in the picaresque. The division of Vitoria's work into treatises may, in addition, help explain the ironic designation of the chapters in the *Lazarillo* as *tratados*.[39]

Santo Tomás de Villanueva

Well known as an excellent preacher throughout Castile, Santo Tomás de Villanueva (1486-1555) also made recommendations for bishops. His character lends support to the idea that the reformers who wrote on this topic were often as energetic in their pursuit of virtue as they were in the denunciation of vice. According to Antonio Cañizares Llovera, "Socorrió con inagotable caridad a toda clase de menesterosos; recogió y sostuvo en la vida a centenares de huérfanos o abandonados; libró de la ruina a muchas jóvenes en peligro de perderse."[40] Yet he takes us a step closer to the picaresque in that his advice often comes in the form of criticism of ecclesiastical corruption. Llovera finds "una cantidad enorme de paralelismos con Erasmo" in his study of the saint's writings.[41]

Of special concern to Santo Tomás was the increasing worldliness of priests: "Los religiosos y los clérigos, que deberían estar ante Dios orando por el pueblo, se han hecho seculares y negociadores."[42] Rather than passing time in the plazas and visiting women, Santo Tomás recommends a

---

[36] Vitoria 1932-1952, vol. 5, p. 101.
[37] Vitoria 1932-1952, vol. 5, p. 117.
[38] Vitoria 1932-1952, vol. 5, p. 131.
[39] See Colahan-Rodriguez 2000.
[40] Cañizares Llovera 1973, p. 22.
[41] Cañizares Llovera 1973, p. 64.
[42] Cañizares Llovera 1973. p. 41.

more solitary religious life: "Para la pureza de corazón y la contemplación son necesarias la soledad, el silencio y la paz, que no están en el foro, sino en el monasterio."[43] Furthermore, the saint points to the moral failure of those who become priests for selfish reasons, only to satisfy their appetite "por el pan."[44] This image, although it goes back to the New Testament, reminds us that Lazarillo's struggle for bread in the first three tratados, when read on the level of metaphor, is only ambiguously innocent, coming from a church tradition in which the desires of the belly stand for materialism.

As a result of such abuses by religious leaders, Spanish society "abunda en tantos vicios y males."[45] In line with the Spanish emphasis on the clergy setting an uplifting example, he stresses that social corruption results from immoral priests: "Ciertamente es terrible que nosotros, que debemos ser luz en el pueblo para mostrar el camino de la salvación, ofrezcamos las ocasiones para pecar. Si los hermanos y los clérigos fuesen tales cuales deberíamos, ¡cómo nos respetarían los pecadores y temerían! Pero si yo, que soy monje, no hago otra cosa que visitar mujerzuelas y pasarme todo el día hablando con ellas, si el clérigo camina vestido de seda y con sonajeros femeninos, ¿no será escandalizado el pueblo? Si el clérigo se ocupa en gran grado en reverencias a las mujeres, ¿el mundano qué hará? Si continuamente se dedica a los juegos, si sigue las litigiosas fraudulencias, si publica y libremente actúa como un villano, qué hará el del mundo? De ahí que cada día la vida pública va corriendo hacia situaciones peores y al final perezca."[46]

In Llovera's view, the saint maintains in his sermons a realistic rather than a pessimistic attitude, "esperanzado y operante."[47] As a model for others, Santo Tomás mentions "los obispos de San Martín [quienes] no gastaban dinero en caballos, en mulos, en palacios, en vestidos, como hacen nuestros pontífices, sino en los pobres, en hospitales para los pobres."[48] Here one must bear in mind the impact on the message of the medium: sermons. In comparison with a novel, designed primarily to be read alone and with time for reflections of various sorts, a sermon is designed to be immediately uplifting, stressing positive statements and

---

[43] Cañizares Llovera 1973, p. 42.
[44] Cañizares Llovera 1973, p. 60.
[45] Cited in Cañizares Llovera 1973, p. 42.
[46] Cited in Cañizares Llovera 1973, p. 42.
[47] Cañizares Llovera 1973, p. 64.
[48] Cañnizares Llovera 1973, p. 62.

examples to be followed. A picaresque sermon, designed to elicit not a clear course of virtuous action but a knowing laugh with sobering undertones, would be a contradiction in terms. Santo Tomás, like Vitoria, could not overlook the prevalent corruption of the time, but he had enough faith in the institutions of the church to channel his observations through them.

Erasmus

As commented above, several works by Erasmus were for a few years highly influential in early sixteenth-century Spain.[49] In the *Paraenesis ad Litteras* which Maldonado wrote for the young Guterius Cardenatus in 1529 (and which is mentioned in the *Pastor Bonus,* e 1 v) Maldonado sets forth a curriculum of recommended Latin authors which includes a prominent section on Erasmus, recommending in particular the reading of *De copia, De conscribendis Epistolis,* and the *Encomium Moriae.* In outlining a curriculum of acceptable Latin authors, Maldonado includes Erasmus along with Quintilian and Cicero as an authority on the writing and speaking of Latin, and exclaims, "He is certainly a man skilled in both languages and most diligent and extremely happy in his restoration of Latin letters," while his commentaries on scripture benefit not only theologians, but the entire Christian population.[50] Although Erasmus did not systematically focus his thought on defining bishops' duties and is justly famous as a passionate critic of corruption in the church,[51] he did hold up an episcopal ideal in statements scattered throughout his lesser-known works. Like other writers on the subject he affirms that a model bishop, following the example of Christ's absolute love for his flock, should demonstrate a scorn for worldly honors, for riches, and for the priorities of the flesh, a scorn that is "absolutae caritatis certissimum argumentum," 'a most definite verification of his unbounded love,'" and at the same time the necessary spiritual condition for doing the apostolic work.[52]

---

[49] Bataillon 2002, p. 773.

[50] See Asensio and Rovira in Maldonado 1980; the quotations regarding the importance of Erasmus are in section 23, pp. 114-115.

[51] For a summary of the major points of contact that have been noted between his work and the *Lazarillo*, and of the criticism on the subject, see F. Márquez Villanueva's chapter on Erasmus in his 1968 work and Ricapito's introduction and notes to *La vida de Lazarillo de Tormes* (Ricapito 1976).

[52] Erasmus' *Paraphrase on John* in Erasmus 1991, p. 224.

In his paraphrase of John 10.1-18, a Biblical passage frequently used by Maldonado in the *Pastor Bonus*, Erasmus writes: "You must beware of one who does not believe in me and yet makes himself out to be a shepherd of the people...But if the voice is not a clear enough proof, watch what they do. A thief comes for no other purpose than to steal, and to get a dishonest profit for himself from the misfortunes of a flock not his own." In the Paraphrase on John 21 Erasmus adds, "...he was well aware that some would arise who not out of love for Jesus but for the sake of their personal advantage would undertake the care of the Christian people — or rather would snatch it up, for they would be tyrants and thieves rather than shepherds."[53] For Erasmus, Saint Augustine personifies the ideal bishop and his necessary virtues, including seriousness, vigilance, activity, zeal, and chastity, "praecipuum espiscoporum decus et ornamentum," 'which is most seemly and attractive in bishops,' poverty, charity, the living example of his life, teaching and preaching, "quae potissimum functio praesulum est," 'which most certainly are part of a bishop's duties,' and the gentle compassion of a father.[54]

Erasmus stresses that bishops should appoint good ministers. Nonetheless, like his contemporaries writing on the subject, he emphasizes a bishop's responsibility to do, as far as possible, his pastoral work personally instead of delegating the tasks to others, who may prove unsuitable: "Ceterum docere populum, hortari, consolari, monere, redarguere, proxima maximeque splendida est Episcoporum functio quam nunc multi libenter cedunt aliis quamlibet sordidis," 'What's more, bishops' first and most splendid duty is to teach the people, encouraging, comforting, warning and reprimanding them, a duty that now many bishops hand over to persons of exceedingly sordid character.'[55]

But in spite of these instructive precepts, Erasmus devotes much more space and energy to his famous anger at immoral prelates. In the *Adagia*, especially in the popular section called *Sileni Alcibiadis* that was later reprinted separately, the primary admonition for bishops is the same as for members of other social groups: to be inwardly what one claims to be in the world. Above all, the common participation of bishops in making money and war is denounced as the opposite behavior of what should be found in Christ's representatives. The church as an institution is

---

[53] Erasmus 1991 pp. 131, 224.
[54] Letter to Fonseca in May of 1529, cited in Tellechea 1963, p. 36.
[55] *Novum Testamentum,* commentary on I Timothy III, 8; cited in Tellechea 1963, p. 32.

corrupt from top to bottom, with the best dioceses going to the most materialistic clergy instead of the few who are spiritual, while a concern for the externals of worship is rewarded.

Ecclesiastical problems receive even more detailed attention in the famous *Moriae Encomium*, but again it comes in the form of condemnation and satire directed against all levels in the church hierarchy, not as supportive recommendations to them. Bishops are roasted, but so are theologians, monks, friars, preachers, popes and cardinals. The sweeping nature of the condemnation can be illustrated by his description of the church's avoidance of its true saving work: "Itidem pontifices in messe pecuniaria diligentissimi, labores illos nimium apostolicos, in episcopos relegant, episcopi in pastores, pastores in uicarios, uicarii in fratres mendicantes. Hi rursum in eos retrudunt, a quibus ouium lana tondetur,"[56] 'In the same way those popes who are busiest getting in the money harvest delegate their properly apostolic labors to the bishops, the bishops to the priests, the priests to their vicars, the vicars to the mendicant friars, who finally pass the job along to those who will be shearing the sheep."[57] The last group mentioned in the chain seems to be an ironic reference to the selfish labors of the unscrupulous ecclesiastical tax farmers, whose shearing of the flock also looms large in Maldonado's *Pastor Bonus*. The image of the bishop as a shepherd occurs elsewhere in the *Moriae Encomium,* and again in a tone of reproach for dereliction of duty:"Quid pedum, nimirum, crediti gregis uigilantissimam curam... At nunc belle faciunt, cum sese pascunt. Ceterum ouium curam aut ipsi Christo mandant, aut in fratres quos uocant ac uicarios reiiciunt. Neque uel nominis sui recordantur, quid sonet Episcopi uocabulum, nempe laborem, curam, sollicitudinem."[58] 'Why does he carry a crozier, if not to take vigilant care of the flock entrusted to him?... But now they're perfectly content, as long as they've pastured themselves. As for watching over the flock, they either let Christ take care of that chore or put it off on curates and the 'Brethren,'as they call them. They never even think of the meaning of their title 'Bishop,' which means 'overseer,' and implies work, caring, taking pains."[59] The importance of the work involved in caring for the

---

[56] Erasmus 1980, p. 33.

[57] Erasmus 1989, p. 73.

[58] Erasmus 1980, p. 31.

[59] Erasmus 1989, pp. 68-69. We have slightly modified the wording to preserve the pastoral imagery of the original Latin.

sheep, and the protest that it goes undone, will also reappear in Maldonado, as will Erasmus' emphasis that the corrupt bishops are more interested in milking profits out of their flock than in protecting them.

Like Santo Tomás, Erasmus dwells on the primary responsibility of a shepherd to provide food, condemning self-serving and worldly bishops who neglect to feed their sheep in order to pursue personal pleasures: "Quem igitur Paradisum sibi promittunt isti qui multorum ouilium suscepta cura, quatuor aut quinque Episcopatibus onusti, ne cogitant quidem de pascendo, sed pro pastoribus agunt depastores, ac de prouentu ouium erigunt Satraparum palatia, apparant quotidie mensas siculas," 'Therefore that sort of bishops, who have taken on the care of many flocks and are laden with four or five bishoprics, promise themselves Paradise but give no thought at all to feeding the sheep. Instead of acting as shepherds they themselves gobble up the pasture, and with what the sheep produce build palaces fit for satraps, and daily set Sicilian tables.'[60]

Though not as loudly or as often, Erasmus also sounds the note, which we have seen in Spanish writers, that calls ecclesiastical corruption the source of unchecked social disease. He notes ironically in his commentary on Romans that some Bishops sign their title as *uocatus Episcopus*, "called a Bishop," as though tacitly acknowledging that they are bishop in name rather than in fact, and that they wrongly claim authority on the strength of their mitres, staffs, and robes rather than their good deeds.[61] He denounces the foremost clergy and laity as having become equally immoral: "At hodie haud scio an ullum hominum genus magis seruiat omnibus affectibus, siue prophanos spectes Principes, siue sacros," 'But today I can't tell at all whether any group of people is more enslaved by their passions, whether you look at the secular princes or those of the church."[62] And he adds that the materialism of God's ministers, who have "cutem unctam, mentem inunctam," 'their palms greased and their minds bone dry,' affects the poor — as the plight of the young Lazarillo might well illustrate — like a divine punishment.[63]

In such a fetid atmosphere, talent strives for distinction in all that is wrong instead of all that is right. One is reminded of the sort of inverted

---

[60] *Ecclesiastes, sive De ratione concionandi* (Le Clerc edition V.802.C) cited in Tellechea 1963, p. 22.

[61] Erasmus 1995, pp. 5, 408.

[62] *Novum Testamentum*, commentary on Titus II, 23: cited in Tellechea 1963, pp. 21-22.

[63] *Enarrationes in Psalmos*, Ps. 2; cited in Tellechea 1963, p. 26.

honor prevalent in contemporary Spanish society — as revealed through the irony of the *Lazarillo* — and the kind of "cumbre de toda buena fortuna" toward which bright young men strive: "Ille demum pessimus sit oportet, qui cum plurimum prodesse possit, si bonus sit, summo omnium malo malus est…Tantum autem est in his (de malis loquor) ambitionis, tantum auaritiae, tantum stultitiae, tantum impietatis, ut qui magistri pietatis esse debuerunt, apud hos paene sit haereticus qui pure studeat esse christianus," 'In short, he who, if he were good, could be the most useful to society, is practically required to be the worst, and so is bad with the worst sort of evil… In these (and I am speaking of the bad ones) there is so much overreaching ambition, so much greed, so much stupidity, so much immorality, that among those who should be teachers of religious devotion there is scarcely any heretic who strives sincerely to be a Christian.'[64]

Tellechea sums up the view of society communicated by Erasmus in his reformer's admonitions for bishops as "sombría y pesimista,"[65] a phrase that matches the aptly-called "worm's-eye view of the world" frequently said to be typical of the picaresque.

Díaz de Luco

With Juan Díaz de Luco we come to the next generation of reformers and a work focused entirely on bishops and the sorts of social corruption they face. His *Libro de instrucción para los perlados* (1530) is, as we shall see, the closest in form and content to the exactly contemporaneous *Pastor Bonus*, and in addition offers a number of parallels to the *Lazarillo*. Díaz de Luco feels there is a dire state of affairs, asking that his readers — especially Francisco de Mendoza, bishop of Zamora, to whom he addresses his thoughts — "desculpen mi ignorancia y atreuimiento con la necessidad que la fee y experiencia les obliga a confessar que ay en estos tiempos de escreuir semejantes cosas."[66] Reflecting the Erasmian idea of the presence of an inversion of values in the society of the time, he writes "en nuestros tristes y peligrosos tiempos no sabe [la costumbre] sino derogar lo bueno e introducir lo malo."[67]

---

[64] *Ecclesiastes, sive De ratione concionandi*; cited in Tellechea 1963, p. 26.
[65] See Tellechea 1963 p. 26.
[66] Díaz de Luco 1530, p. v verso.
[67] Díaz de Luco 1530, p. xiii.

According to Díaz de Luco, many pastors doze instead of keeping vigil over their flocks, and he writes to sound the alarm and call for universal improvement.

Díaz de Luco emphasizes the responsibility of bishops to render an account of themselves and of their sheep on the day of judgment, again linking the specialized literature of advice to bishops to the Inquisition confessions studied by Gitlitz: "de las almas tienen obligacion de dar cuenta a Dios dellas el dia del juizio."[68] Like his contemporaries, he cites ecclesiastical corruption as the source of prevailing social ills: "suelen mucho seguir los subditos al superior, y si el mal biue, casi siempre suelen ellos biuir assi mismo mal"[69] y "de los principales desciende todo exemplo a los otros ecclesiasticos y por consiguiente a los seglares."[70] Summing up one of the central ideas of Spanish writers for bishops, Díaz de Luco observes, "Porque conoscidamente se vee que tal es el pueblo, qual es el clero,"[71] and "los perlados que viven mal son como las piedras grandes que caen de las tierras altas, que aunque al principio comenzaron a caer solas, llevan siempre muchas de las pequeñas que encuentran consigo."[72]

As the *Lazarillo* vividly demonstrates, improper education of youth leads to social corruption, and Díaz de Luco advises bishops to take "especial cuydado de enseñar a todos los niños todo lo que para ser buenos Christianos deuen saber, para que desde pequeños comiencen a amar y temer a Dios."[73] While Lazarillo expresses satisfaction at having reached the height of good fortune, the ugly truth of his situation aligns him with the many who live immorally, characterized by Díaz de Luco as follows: "Que si en estos tiempos se preguntasse a todos los hombres que viciosamente biuen y estan tan oluidados de lo que a de ser dellos perpetuamente que a sido la causa de sus malas costumbres, no ternan otra respuesta mas verdadera que dar: Saluo que la poca doctrina de virtud que tuuieron quando pequeños y mal exemplo que vieron en el mundo quando començaron a tener discrecion les ha traydo a tan vicioso estado."[74]

---

[68] Díaz de Luco 1530, p. vii.
[69] Díaz de Luco 1530, p. vi.
[70] Díaz de Luco 1530, p. xvi verso
[71] Díaz de Luco 1530, p. xvii.
[72] Díaz de Luco 1530, p. vi verso.
[73] Díaz de Luco 1530, p. xv verso.
[74] Díaz de Luco 1530, p. xv verso.

Although his examples of social corruption are less detailed and developed as anecdotes than those found in the *Pastor Bonus*, Díaz de Luco comments in some depth on a variety of ecclesiastical abuses in need of correction. For example, he rebukes bishops who jump from post to post seeking more prestigious positions as though a diocese were to be used as a servant girl instead of loved as a wife: "ay algunos que desde que comiençan a ser perlados hasta llegar a summos pontífices, o a lo menos a la mas principal dignidad del Reyno, siempre creen que las yglesias que Dios les da no son esposas sino criadas, y asi las tratan, y tienen las por medios con los quales an de alcançar las otras mayores, y ninguna por ygual para hazer vida con ella, como con legitima esposa."[75]

Díaz de Luco also remarks on church officials who take unethical advantage of their role as dispensers of sacraments who are paid by the recipients for services received, comparing them to merchants who overcharge their customers: "lleva[n] y roba[n] alguna cosa demasiada a los que a ellos vienen sin poder escusar de venir a sus manos y porque las mas vezes esto se lleva secretamente y so color que ay costumbres... suele auer muchas vezes un gran robo, y los negociantes son muy opprimidos, y como son negocios necessarios y de qualidad que no tienen libertad para escoger la tienda como en otros officios, ni pueden tener noticia todos, de lo que meresce lo que por ellos se haze, y ya que la tengan no osan ir a la mano a los officiales, danles lo que piden, teniendo por mayor el inconueniente que se siguiria en sus negocios."[76] Although nothing in the Lazarillo parallels this precisely, the image of priests as merchants recalls the cleric who sets the protagonist up in business as a water carrier, keeping much of the profits himself from traffic in a basic necessity.

One of the most detailed examples of ecclesiastical wrongdoing presented is bishops without dioceses who accept compensation for blessing religious articles that will later be sold, somewhat reminiscent of the upper-level church corruption made use of by the Lazarillo's *buldero*: "se venden en las ferias y tiendas de mercaderes calices y aras consagradas, y ornamentos y otras cosas bendezidas como otras mercaderias. Y acaece asi mismo, que los mismos que hazen calices y patenas para vender van a llenarlos a dozenas a obispos de anillo[77] que se los

---

[75] Díaz de Luco 1530, p. ix verso.
[76] Díaz de Luco 1530, p. xxi verso.
[77] "Obispos de anillo" were those who had through underhanded methods managed to have themselves ordained as bishops, although they did not have a position in a diocese. They traveled frequently, taking whatever assignments they might be given by the bishop

consagren y lleuanles dineros por ellos, y despues quando los venden ponen por precio por si lo que costo a consagrar, y lo mismo en los ornamentos y otras cosas semejantes."[78] Díaz de Luco is more specifically like the author of the picaresque novel in his moral rejection of the fraudulent sale of papal bulls, insisting that they must be approved by the appropriate authorities: "estan suspensas todas las indulgencias, facultades y questas, hasta que sean vistas por el ordinario del lugar donde se an de publicar, y por el Nuncio que por tiempo vuiere, y por el capellan mayor del Rey, y por uno o dos perlados que el Rey para ello diputare, deben tener los perlados aviso que no consientan que algunas bulas se prediquen sin que preceda esta solemnidad y examen."[79]

Bishops must also be wary of the corrupt custom of their lieutenants arranging for sweet deals for their cronies, i.e., of showing self-serving favoritism in giving out the business generated by church purchases.[80] We also see passing mention of priests "ocupados en otras cosas viles e ilicitos tratos,"[81] especially offers to say numerous masses each day for money, and new church officials who appoint their former teachers to ecclesiastical posts.[82] Finally, Díaz de Luco laments the selling of church positions for money or favors, "que las mas vezes los compran los menos habiles y personas de mala conciencia,"[83] a situation that recalls Lazarillo's "purchase" of his job of wine salesman through the archpriest of San Salvador.

Díaz de Luco's treatise is remarkable for its composition in the vernacular instead of Latin, uncommon in ecclesiastical and scholarly writing of the time, and especially when criticism of the church was involved. He explains his choice of language in terms of convenience for his readers, although one wonders if a hope for a larger audience may have been in his mind as well. Certainly there is an informal, sermonlike quality to the work that may also have influenced the decision to write in Spanish. That quality is reflected, too, in the use of the first-person and a colloquial

---

holding the local jurisdiction. They often conducted rituals such as confirmations, ordinations, and lived from the fees thereby collected. They became so common, and their activities so close to simony, that even the Spanish crown protested. See Azcona 1530, p. 122.

[78] Díaz de Luco 1530, p. xxix verso.
[79] Díaz de Luco 1530, p. xxx verso.
[80] Díaz de Luco 1530, p. xi.
[81] Díaz de Luco 1530, p. xix.
[82] Díaz de Luco 1530, p. xx verso.
[83] Díaz de Luco 1530 p. xxii.

syntax. As for the ordering of the work, although he comments on many of the same duties as Maldonado, Díaz de Luco, like Vitoria, organizes his recommendations for bishops more didactically — into clearly delineated chapters, each focusing on a single theme. A further difference is that while Maldonado relies extensively on contemporary anecdotes from life in Burgos to illustrate his points, Díaz de Luco is more orthodox in primarily referencing — and in Latin — the writings of saints and religious scholars such as St. Chrysostom, St. Gregory, and Thomas Aquinas. In part due to his clearly committed efforts to make his book readable and accessible to all, and even more because it is written — in seeming contradiction to that zeal — with only an attenuated belief in the possibility of thoroughly reforming the church's deep-rooted corruption, Márquez Villanueva appraises the book as an expression of protest: "Don Bernal da la impresión de escribir su librito mucho más como denuncia y protesta (centrada en lo que debiera ser) que no con esperanza de que resulte medio adecuado para una renovación tan radical del estado eclesiástico."[84] On the other hand, Tellechea deems Díaz de Luco's work "llena de entusiasmo y de prudente sencillez… un elemento que no lo encontramos fácilmente en autores de este tiempo."[85] That characterization, though, is overly cheerful, attributing an optimism to Díaz de Luco that his book scarcely demonstrates.

Alfonso de Valdés: A change of literary venue

The *Diálogo de Mercurio y Carón,* written by the well known secretary to Carlos V and disciple of Erasmus, has been dated between 1528 and 1530,[86] and so is also contemporaneous with Maldonado's *Pastor Bonus.* Both Valdés and Maldonado were born in the province of Cuenca about 1490. Valdés came from a converso family, Maldonado may have as well, and both corresponded admiringly with Erasmus.[87] *Mercurio y Carón,* in spite of being an Erasmian colloquy based on Lucian expressing broad

---

[84] Márquez Villanueva 1968, p. 134.

[85] Tellechea 1963 p. 50.

[86] Alfonso de Valdés 1986, Introduction, p. xv.

[87] For biographical sources on Valdés, see Ricapito's introduction to the *Dialogue of Mercury and Charon* (Valdés 1986, pp. ix-xii). For studies on Maldonado, see Colahan-Rodríguez 1995, pp. 290-291, 294, 307, n. 16.

social criticism instead of a treatise centered on bishops' problems, still contains many of the elements of the latter.

Its thematic ties to the *Lazarillo* have been thoroughly analyzed,[88] but of particular interest to the tradition we are considering — and to the *Lazarillo* — is the sarcastic condemnation of clergy who do not feed the poor. A bishop is asked, "De manera que si viniera Jesu Christo a comer contigo, ¿no lo sentaras a tu mesa porque era pobre?" The bishop replies, "No, si viniera mal vestido."[89] Similar parallels and tone are visible in the passage where a bishop asks Carón to be on the lookout for a lady named Lucrecia, of whom he remarks, "Teníala yo para mi recreación, y soi cierto que como sepa mi muert[e], luego se matará." To which Carón quips, "Calla ya, que no le faltará otro obispo."[90] The character study of the bad bishop is, in fact, arguably the work's most forceful in its moral condemnation, and simultaneously the funniest. Ricapito's praise for it rings true: "Es aquí donde la nota sarcástica y satírica sale a primer término. Todo Erasmo, e incluso Lutero si se quiere, está en este retrato religioso, moral y ético que es, a mi parecer, uno de los cuadros satíricos más sabrosos y más llenos de savia erasmista en toda la obra, si no la época."[91]

Unstudied, though, is the extent to which the work makes use of the theme of the good shepherd — and the bad. In each of the two halves of the work, among the souls who tell their story while on the road to hell or heaven, one of the longest sections is devoted to a bishop. The admirable one, bound for glory, even resembles the works of Díaz de Luco and Maldonado in that he quotes, in Latin, St. Paul's recommendations for selecting a good bishop.[92]

But the image of the good shepherd also plays an important role in the long story of the good king. In a newly dramatized shape, it expresses the familiar concept of the shepherd as symbol of the responsibilities to their subjects of those highly placed, now even of those outside the church hierarchy:

> vn día, passeando solo en mi cámara, vino vn criado mío con quien yo tenía poca y aun quasi ninguna con[u]ersación, y trauándome por el hombro, me remeció diziendo, torna, torna en ti, Polidoro. Yo, espantado de ver vn tan

---

[88] See the introduction and notes to Ricapito's edition, 1997.
[89] Valdés 1993, pp. 124-25.
[90] Valdés 1993 p. 127.
[91] Ricapito in Valdés 1993, p. 29.
[92] Valdés 1993, p. 234.

grande atreuimiento, no sabía qué dezir. Por vna parte me quise enojar, y por otra me parecía no ser sin algún misterio aquella nouedad. A la fin, viendo él que yo no hablaua, me tornó a dezir, — veamos, ¿tú no sabes que eres pastor y no señor y que has de dar cuenta destas ouejas al señor del ganado que es dios? — Diziendo esto se salió de la cámara y me dexó solo y tan atónito que no sabía adónde me estava. Mas luego torné en mí y comencé a pensar en las palabras que me dixo, que era pastor...."[93]

Inspired by this exhortation, the king utterly reforms his formerly oppressive regime, much like a good bishop spreading the benefits of his virtue and pastoral care throughout the kingdom, and the image of the shepherd continues for several pages.

From the perspective of literary form and content, the positive second half of the work, in which all of the characters who speak are admirable models counterbalancing the negative ones presented in the first half, reflects a didactic intent similar to that of the treatises for bishops and unlike the despairing rage of the *Lazarillo*. Yet the theatrical format does point toward the picaresque in that it brings common abuses to life through a closeup, first-person perspective on corruption, together with the humor of comedy. But for the full picaresque combination of lively characters and a systematic review of ecclesiastical/social abuses — all placed in the framework of an epistolary narrative with a self-serving narrator — we have to go to the *Pastor Bonus*.

Maldonado

Maldonado's contribution to this group of writings is, like others, directed broadly to those who should be spiritual shepherds at a time when the sheep have gone terribly astray, but like Díaz de Luco's it differs from most of the works previously discussed in that it is addressed to a specific bishop, Don Iñigo López de Mendoza of Burgos. Burgos was the center of a diocese which was perhaps the most important in Spain,[94] and, though it lacked a university, it was also a major center for trade. Having become a priest, Maldonado took up residence in Burgos thanks to the favor of Juan de Fonseca, Bishop of Burgos, whose habits as Bishop

---

[93] Valdés 1993, p. 207.
[94] Much of the following paragraph is indebted to Bataillon-Margolin 1998, pp. 231-232.

and whose moral reform are described in some detail in the *Pastor Bonus* by his protegé Maldonado, who clearly knew him intimately. Fonseca made Maldonado an examiner of candidates for the priesthood, no doubt partly because of his fluency in Latin, and he acquired a first-hand knowledge of the inadequacies of education of many candidates for the priesthood which he details in the *Pastor Bonus*. For some years he carried out this position of central importance in the administration of the diocese, a position which clearly enhanced the knowledge and authority with which he addressed the new bishop in the *Pastor Bonus*. At the same time Maldonado continued his work as a Latinist for another of his patrons, Don Diego Osorio, a gentleman and lover of humanities, who commissioned him to put together a collection of passages from Latin authors including Pliny and Livy.

Fonseca died in 1524 and was replaced the following year by Antonio de Rojas, who in turn died in 1529. Brother of a highly placed counselor to the emperor, Juan de Zúñiga y Avellaneda, and of Francisco de Zúñiga, the third count of Miranda, López de Mendoza was appointed bishop of Burgos while in England on a diplomatic mission on March 2, 1529. As mentioned above and as Maldonado himself mentions in the *Pastor Bonus*, he served as a tutor to Francisco de Zúñiga's son, Gutierre de Cárdenas, for whom he put down his thoughts on pedagogy in a short treatise. In addition to his learning — to be expected in a classics teacher — Maldonado's letter to López de Mendoza reveals an exceptional ability for observation and a graphic rendering of the current ecclesiastical and social landscape.

The biblical image of the priest as a shepherd whose primary duty is to feed his sheep is naturally the organizing theme in the *Pastor Bonus*. Maldonado stresses that bishops should fulfill Christ's command to feed his sheep, especially the poorest of the flock. The good shepherd works fully for the feeding of the poor; "quos summa uexat pauperies in uicis paganis, solaretur, ac cibaret," 'those whom poverty weighs on most heavily in the peasant villages, he should console and feed.'[95] The emphasis on eating and food — and especially on whether or not it is provided to the hungry — is given a similar prominence in the *Lazarillo*, the first three tratados of which offer prime examples of failure to live up to this first demand of being a care giver.[96] When Lazarillo's father, a miller,

---

[95] Maldonado, *Pastor*, p. g iiii verso.
[96] Critics of the novel who have stressed hunger as central to the work's themes, along with the responsibility of meeting this basic human need, include Cruz, Márquez Villanueva, and Maravall. See Cruz 1999, pp. 18, 29, 30.

dies, he leaves his son quite literally without bread. From that point on, the protagonist is consumed by intense hunger, and he appraises his masters by the quantity and quality of nourishment they offer.

In the case of Lazarillo's second master, who hoards his store of bread in a locked chest, the failure of masters to feed servants and priests to feed the needy becomes particularly clear. Lazarillo quickly determines that "en toda la casa no había ninguna cosa de comer, como suele estar en otras: algún tocino colgado al humero, algún queso puesto en alguna tabla o en el armario, algún canastillo con algunos pedazos de pan que de la mesa sobran."[97] The exaggerated barrenness of the cleric's house, and his reluctance to feed his starving servant boy, seem to point to a generalized failing among the clergy. Lazarillo makes it explicit with the remark, "no sé si de su cosecha era [la avaricia del clérigo] o lo había anejado con el hábito de clerecía."[98] As Ricapito observes, "El hambre de Lazarillo proviene de la avaricia y mezquindad de su amo; y esto está ligado a la iglesia."[99]

Even more reprehensible than priests who neglect to feed their sheep, priests who consume their own flock receive sharp criticism from Maldonado: "tondent hodie pastores diligentisime suas oues atque detondent; mulgent ac immulgent," 'Today shepherds most diligently clip their sheep, and shear them very close. They milk them, and they milk them dry..'[100] Especially when underpaid, priests commonly "ex ouibus utilitatem, ac emolumentum… sibi capere," 'take for themselves the value and profit from the sheep.'[101] Often the shepherds become ravenous beasts, "minus studere commoditatibus ouium, ut sunt cum conducebantur polliciti, sed uulpibus ac lupis esse nocentiores," 'are not as eager for the well-being of the sheep as they promised to be when they were hired, but are in fact more harmful than foxes and wolves.'[102] In fact, "multi sunt pastores mercenarii quam plurimi pascunt utrique non equidem oues, sed suos affectus, uota, studia, cupiditates, trahunt oues et retrahunt, ducunt atque reducunt, earum ut ex pinguedine pinguescant, uel potius turgeant ipsi," 'There are many shepherds and a very great number of

---

[97] *La vida de Lazarillo de Tormes*, ed. Antonio Rey Hazas 1993, p. 85. All quotes from the novel are from this edition.
[98] Rey Hazas 1993, p. 84.
[99] Ricapito 1973, p. 146.
[100] Maldonado, *Pastor*, p. a iiii i verso.
[101] Maldonado, *Pastor*, p. a iiii i-a iiii i verso.
[102] Maldonado, *Pastor*, p. b iiii iii.

mercenary shepherds, and on all sides they pasture not, indeed, the sheep, but their own emotions, wishes, pursuits, and desires, taking them, like sheep, first here and then there, leading them places and then back, so that from the fatness of these they themselves may grow fat, or rather bloated.'[103]

In these cases the bishop should intervene on behalf of the sheep, for it is better that "lupis oues non nunquam expositas errare, quam a canibus et mercenariis custodiam simulantibus passim trucidari," 'the sheep sometimes to wander exposed to the wolves than to be slaughtered left and right by dogs and hired hands that only pretend to care for them.'[104] Although Lazarillo's third master, the hidalgo, does not belong to the religious establishment, he represents the inversion of the proper shepherd-sheep, master-servant relationship. Instead of providing Lazarillo with food, the proud gentleman consumes the fruits of his servant's begging. While he pities his destitute master, Lazarillo articulates the impropriety of the situation: "Contemplaba yo muchas veces mi desastre, que escapando de los amos ruines que había tenido, y buscando mejoría, viniese a topar con quien no sólo no me mantuviese, mas a quien yo había de mantener."[105]

Lázaro Carreter has argued convincingly that the moment when servant feeds master is the culminating point of the first three, best-developed chapters of the novel, a symbolic denunciation of society's failure to provide physical and spiritual sustenance. So central to the novel's criticism of society is that inversion that in the third tratado the moral character of the protagonist has had to be improved to make plausible such a turn in the plot. The critic refers to "el plan paradójico previsto por el autor: hacer que el criado alimente al amo. De que tal plan preexiste a su solución, no cabe duda: el escritor ha partido de un proyecto estructural."[106] In essence, the theme of "Feed my sheep" is at the heart of the *Lazarillo* as well as the *Pastor Bonus*.

But in addition to the failure to provide necessary food, other ideas stand out in the *Lazarillo* that parallel Maldonado's criticisms, particularly his condemnation of excessive ambition: the desire to ascend in the social and ecclesiastical hierarchies. As Márquez Villanueva — and practically

---

[103] Maldonado, *Pastor*, p. f iii verso.
[104] Maldonado, *Pastor*, p. e iiii i verso.
[105] Rey Hazas 1993, p. 110.
[106] Carreter 1969, p. 103.

all the most recent generation of *Lazarillo* critics — has explored in depth, Lazarillo is as much sinning as sinned against. Lazarillo's sin consists in his attempt to ascend the social ladder by immoral means from beggar to royal/ecclesiastical official. Although the narrator presents himself as a self-made man who has worked his way up to "la cumbre de toda buena fortuna" through a variety of endeavors that give the outward appearance of increasing respectability,[107] Márquez Villanueva contends that his desire to rise in society is in itself criminal from the author's perspective.[108] But it seems more accurate to say that the novelist qualifies that judgment, as Maldonado does, with evaluation of the specific moral costs involved. Aspiring to responsible positions is not, in itself, condemned in the *Pastor Bonus*. What is considered to be overly ambitious behavior is made clear by the detailed accounts of the schemes used to obtain positions in the church. An outraged Maldonado, like the anonymous author of the novel, describes such unethical measures as the norm, e.g. "hic tritus mos est uenandi maiora sacerdotia," 'the old and common way of hunting for the bigger positions among the clergy,' and contends that "nullum apud collegium urbanum sedentem in altis hemicyclis propemodum uideas qui arte consimili non conscenderit, nisi perpaucos sane nobiles aut litteratos," 'almost no one sitting in the city college in circular seats who has not risen through similar tactics, except, of course a very few nobles or learned men.'[109]

In conjunction with the corrupting force of ambition, Maldonado emphasizes the danger of desires for worldly gain and profit, both among clerics and laymen. López de Mendoza should exhort rich merchants in his diocese, saying "tempera, reprime, moderare cupiditates effrenes," 'Temper, control, and moderate your unrestrained desires,'[110] addressing especially those who "posthabita caritate, quaestui se deuouent," 'who put charity second and instead devote themselves to profit.'[111] As for greed among the clergy, he writes, "si episcopis cura quidem esset ouium, prohiberent uel inter clericos impia saltem lucra," 'If the bishops' concern were for the sheep, they would prohibit, surely among the clergy,

---

[107] Rey Hazas 1993, p. 141.

[108] Márquez Villanueva 1968, p. 95. In reply to this view Truman has pointed to the 16th-century tradition of the homo novus, in which social rise through virtue and effort is praised. See Truman 1975, p. 43.

[109] Maldonado, *Pastor*, p. c iiii i.

[110] Maldonado, *Pastor*, p. b iiii verso-b iiii i.

[111] Maldonado, *Pastor*, p. b iiii iii.

immoral profiteering.'[112] As noted earlier, the idea of priests as business-men immediately recalls the business involvement of the cathedral chaplain for whom Lazarillo sells water. This master illustrates Maldonado's category of priests who "diuertunt ad artes seruiles, non nunquam ad impias, emptitando quod carius uendant," 'turn to devices typical of slaves, sometimes to immoral ones, by buying what they can resell at a higher price.'[113]

Maldonado also attacks the manipulation of wheat prices by the clergy, priests who "triticum sacrum pluris uendunt quam impii foeneratores, bonas collocant horas in defraudandis pauperculis, laute scilicet ut ipsi uiuant et amplissimum haeredibus relinquant patrimonium," "sell the holy wheat for more than the unscrupulous usurers charge, spend good hours cheating the little guy who has no money, and all so that, of course, they themselves may live elegantly and leave a huge legacy to their heirs.'[114] He continues: "Famelicis alii ciuibus et agricolis triticum decimae iure sacrum foenori dant, milleque modis imponunt, quibus oportuisset ex officio consulere," 'Others loan out at interest to starving farmers and townspeople the wheat which has been hallowed by the law of the tithe, then impose in a thousand ways on the same people whose interests they should have consulted as part of their duties.'[115] Such practices condoned by the clergy resemble the harsh decree in the novel driving the poor out of Toledo under similar conditions: "el año en esta tierra fuese estéril de pan."[116]

Like other contemporary would-be advisers to bishops, Maldonado argues that ecclesiastical corruption engenders cheating and stealing as a way of life in society at large. As a group, priests have come to serve as negative role models for society. Corrupt laymen defend their ways saying: "nobis ne uitio uertetur, aut summum ante iudicem crimini dabitur, sacrosanctos sacerdotes imitari studuisse? Qui nobis in exemplum propositi sunt et tanquam scopus praefixi in quem actiones nostras dirigamus?" 'Will our life be called sinful, or be denounced as crime before the highest judge, when we have striven to imitate the most holy priests, who have been held up to us as examples and set before us like a marker

---

[112] Maldonado, *Pastor*, p. f ii verso.
[113] Maldonado, *Pastor*, p. c iiii iiii verso.
[114] Maldonado, *Pastor*, p. e iiii iiii verso.
[115] Maldonado, *Pastor*, p. e iiii iii verso.
[116] Rey Hazas 1993, p. 111.

by which we should guide our own actions?[117] Márquez Villanueva makes the same point concerning the Lazarillo: "el 'anticlericalismo' del Lazarillo trasciende con mucho el alcance normal del término, pues no se limita a señalar la depravación de los eclesiásticos, sino que los presenta como puntales y fuentes del mal en la sociedad."[118]

The results of priestly misconduct throughout society, as depicted by Maldonado, are similarly harmful. His analysis of the gritty details of social interaction conveys the atmosphere of universal deception characteristic of the picaresque: "Enimuero tam celebris est imponendi consuetudo ut socordes, hebetes, somniculosi iam habeantur, qui mentem gerant sinceram. Nec facile nubunt simplices feminae, uiri difficile ducunt uxores qui fraudes non admodum callent, qui non uulpinam quandam in uicinum uafriciem exercent. Primam iam dicunt dotem, scire uiuere, uidelicet fraude nosse duplicare rem, fallere semper emptorem, uitiare obsonia, adulterare quidquid ad manum uenerit…uiuitur ex rapto, uel potius ex mutuo laniatu," 'For in fact the custom of cheating is so common that those who have moral integrity are now considered lazy and weak minded, and as if in a daze. It is not easy for pure women to marry, and men with difficulty find brides if they are not great experts in deceit who practice a kind of foxy cunning against their neighbor. It is said that the primary dowry is to know how to live, such as to know how to double your possessions by trickery, always deceive the buyer, sell tainted victuals and adulterate whatever comes to hand… everyone lives by theft, or rather, by mangling each other.'[119] As Bataillon remarks of Maldonado's damning overview, "La rapacidad de los sacerdotes parece ofrecer una justificación a la rapacidad de los agentes de la autoridad y de los simples particulares, comerciantes, usureros, artesanos. En consecuencia, ¡qué espectáculo ofrece a los ojos de Maldonado ese mundo en compendio que es el obispado de Burgos!"[120]

Indeed, the immoral world so thoroughly documented by Maldonado appears remarkably similar to that of the *Lazarillo*. In both works deceit pervades not only the social relations of commerce, but grows to a generalized self-misrepresentation. Maldonado asks, "An est qui noceat uerius frequentius, perniciosius, quam qui uiri boni speciem gerit?" 'Is there anyone who does harm more truly, more frequently and more

---

[117] Maldonado, *Pastor*, p. f i verso.
[118] Márquez Villanueva 1968, p. 129.
[119] Maldonado, *Pastor*, p. b iiii i verso.
[120] Bataillon 2002, p. 335.

perniciously [b i] than a person who only takes on the appearance of a good man?'[121] He advises Bishop Mendoza to prevent priestly hypocrisy by investigating "cunctane sint intra sacras aedes pure suis decenterque constituta locis, linteamina tersa, uasa pura nitidaque, sed an sit sacerdotibus integritas uitae, morum sinceritas, eruditio tandem congruens professioni," 'not only whether all things in the holy buildings are cleanly and appropriately stored in their proper places, the linen cloths neat, the vessels shining clean, but rather whether there is in the priests an integrity of life, a purity of character, and finally, a learning which is appropriate to their profession.'[122] With regard to the *Lazarillo*, Ricapito finds that "all the clerical characters represent a break between the outer profession and the inner lack... the depiction of hypocrisy to which the reader infers the inner emptiness of values."[123] The same kind of hypocrisy appears in the case of the squire, who projects the image of a nobleman, retaining his upper-class manners and referring to his family estate while living in utter misery sprung from a foolish arrogance.

To prevent such degradation of morals on both the individual and social levels, the *Pastor Bonus* and the *Lazarillo* suggest the importance of proper role models and education for youth, a campaign in which bishops should lead the way. While Maldonado focuses a great deal on the literary education of prospective priests, he also calls for early moral training for all members of society: "A pubertate impietas est omnis dediscenda, boni mores imbuendi, christianus candor imbibendus, caritas in genus omne mortalium exprimenda, tum annis accedentibus solidanda," 'From puberty on all immorality must be unlearned, good character must be impressed on him, Christian purity must be absorbed, brotherly love expressed toward every sort of mortal and, in the years when one enters public life, solidified.'[124] Lazarillo, of course, receives exactly the opposite kind of education, learning how to swindle his way in the hostile world under the tutelage of depraved masters who act as corrupting surrogate fathers. Similarly, as García García points out, Maldonado believes "el poder del obispo no es el de un amo, sino el de un padre."[125] In addition to feeding their flocks, bishops and priests must

---

[121] Maldonado, *Pastor*, p. a iiii iiii verso-b i.
[122] Maldonado, *Pastor*, p. g iiii i verso.
[123] Ricapito 1997, p. 27.
[124] Maldonado, *Pastor*, p. g i.
[125] García García 1983, p. 267.

administer fatherly instruction to their sheep rather than allowing them to
wander in ignorance of true principles. When "cum uero functio aliqua
siue sacra, siue profana, obuenerit," 'some position, whether sacred or
profane, falls to his lot,' the appropriately educated person makes every
effort that it "ex Christi dogmate geratur, administretur, obeatur," 'be
managed, administered and performed in accordance with the teaching of
Christ.'[126] This stands in stark contrast with Lazarillo, who follows his
masters step by step in the paths of vice.

The overall direction of moral decline in Lazarillo's life is touched on
in Maldonado's remark on the uncommon nature of real character reform:
"Nullum denique uitium momento insperatoque relinquitur, ni paulatim
turpitudinem quis agnoscens, aut a uiro pio sapienter admonitus, pedem
ipse referat, uel ictus (quod aiunt) cum piscatore sapiat," 'no vice is given
up in a sudden moment unless someone, gradually recognizing his moral
degradation or, wisely admonished by a religious man, himself takes a
step back, as though, like a fisherman, he feels the strike [coming], as the
saying goes.'[127] In Renaissance Spain the biblical Lazarus raised from
the grave was at times symbolically interpreted as the moral putrification
of sinners who steadfastly refuse to repent and so become hardened in
sin.[128]

In the style of the picaresque novel, and unlike the treatise writers we
have looked at until now, Maldonado employs several anecdotes in the
Pastor Bonus that are often developed, as in Valdés' colloquy, with characters, dialogue, and explanations of the motives behind the actions. Setting the tone for the rest of the epistle, Maldonado immediately inserts
the story of his boyhood time "frugalissimos ac diligentissimos inter pastores," 'among highly virtuous and diligent shepherds' who demonstrated
ideal care of their sheep.[129] Just as in the *Lazarillo*, where only prostitutes
and those of lower social standing extend any kindness toward the protagonist, the humble shepherds are one of very few positive examples
Maldonado provides. Next, he includes a lengthy section written in the
first-person voice of a bishop addressing wayward sheep in his flock.
Here is another positive role model, but it is thoroughly picaresque in
detailing and decrying corruption.

---

[126] Maldonado, *Pastor*, p. g i.
[127] Maldonado, *Pastor*, p. f iiii iiii verso-g i.
[128] See Colahan 2001, p. 560.
[129] Maldonado, *Pastor*, p. a iiii verso.

Other well-rounded anecdotes follow, including an account of a street brawl between monks and priests over the right to conduct the funeral of a citizen who had left his body to a monastery. While Maldonado seems to chuckle at the avaricious foolishness of both sides, he takes care to mention that the monks' cross "interim aut iacet aut uicem conti praebet," 'was either lying unused or served as a pike' during the battle,[130] indicating the serious problem of clergymen who neglect their true duty in service of personal gain. The work's most elaborate example is an interpolated tale involving a father's instructions upon sending his son off to Rome to buy a high ecclesiastical position. The father's long speech shows that buying church titles has been refined to a science. But even more disturbing than the means of securing appointments is the cynical goal, not unlike the immoral situation of Lazarillo's last master: 'nobilibus adaequaberis, salutaberis canonicus et archidiachonus, sedebis in altis ac primis hemicyclis, nunquam sacrificabis; ad haec, si quid humane designaueris, filios forte procreaueris, nullum in te ius habebit episcopus, libere uiues et laute," 'You will be considered the equal of nobles, greeted as a canon and archdeacon, sit in high and prominent circular chairs, and never have to say mass. Add to all this the advantage that if you should get ideas in some very human way, if you should by chance father some children, the bishop will have no legal power over you, and you will live freely and splendidly.'[131]

Later in the work, Maldonado examines the thoughts and feelings of a victim of corruption rather than those of its perpetrators. Discussing the characteristic vices of scribes, Maldonado expresses his outrage at unjust lawsuits through the story of a priest from the mountains who has undergone a protracted lawsuit in order to take possession of a benefice that is rightfully his. Although he ultimately wins the case, he must pay additional fees and bribes to obtain the official document containing the judge's decree. Already bankrupt, the priest curses the entire ecclesiastical establishment and commits himself instead to a life of societally sanctioned violence: "iugulandisque hominibus deuotus, strenuum militem agam," 'committed to butchering people, and act the part of a vigorous soldier.'[132] Maldonado also relates his personal experiences in a similar lawsuit. Like the clergyman from the mountains, he prevails, though not

---

[130] Maldonado, *Pastor*, p. c ii verso.
[131] Maldonado, *Pastor,* p. c iiii verso.
[132] Maldonado, *Pastor*, p. e iiii.

by "aequitate aut gratia," 'justice or favor,'[133] but by taking a friend's advice to bribe the judge's secretary.

While there is no real element of confession in Maldonado's letter, other incidents taken from his own life appear throughout, including his interaction as tutor with the bishop's nephew and his relationship with his late protector, the former bishop of Burgos, Juan de Fonseca. Maldonado takes advantage of his intimacy with Bishop Fonseca to present the latter's thoughts as he nears the end of his life, reflecting on his luxurious lifestyle and repenting of his improper conduct: "Ubi mea mens erat? Ubi iudicium? Ubi ratio?" 'Where was my mind? Where my good judgment? Where was my reason?'[134] Maldonado copiously describes and warmly applauds Fonseca's repentance and commitment to charity at the end of his life, but he stresses that "rari sunt eiusmodi successus," 'such successful outcomes are rare,'[135] again recalling Lazarillo's inability to renounce vice.

Given the wealth of anecdotes and dialogue that appear in the *Pastor Bonus*, it is not surprising that Bataillon writes, "Maldonado nos muestra cómo el Coloquio erasmiano podía transformarse en un género de pasatiempo, capaz de hacer la competencia a la literatura novelesca y de preparar la renovación de ésta en más de una dirección."[136] However, although he saw parallels to the *Guzmán*, Bataillon did not connect the *Pastor Bonus* with the *Lazarillo*, very probably due to his hesitancy to accept an Erasmian perspective in the novel.[137] Lázaro Carreter concurs about the authorship, arguing that the theory of an Erasmian author is at odds with "un rasgo constante del libro: su aplicación de formulas y expresiones religiosas, a mal fin. Un erasmista sincero, Luis Vives, condenaba enérgicamente tal práctica."[138] Nonetheless, even if we put aside all the subsequent criticism of the novel that explores its parallels to Erasmus' work,[139] it is clear that sacrilegious jokes appear in the work of some Erasmian writers. O'Reilly has responded directly to Lázaro

---

[133] Maldonado, *Pastor*, p. e iii verso.
[134] Maldonado, *Pastor*, p. f iiii iii.
[135] Maldonado, *Pastor,* p. f iiii iiii.
[136] Bataillon 2002, p. 648.
[137] Bataillon 2002, p. 611. Toward the end of his career, however, he did point out that the over-all form of the novel, if not the specifics of the ecclesiastical satire, may have been inspired by Erasmus' *Praise of Folly*. For a discussion of the question see Truman 1975, pp. 33-34.
[138] Carreter 1969, p. 129.
[139] See O'Reilly 1984, pp. 91-100.

Carreter's objection by pointing to "the diversity in the Spanish movement of reform. Many Spaniards who admired Erasmus drew inspiration
also from other traditions...."[140] One of those was the contemporary converso playwright Miguel de Carvajal, whose play *Cortes de la muerte* we
will examine below for his portrayal of a hypocritical bishop. That character, for example, attempting to justify his worldly attire and soldierlike
appearance, is the vehicle for an irreverent joke about Christ's transfiguration: "y por no tardarme / he mudado así el vestido / y esta causa me
a mouido / a querer transfigurarme."[141] In the same impious vein is a
remark about Sancha by her niece, the older woman having been
described as another Celestina who retains her youthful appearance inspite
of old age: "Vegezuela la ternan/ por cierto que me paresce/ si bien la
miran diran/ que en el agua del Jordan/ se laua y se remocece" (xliii). The
sacred baptisms into new life performed by John in the Jordan River,
including that of Jesus, is compared with the tricks a whore uses to stay
looking young.

The one extensive study devoted to the *Pastor Bonus*, the book chapter by Heliodoro García García, emphasizes the detailed social criticism
of Maldonado's work, although without linking it to the picaresque:
"Maldonado, lejos de encerrarse en cuestiones metafísicas, nos da a cono-
cer las cuestiones cotidianas con su sello personal";[142] that is, his "aguda
y fina observación."[143] More sharply realistic than the works of his fellow writers for bishops, Maldonado's letter to Bishop Mendoza, in his
view,"está exento de todo idealismo extremado, no pierde el contacto
con la realidad presente.[144] But while García García observes that Maldonado's works usually include a character that presents the correct view
of the subjects,[145] the exemplary figures in the *Pastor Bonus* are few and
far between. More representative is Maldonado's own comment within
the work: "quo malo mortalium fato plerunque fit, ut frequentiora sint
exempla nequitiae quam alicuius eximiae uirtutis," 'by some evil destiny
of mortals, it usually happens that examples of iniquity are more frequently encountered than of any outstanding virtue,"[146] a disillusioned

---

[140] O'Reilly 1984, p. 98.
[141] Luis Hurtado de Toledo 1964, p. f vi.
[142] García García 1983, p. 11.
[143] García García 1983, p. 245.
[144] García García 1983, pp. 246-7.
[145] García García 1983, p. 9.
[146] Maldonado, *Pastor*, p. g 6 verso.

sentiment that might well have been expressed by the author of the Lazarillo.

As noted earlier, the element of self-justification in the sixteenth-century personal accounts addressed to the Spanish Inquisition recently documented by Gitlitz[147] is present in the *Pastor Bonus* as well. Although lacking the ironic distance between narrator and author found in the *Lazarillo*, Maldonado's open letter also betrays self-serving motives, and similarly attempts to contrast his relative innocence with that of the social decadence that surrounds him. When reviewing for his new superior the abuses plaguing each and every one of the several ecclesiastical positions in the diocese, Maldonado doesn't hesitate to emphasize the importance of reform for the position of examiner, the post he held at the time of writing the Pastor Bonus: "magnum hoc nimirum munus atque sanctissimum est iudicandum... Vertitur siquidem in eo uelut regionis totius harmonia," 'there is no doubt that this office must be judged as great and most holy.... Indeed the harmony of the whole region turns on this.'[148] Indeed, he makes it clear that he is asking Mendoza to reappoint him to the post: "Putabis optime praesul, negotium me agere meum, cum prorsus habueris compertum functionem me hanc aliquot annos gessisse... sed cum rem penitus noris, intelliges tandem opinor, me cum candore gessisse," 'You will think, most excellent superintendent, that I do my job when you have thoroughly verified that I have carried out this duty for several years.... When you have become thoroughly informed about the subject, I think you will conclude that I have done it honestly.'[149] In short, as Bataillon observes, Maldonado makes use of rhetorical strategies to highlight the evils of society[150] and, we can add, his own goodness.

Carvajal

Another work from the first half of the century, or in this case shortly thereafter, dedicates an extensive section to episcopal tasks and typical abuses of the position. Although written, like Valdés' dialogue, in a theatrical form that blends allegory with social criticism, it was composed

---

[147] Gitlitz 2000, p. 71.
[148] Maldonado, *Pastor,* p. d 5.
[149] Maldonado, *Pastor,* p. d 8.
[150] Bataillon 2002, p. 335.

some twenty years after the last three pieces we have looked at. Nonetheless it resembles the *Pastor Bonus* in weighting the thematic balance toward exposé more than teaching, It illustrates, too, how the beginnings of the picaresque novel could well have fused the lively character development and dialogue of theatre — often set in a context of authorial irony toward those characters' words — with the sometimes despairing review of generalized social corruption found in treatises of advice for bishops. It is also important for its relation to the *Lazarillo*, in that it appears very possibly to have received influence from that novel, and for its series of sinners who tell the stories of their lives.

Micael Carvajal's morality play *Cortes de la muerte*, like the *Lazarillo,* was probably composed close to 1550; possibly it was retouched by Luis Hurtado de Toledo for its publication in 1557. It features a hypocritical bishop who appears as a spokesman for the clergy in a parliament convoked by Death to hear complaints and pass judgments. Arguments about clerical virtues and corruption take up all of the lengthy fourth scene. After a self-serving description by the bishop of the difficult life of the clergy, St. Augustine, present as friend of the court, summarizes the ideal behavior prelates should emulate: "Sean honestos y templados / castos y caritatiuos / prudentes bien atauiados / diligentes concretados / no litigiosos ni altiuos / No de renta cobdiciosos / vinolentos comedores / no crueles mas piadosos / sufridos no sediciosos / ni simples enseñadores."[151] These precepts, which could easily be inserted in Vitoria's treatises, are also brought out by the customary good shepherd imagery, which is still emphatic and more fully fleshed out than ever. The church's shepherds should watch over the flock, protecting it from hungry wolves. They need a good sling and a good staff, a good whistle and good pasture. They should station themselves on top of a hill as a lookout, anoint the sheep's wounds and diseases, and keep them from wandering off where they don't belong.[152]

But after this compact evocation of utopia, Satan, acting as prosecutor, rebuts the bishop's claims to moral integrity with a long list of charges, beginning with hypocrisy: "Que todo lo que ha contado / el perlado reuerendo / todo es fingido y forjado."[153] This issue is also

---

[151] Hurtado 1964, p. f x verso.

[152] Hurtado 1964, p. f x verso.

[153] Hurtado 1964, p. xi. The on-going attempts after 1530 to reform bishops, and their ineffectiveness, can be seen in what was yet another prohibition against concubinage pronounced in the Toledo Synod of 1536. The decree was written by the eminent reformer

paramount in the abuse that takes up much more space than any other: clergymen providing dowries and making arrangements for young women to marry. In a passage loaded with double meanings that recall the sexual relationship — fundamental to the novel — between the archpriest and Lazarillo's wife, the bishop testifies that, "En el remedio y amparo / de los pobres y biudas / y en el aliuio y reparo / de otros muchos que muy claro / padeseen passiones crudas / y en buscar secretamente / muchas huerfanas donzellas / y en casallas largamente / y en pagar entre la gente / muy muchas deudas por ellas // Inquirir con diligencia / parientas necessitadas / y como hombres de prudencia / dotallas en mi pressencia / porque biuan mas honrradas…"[154] The author's irony in the bishop's use of the word "honrradas" recalls Lazarillo's statement that his wife is "tan buena mujer como vive dentro de las puertas de Toledo,"[155] and alludes to the practice of high-ranking churchmen of keeping concubines and then marrying them off to other men. Exposing the true meaning of this supposedly charitable act by the clergy, Satan charges, "Y essas huerfanas donzellas / no saben que he yo notado / lo que suelen hacer dellas / ay tristezicas de aquellas / quantas vereys que an cassado / y si fuere menester / yo trayre aquí la minuta / y el registro y podrán ver / que conellos no ay mugger / que no quede dissoluta."[156] Further emphasizing the bishop's failure to practice what he preaches, Death makes an irreverent joke, cited above, about Christ's transfiguration as part of his sarcastic criticism of the bishop's secular clothing: "Vuestro puñalico al lado / el roquete tan vistoso / el gorjalico labrado /… Cierto embiaron aquí / un galan procurador / y anda ansí todo el Ganado / eclesiástico vestido / tan apunto repicado / Papagayo tan pintado / de la India no a venido."[157]

In addition to unmasking episcopal vice in order to criticize churchmen in general, the play makes a broader accusation of hypocrisy in the Spanish church by means of one of the basic images in the Lazarillo. If one keeps in mind that the allegorical *Cortes de la muerte* was written to be performed in honor of Corpus Christi, which celebrates the miracle of

Cardinal Juan Tavera, who was also Inquisitor-General and Archbishop of Toledo. Cruz points to this decree in connection with the mistress of the Archpriest of San Salvador in the *Lazarillo* and suggests that Tavera could be the model for the "Vuestra Merced" to whom the narrator explains his marital situation. See *Discourses*, pp.18-19.

[154] Hurtado 1964, p. vi.
[155] Hazas, p. 141.
[156] Hurtado 1964, p. xi.
[157] Hurtado 1964, p. v verso.

the communion wine becoming Christ's blood, a bitter complaint — lodged by an Indian denouncing the treatment given New World peoples by Christians — can be seen to parallel the sacrilege of Lazarillo's triumphal entry into respectable society through his corrupt job announcing the sale of wine for the church: "también alla an bozeado / que la ley y los prophetas / penden en que dios sea amado / y el próximo no unjuriado / y estas son las vias rectas / Pues como es esto señora / y estos apregonan vino / y venden vinagre agora / despojando cada ora / al indio triste mezquino."[158] Gitlitz feels that the vinegar refers to the persecution of Spanish conversos as well as Indians,[159] as well it may, but the context of the phrase seems to point out the inconsistency of the Christian church's failing, in general, to love God while harming its neighbors. In relation to the first picaresque novel, this passage gives new force to the presentation of the protagonist's hypocrisy. As a wine salesman for the church, Lazarillo has finally achieved an enhanced outward appearance of respectability, but he is now morally worse than ever, metaphorically delivering vinegar in place of Christ's blood.

It should not be forgotten, of course, that the date of composition of the play is uncertain, and it is not clear which work may have come first. Still, the close parallels in subjects and imagery show how easily the novel could have drawn on — and subsequently been incorporated into — such works ironically but systematically damning the vices of the ecclesiastical establishment and its corrupted flock.

[158] Hurtado 1964, p. liii.
[159] Gitlitz 1989.

PASTOR BONUS Latin text
PASTOR BONUS Translation

Bishop with Sheep (R. Simmons)

PASTOR BONUS LATIN TEXT

Pastor Bonus per Ioannem Maldonatum. Libellus sane dignus quem praesules legant et suis legendum propinent.

A 2   Illustrissimo ac Reuerendissimo in Christo Patri Domino. D. Inacho Mendozae Episcopo Burgensi Ioannes Maldonatus.
S[alutem] P[lurimam] D[icit].

Antequam ingrediar promere, pater amplissime, meum in his litteris princeps institutum atque propositum, admiratione, quae te forte iam tenet, omnino conabor absoluere. Miraberis haud quidem immerito, cur ego, uir nequaquam sane percelebris, sed neque de facie tibi notus, ausim te literis in uoluminis prope mensuram porrectis, interpellare, uirum maiorum imaginibus celebrem, episcopatu conspicuum, uirtutibus clarum, eruditione praestantem, longe praeterea renotum, maximis negotiis inuolutum,
A 2v /seriis apud Caesarem rebus occupatum. Ceterum si me audis, mirari iam desines.

Cum mecum animo uoluerem demandandi praesulatus et sacros honores in te morem omnino fuisse mutatum propterea quod soleant plerumque reges in Hispania per gradus quosdam euehere, quos sacra dignos initiatione uiros diiudicant minoribus nimirum episcopatibus primo

Editorial note: The *Pastor Bonus* was an addition to the 1549 edition of the collection of works by Maldonado; the call number at the National Library in Madrid is R 5848 (it

PASTOR BONUS TRANSLATION
THE GOOD SHEPHERD

BY JUAN MALDONADO

A little book truly worthy of being read by bishops, and worthy of their furnishing to their people for reading.

A 2   To the most Illustrious and Reverend Father in Christ, Señor Don Iñigo Mendoza,[1] Bishop of Burgos, Juan Maldonado sends warm greetings.

Personal Appeal to Bishop Mendoza

Before beginning to set forth, most honorable father, my chief plan and proposal in this letter, I shall attempt to dispel thoroughly the surprise that you may be feeling. You will be surprised, and with good reason, that someone like me, neither famous nor known to you by sight, should dare to speak in a letter almost as long as a book, on the subject of the good shepherd, and to a gentleman like you, famous for the busts of his ancestors, outstanding among the bishops, a shining example of virtue, distinguished for his learning, and in addition renowned far and wide as being

A 2v   involved in affairs of the highest importance, / busy with earnest matters on behalf of the emperor. However, if you will listen to me, you will soon cease to be amazed.

I was pondering in my mind that the custom of entrusting bishoprics and holy honors in you has been altogether changed — especially because most kings in Spain promote by a kind of steps those whom they judge worthy of holy consecration, namely by first setting them over smaller bishoprics. Then soon, one step at a time, if they prove to be good men, they transfer them to bigger dioceses. But in fact you, though you had

---

[1] After receiving his education at Salamanca, Iñigo López de Mendoza y Zúñiga, son of Pedro de Zúñiga y Velasco, second count of Miranda, was named bishop of Extremadura in the 1520s. Carlos V sent him to England as a negotiator for peace in 1526, and while there, on March 2, 1529, he was appointed bishop of Burgos. Although he returned to Spain in May of 1529, he soon departed for Italy with Carlos V. In March of 1530, Pope Clement VII secretly named him cardinal, and he returned to his diocese in 1533, where he established the college of St Nicholas at Burgos. See Bietenholz and Deutscher 1985-87, vol. 2, p. 346.

praeficiendo, mox gradatim, si bonorum uirorum specimen ferant, ad maiores traducendo; te uero privatum adhuc, longinqua legatione peregrinantem, nil minus ambientem (quod raro uidimus) ad opulentissimum episcopatum Caesar uocarit, non mihi potui tandem imperare, quin ad te de boni pastoris officio perscriberem et quod prioribus quibusdam in pastoribus, et in urbano collegio per interregnum (ut ita dicam) fuerit

A 3   desideratum, ob oculos tibi ponerem. Nam etsi nusquam non praedica/tur, haud quidem ob splendorem solum generis et familiae, sed ob egregias [1]quas in te clarescere uidet orbis, uirtutes, ob candidissimos mores, ob pietatem uere Christianam ad amplissimam fuisse dignitatem non tua plane sponte sublatum.

Multa sunt tamen in functione tam late patente, quae, ni rem in praesentem ueneris, diuinare uix potes. Praeterea quae diuus Paulus, clarissimum nostrae persuasionis oraculum, suis Timotheo et Tito, de cooptandis bonis episcopis praescribit, nihil in te profecto desideramus. Fama constans laudum tuarum implet abunde nostros affectus. Tum chorus ille uirtutum, quem commendat apostolus et plane exigit ab iis, qui sunt

---

is not included in the 1541 edition). The title page in 1549 reads: *Ioannis Maldonati Opuscula quaedam docta simul et elegantia, De Senectute Christiana. Paradoxa. Pastor Bonus. Ludus Chartarum, Tridunus, et alii quidam. Geniale Iudicium siue Bacchanalia.* Burgis excudebat Ioannes Giunta. Anno. 1549. (See further Asensio and Rovira's edition of the *Paraenesis ad Litteras*, 1980, pp. 22-25.)

In a few instances someone made an attempt to correct the Madrid copy, sometimes blotting out entire words; for such passages we have benefited greatly from the aid of Dra. Esther Ortas who kindly consulted the copy in the Biblioteca General Universitaria de Zaragoza (Signatura: H-11-206) and made detailed collations. The corrections mostly relate to small points of grammar or style. The Madrid copy is cited as M in our notes, and the Zaragoza copy as Z. What are cited in our notes as differences between these two copies actually refer to post-publication corrections in M by this unknown hand.

We have standardized this copy to conform, as far as possible, with the orthography acknowledged by the *Oxford Latin Dictionary*. Thus we write (to give a few examples) *u* everywhere for *v*, *plerumque* for *plaerunque*, *initiatos* for *initiacos*, *famae* for *fame*, *sinceram* for *synceram*, *profani* for *prophani*. The punctuation has also been changed to conform more to modern practice.

held no office in the church up until then,[2] while traveling abroad on a diplomatic mission and in no way soliciting the richest bishopric (how rare it is to see this), were named to it by the emperor. Therefore I couldn't stop myself from writing to you at length about the duties of a good shepherd and to place before your eyes what we missed in some former shepherds and in the city college during the interregnum (so to speak).[3]

A 3 For, as is everywhere being pointed out,/ it is not only due to the splendor of your lineage and family, but to the outstanding virtues which the world sees shining in you, to your unblemished character and to your true Christian piety, that you have been lifted up to the highest honor — though certainly not because you sought it.

Still there are many aspects to such a broad and wide-ranging charge, things that without entering into the actual situation you can scarcely guess at. What's more, of those things that St. Paul the most famous oracle of our persuasion wrote out in full to his disciples Timothy and Titus[4] about choosing good bishops, we find absolutely nothing to be desired in you. Unceasingly the report of your praises fully satisfies our desires. So, since that chorus of virtues that the apostle recommends and

---

[2] Apparently Maldonado was not aware of Mendoza's previous appointment as bishop of Coria.

[3] After the death of Bishop Juan Rodríguez de Fonseca in November of 1524, the diocese of Burgos remained empty until the appointment of Antonio de Rojas on July 3, 1525. Upon his death, Iñigo López de Mendoza was appointed bishop on March 2, 1529, but did not take up residence in Burgos until 1533, as noted above. See "Burgos" by D. Mansilla in *Diccionario de Historia*, vol. 1, p. 294.

[4] Saint Paul's first letter to Timothy contains a list of qualifications for church officials: "If a man desires the position of a bishop, he desires a good work. A bishop then must be blameless, the husband of one wife [as the mandate of celibacy for clergy did not exist in the early church], temperate, sober-minded, of good behavior, hospitable, able to teach; not given to wine, not violent, not greedy for money, but gentle, not quarrelsome, not covetous; one who rules his own house well, having his children in submission with all reverence (for if a man does not know how to rule his own house, how will he take care of the church of God?); not a novice, lest being puffed up with pride he fall into the same condemnation as the devil. Moreover he must have a good testimony among those who are outside, lest he fall into reproach and the snare of the devil. Likewise, deacons must be reverent, not double-tongued, not given to much wine, not greedy for money, holding the mystery of the faith with a pure conscience. But let these also first be tested; then let them serve as deacons, being found blameless." See 1 Timothy 3.1-10. Similarly, in his letter to Titus, St. Paul enumerates the qualities necessary in a bishop: "For a bishop must be blameless, as a steward of God, not self-willed, not quick-tempered, not given to wine, not violent, not greedy for money, but hospitable, a lover of what is good, sober-minded, just, holy, self-controlled, holding fast the faithful word as he has been taught, that he may be able, by sound doctrine, both to exhort and convict those who contradict." See Titus 1.7-9.

episcopi designandi, semper eluxit in te; non est quod immoremur in hac parte: doctissimus es et sine fuco pius, nunquam committes ut immerito praepositus esse uidearis.

Geris tamen prouinciam maxime negotiosam per proconsules, per prae-
A 3v tores, per le/gatos, per quaestores, per tribunos: et per quos non? Multa te fugiant necesse est, quae si percognita prorsus intellectaque satis haberes, omnino tolleres aut certe pro uiribus emendares. Et magnis in tempestatibus summi gubernatores a uectoribus non grauantur admoneri.

Quam ob rem unus ego tua ex cohorte nescio quis, non forte tribunus, sed neque lixa quidem aut uector, facturus mihi pretium operae uideor, si boni pastoris officium, functionem nimirum a te nunc primum initam, ex parte saltem deliniem. Non quidem iuris quid habeas in uitam necemque mortalium explicare nunc mihi mens est, nec qui tuo, qui regio sint foro peragendi rei, quid aeris tuo fisco accrescat ex profanorum com-missis in uiros initiatos et sacras aedes, quid ex clericorum in uiros sacros, aut profanos; nec etiam quid tibi census ac decimarum pendant fundi et
A 4 latifundia cuiusque regionis, siue montanae siue campestris; multo mi/nus quid uisitationes annuae, quid sepulturae, quid tabularum, quid diploma-tum sigillatio conducat ac lucrifaciat, quid exactionum genera sescenta, quae uelut capita Hydrae alia ex aliis quotidie suppullulant. Nam de his

fully demands of those who are to be chosen as bishops has always shone out in you, there is no need for us to linger on that part. You are most learned, pious without deceit, and will never do anything to make it seem that undeservedly you were promoted.

Still you manage a district that is busier than any other, with royal
A 3v governors and magistrates,[5] envoys,/ finance judges, and tribunes.[6] Indeed, who *isn't* here? So, many things will necessarily escape your attention, things which if you had the power to know about thoroughly and understand them sufficiently, you would entirely remove them, or at least you would correct them to the best of your ability. In big storms, too, the chief helmsmen are not reluctant to receive advice from passengers.

True, I am only one of your company, an unknown, not even by chance a tribune, but certainly not a camp follower or a passenger, but I believe I will be doing something worthwhile if I sketch out at least partially the duties of a good shepherd, namely, the role you are now taking on for the first time. It is certainly not my intention here to explain what your legal power is in cases of the life and death of mortals. Nor which defendants should be prosecuted in your court and which in the king's, or how much money will come to your purse from the crimes of laymen against clergymen or churches, or from those of clergy against sacred or profane men. Nor, indeed, how much in wealth and tithes the estates and latifundia pay out to you from each region, whether in the mountains or on the
A 4 plains. / Much less how much income is produced by annual visitations,[7] and how much by burials, how much brought in by issuing or sealing official documents and letters,[8] how much by six hundred kinds of exactions, which like the Hydra's heads daily sprout one after another. For

[5] In 16th-century Spain the crown often appointed a *corregidor* over a city, and his duties could be both administrative and judicial. The duties of both *proconsules* and *praetores* could have been carried out by a *corregidor*, but precisely what royal offices Maldonado intended with those two words is not clear.

[6] In the Latin, *tribunos*, by which Maldonado may have meant members of the city council, an institution that was very powerful in Castilian cities of the period, or members of the *Cortes*, the weak national parliament.

[7] A bishop was required to visit every parish in his diocese at least once a year (unless he chose to send a priest in his place), and he could receive a payment in exchange.

[8] The official seals of Spanish bishops and archbishops were made of wax, often red in color, circular, and bearing an impress of the bishop, sometimes in bust and sometimes standing, dressed in pontifical ornaments, a staff in the left hand and the right hand in an attitude of blessing. The seals of the clergy were usually made of green wax, round or almond-shaped, and bore religious symbols or heraldic emblems. See *Diccionario de Historia*, "Sigilografía," vol. 4, pp. 2461-2467.

et huiusmodi sunt iura, sunt constitutiones, sunt iurepiti, qui blandientes tibi nec teruncium decedere fisco patientur.

Sed quam late pateat tua dicio spiritualis, quam tuum quaquauersum diffundas imperium in animas cunctorum, nimirum in internum hominem; et quantum tibi ceterisque episcopis detulerit Christus optimus maximus, quantum a uobis exigi uoluerit, quantae uos curae reddiderit obnoxios, cum dixit, "Ego sum pastor bonus, bonus pastor animam suam dat pro ouibus suis. Mercenarius autem et qui non est pastor, cuius non sunt oues propriae, uidet lupum uenientem et dimittit oues, et fugit, et lupus rapit et dispergit oues." Enimuero bonus episcopus (nam ii sunt ueri pastores) A 4v / nihilo minorem curam impendet lucrificandis Christo quotquot eius in dicione degunt quam frugi pastores solent in seruandis, pascendis reficiendisque suis pecudibus.

Puer ego sum aliquando frugalissimos ac diligentissimos inter pastores animi causa uersatus et animaduerti primores eorum, quorum erant oues propriae, circuire frequenter peculium, tabentes ac morbidas denotare, pro tempore mederi aut segregare; tum mercenariorum negligentiam coarguere, castigare, rationem languentium subducere, pelles reposcere; et si quam uiderant tardius subsequentem, pedites ipsi adiutare, nonnumquam asini tergo imponere et quouis modo ad caulam perducere. Si sunt ad hunc Lydium lapidem episcopi prorsus explorandi, ut uere sunt ex praescripto Christi, nescio qua dormitatione, quo tenentur lethargo praesules A 5 quamplurimi, ut iudicium vel supremum Dei non uereantur, / in quo districte subducetur ratio bene gestarum functionum, ac secus, praesertim earum, quae curam magis respiciunt animarum quam corporum.

regarding these and other such things, there are laws, charters, and legal experts, who, in their coaxing of you, will not allow a single penny to be cut off from your income.

But how widely does your spiritual authority extend, how widely do you pour out your power in every direction into the souls of all, that is, into the inner person? But with how much has Christ, best and greatest, charged you and the other bishops, how much will he want to be demanded of you, and for how much careful management has he made you liable? For he said,

"I am the good shepherd. The good shepherd gives his life for his sheep. But the hired man, who is not a shepherd and whose sheep are not his own, sees the wolf coming and leaves the sheep and flees, and the wolf steals and scatters the sheep."[9] Truly the good bishop (for those are A 4v the true shepherds) / puts no less care into making profitable for Christ any and all who live under his authority than virtuous shepherds are used to doing in order to save, pasture and restore their flocks.

Follow Positive Examples of Shepherds

I once as a boy spent my pleasure among highly virtuous and diligent shepherds, and I observed the meticulous care of the best among them, whose sheep were their own, as they frequently went around the flock, noting which sheep were diseased or sick, then in a timely manner healing or setting them apart. Then they reproached and punished the negligence of the hired hands, totaling up the weary ones, the sick and those about to die and claiming the hides. And if they spotted one trailing along behind the others, they would go on foot themselves to help, sometimes placing it on the back of a donkey, and in some way or another bring it all the way to the sheepfold. So then, if bishops are to be put to the test by the standard of this Lydian stone,[10] as Christ's prescription calls for them to be, then many of them are held fast in some sort of drowsiness or lethargy, as though they didn't fear even the last A 5 judgment of God,/ where a reckoning will be made point by point of good performance of duties, or otherwise, especially of those duties that have to do with the care of souls rather than of bodies.

---

[9] The quote is from John 10. 11-12.

[10] A touchstone. Pliny in *Natural History* 33.126 says that experts can remove a "Lydian stone" from a vein of metal and, from its weight, predict the amount of gold, silver, or bronze in the vein. True bishops must look to Christ, the model of the good shepherd, as their standard.

Tondent hodie pastores diligentissime suas oues atque detondent; mulgent ac immulgent, et quas norunt senes aut inutiles alioquin neglegunt
lupisque deuorandas relinquunt, propterea scilicet, quod nec lana prosunt
nec lacte, et esui caro penitus incommoda est. Hos equidem non appel-
lauerim bonos, quantumuis se iactent ueros pastores, quoniam tondent,
sed non pascunt oues. "Pasce agnos meos" dixit Christus Iesus, hoc est
ale, cibum praesta. Et iterum: "Pasce oues meas," id est rege, et pastorem age. Qui potest bonus esse pastor, peculium atque magalia
numquam reuisens, opes ac uoluptates sollicite quaerens, depascendis
ouibus omni seposita cura? Mercenarios conducunt isti quam plurimos,
qui tondendis ouibus praesint; interdum, immo frequentius qui sine
A5v salario, uel quam mi/nimo norint ipsi ex ouibus utilitatem ac emolumentum, dimenso nihilo pastoris imminuto, sibi capere.

Novum utique pensionis genus eos eligere mercenarios ad curandum
ouile, qui quoniam nulla est ipsis constituta merces, audeant vel potius
cogantur ex rapto uiuere. Quid aliud obsecro clamitat episcopus, cum
functioni uirum praeficit alicuius nominis sine iusto salario, quam ut sibi
quaerat iure quocumque necessaria? Sed quando tu, clarissime candidis-
simeque praesul, nunc primum inis episcopatum absens longeque desitus,
cogerisque per uicarios tantisper ualde nimirum operosam administrationem agere, dum uidelicet peragis legationem Anglicam et eam Caesari
renuncias, uolo summatim percurrere, quam late pateat officium boni Pastoris et quantum fuerit desideratum, quantisque in rebus male praesules
quidam priores audiuerint, uulgatoque fuerint traducti, et nunc post fata
A 6 traducantur. Cum enim eo tu semper / candore, eo uitae morumque splen-
dore peregeris uitam priuatam, ut uiuendi dispensandique redditus ecclesiae, quos uberes et magnos nihilominus adhuc possedisti, norma et

Today shepherds most diligently clip their sheep, and shear them very close.[11] They milk them, and they milk them dry. Those that they know are old or useless they generally neglect, leaving them to be devoured by the wolves, and no doubt for this reason, that they are not useful for their wool or their milk, and their flesh is entirely unsuitable for eating. These I would certainly not call good, no matter how much they boast of being true shepherds, since they shear sheep, but do not pasture them. "Pasture my sheep", said Jesus Christ: that is, nourish them, give them food. And then again, "Pasture my sheep": that is, rule them and fill the role of a Shepherd. Who can be a good shepherd without ever revisiting his little flock and the huts? Is it the one who anxiously seeks wealth and pleasures, and has banished every thought of pasturing the sheep? That sort pay a great many hired hands who are in charge of shearing sheep. Sometimes, indeed even more frequently, these hired hands, while not receiv-

A 5v ing a salary — or only / a very small one — know to take from the sheep what is useful and profitable, without making any reduction in the shepherd's portion.

It is certainly a strange sort of collection system to use hired men to care for the sheepfold, men who, since no wages have been agreed to in cash, dare — or rather they are obliged — to live by theft. What, pray tell, is a bishop indicating plainly when he appoints a man to a position with some sort of title but without a fair salary, what else but that he should seek out what he needs by whatever rights he can claim? But since you, most famous and pure bishop, now for the first time are undertaking a bishopric, and while absent and far away, you will be forced for a while to carry on the exceedingly busy administration required by means of vicars — that is, as long as you are completing the mission to England and reporting on it to the emperor. Therefore I want briefly to review how wide the sweep is of the duties of a good shepherd, how far they have fallen short in the past, and how important were the situations in which prior bishops received bad reputations, were exposed to scorn in public, and now, even after their deaths, are still being scorned. You

A6 have led your private life with such unwavering integrity, providing / such a shining example in your actions and character, that you are held up to the clergy and the common people as the rule and only model, both

---

[11] "Clip...shear very close:" that is apparently the distinction intended between *tondent* and *detondent*; the prefix *de-* may indicate "thoroughness or completeness" (*Oxford Latin Dictionary*).

unicum specimen clericis uulgo proponaris, haud quidem abs Caesare fuisti temere ad maximas subinde legationes et uiro sincero dignas functiones selectus. Non, existimo, tibi uidebitur abs re, si tui te magistratus perpetuaeque dictaturae, quam praesens nondum praesentem adiisti, paucis admonuero.

Primum te igitur facio certiorem, episcopatum te sortitum amplissimum ac opulentissimum. Certe nullus in Hispania tantas tamque uarias regiones amplectitur nec tot terrarum tractus occupat, tot ciuitatibus ac oppidis frequentatur. Mortalium cunctorum qui tuam hanc intra prouinciam sic diffuse porrectam degunt, uerus tu pastor es; an bonus, tua situm in manu. Atqui nemo dubitabit, futurum te bonum in ampla ditione, qui A 6v fue/ris optimus in mediocri, illo ueridico testante tuam fidem elogio, quo uideris ad episcopatum euectus: "Quia fidelis nimium in paucis fuisti, supra multa te construam." Quidquid in tua peccatur ubique dicione tuo peccatur periculo, si quo pacto tuum cessauerit officium, si dormitauerint quos muneribus praeficis, si parum in praeficiendo solers aut in subducenda ratione minus circumspectus ac diligens fueris.

Nec quenquam putes, uel ipsos etiam profanos magistratus atque magnates tua censura liberos: grex sunt, quamuis alio nomine praesint arietumque uices agant. Rex ipse cum tuam in dicionem diuertit, si bellum mouet iniustum, nimirum in Christianos leui de causa, aut si pensiones imponit populis insolitas nulloque praetextu tolerabiles, si pauperculos grauat ac diuexat exactionibus, adeundus est abs te caute sapienterque A 7 quanto faciat illud animae periculo, admonendus, docendus etiam, quid / principis Christiani sit functio, regem esse, commonefaciendus, animam

for the way you have lived and for how you have managed the church's large and fruitful income, of which you have already taken possession. It was for good reason that you were repeatedly selected by the emperor for missions and posts worthy of a sincere man. So I do not think that it will seem to you inappropriate if I counsel you in a few things regarding your magistracy and perpetual dictatorship, which you have taken possession of though not yet on the actual scene.

The Great and Varied Duties of the Bishopric

First therefore I inform you that the bishopric that has fallen to your lot is exceedingly big and wealthy. Certainly none in Spain takes in so many and so varied regions. Nor does any occupy a tract of so many lands, full of so many communities and cities. Of all the mortals who live in this province of yours, which spreads out so extensively, you are the true shepherd, but whether good or not is in your hands. Neverthe-less no one will doubt that you will be a good one in a large dominion, A6v / as you were the best possible when you had a mediocre one, while your faithfulness is attested by that true maxim by which you seem to have been promoted to the episcopate. "Since you were so very faithful in small things, I will place you in charge of many."[12] Whatever goes wrong in any part of your jurisdiction, it goes wrong to your danger, if some-how your dutiful administration should lapse, if those whom you appoint to office should nod off, or if you should prove insufficiently skilled in making appointments, or should you be less circumspect and diligent in reckoning up accounts.

Nor should you think that anyone, even those secular judges and magnates, is free of your censure. They are part of the flock, even though they sometimes take charge under a different name and act like rams. The king himself, when he turns aside into your jurisdiction, if he under-takes an unjust war, that is against Christians and with little cause, or if he imposes payments on his people which are unprecedented and not tolerable by any excuse, if he burdens and plunders the humble poor with exactions, it is incumbent on you to approach him cautiously, and warn him wisely, and even teach him, how much doing that places his soul in A7 danger, and what / the duties are of a Christian ruler. He should be reminded that the king should be the soul of the people, which extends

---

[12] See Matth 25.21, of the slave who invested his master's five talents and made five more talents.

populi, quae singulos in artus uitam diffundit, omnibus ex aequo sese accommodat, omnibus bene uult, saluosque cupit, eorum commodis semper intenta.

Sed raro (dices) usu ueniet, ut in regem episcopus pastorem agat, nec rege sub quolibet fieri tuto. At qui sunt magistratus, sunt proceres; qui multa quotidie designant, quae si cura qualis oportet, esset pastoribus ouium, aut ipsi corrigerent aut pudore nonnumquam dissimularent. Iura uendunt magistratus odio. Et amicitia persaepe ducuntur; sed auaritia potissimum, quae quidem acerba pestis genus hoc homines totos habet occaecatos. Nam cum iuridicendo Caesareo et Pontificio, iure modo consulti praeficiantur; qui patrimonium forte si quid habuere, in scholis absumpserunt, aut inibi mendicato forte uictitarunt, cum prorumpunt ad honores forenses ac iudicarios, lucrum sitiunt, lucrum inhiant,/ lucrum ambiunt, lucrum illis Deus est.

A 7v

Has perditas oues bonus pastor non contemnet, nec lupis, hoc est malis geniis dilacerandas relinquet. Ad se uoce paterna uocabit, uel ipse eas adibit, a pastu messium alienarum deterret, ne tenues in pauperes desaeuiant, atque diuitibus blandiantur commonefaciet. Non pretio sententias ferant, ac pronuntient. Non alant delatores impios. Non lucro inuigilent qualibet ex re atque reo. Meminerint, semel ac iterum dicet, summi iudicis ipsos personam sustinere qui omnibus omnia bona largiuntur immeritis, qui quamlibet reis commissa fatentibus parcit, et nullis non est munificus ac liberalis. Et si forte allegauerint, non sacro, sed Caesareo se foro teneri, pastorem se profitebitur omnium animarum, medelam pa-rentibus impartiturum obstinatas diris manibus deuoturum, atque cetera Deo permissurum.

Hoc si praestiterint magni pastores, minores discent, quid sui muneris sit, et cer/te ciuitatum status melius habebit. Nullus erit magistratus, qui

A 8

life out through each of the limbs and accommodates itself to everyone on even terms. It wishes everyone well and wants them to be safe, always striving for their advantage.

Extend Your Oversight Even to the Civil Authorities

But, you will say that it is rare for a bishop to play the role of a shepherd for a king, nor is it safe for this to happen under every king. But those who are state officials are princes who devise many things every day which the shepherds of the sheep would either correct or cover up out of shame if they had the kind of concern which they ought to have. Magistrates sell people's rights, and are very often swayed by hatred or friendship. But greed has the biggest effect, which is certainly a bitter plague which grips all this kind of men in blindness. For in administering civil and ecclesiastical justice, only those experienced in the law are appointed, who have perhaps consumed their inheritance, if they had any, in schools, or have kept themselves alive there by begging. Then when they burst forth into positions of legal and judicial honor, they are thirsty A 7v for gain, they long open-mouthed for gain, / they go around seeking gain, and gain is God to them.

These lost sheep the good shepherd will not despise, nor will he leave them to be torn apart by the wolves, that is, by evil inclinations. He will call them to him with a father's voice, or go himself to them. He deters them from pasturing in other people's grain, and will remind them not to rage violently against the humble poor or to flatter the wealthy. They are not to give out or issue rulings for money. They are not to encourage unscrupulous accusers. They will not be eager for gain regarding any matter or anyone who has been charged with a crime. And the bishop will say over and over that they are to recall that they themselves represent the person of the highest judge, who gives lavishly all good things to all those who have not earned them. Who spares people even when they confess to having committed crimes, and to none fails to be openhanded and generous. And if by chance they should allege that they are subject to the emperor's courts, not the church courts, he shall declare himself to be the shepherd of all souls, ready to bestow healing on obedient souls, ready to hand stubborn souls over to the dreadful spirits of the dead, and leaving other questions to God.

If the great shepherds will take the responsibility for this, the lesser A 8 ones will learn from them all that falls within their charge, and then / certainly the condition of the cities will improve. There will be no public official who, if he sees a vigilant bishop turning his attention to

si uigilantem uiderit episcopum et ad minima quaeque curas demittentem non erubescat atque prorsus agere perperam plane metuat, praesertim cum intelligat, si censuram episcopi faciat ipse pili, abs rege tandem seuerius, indice praesule, bonis, ne grauius dicam, plectendum. Rectores urbium, quos senatores appellabant Romani, nonne sanctius ac uigilantius publica curarent, si pastoris uel obiurgationem aliquam timerent? Rempublicam isti curare se dicunt, cum nihil plerumque faciant minus. Emunt eorum quam plurimi functiones illas, ut ex publicis commodis corradant aliquid et ut praeficiantur uel publicis aedificiis, uel aedilicio muneri, tum horreo aut aerario; siue procuratores forte legentur in publica concilia, quae solent abs rege frequenter indici (curias nostri uocant), quam quidem in procurationem, siue legationem, propensi sunt omnes, certi, plus inde se pecuniarum semel habituros, quam /distractori magistratus impenderunt.

A 8v

Multae sunt praeterea illis occasiones fallendi uendicandique sibi ius publicum. Agunt curam civitatis, ut uolunt uideri, et proprias curant res: quodque fuerat eis commune cum omnibus, mille captionibus faciunt suum, subornatis iudicibus qui quocumque tandem praetextu ipsis addicant.

Loquor de quibusdam mentis perditae, non utique de omnibus: sed una scabiosa nonnumquam ouis inficit omne pecus. Atqui bonus si pastor inuigilaret omnibusque locis ac horis adesset anxius, ne malis moribus ac uetitis pascuis assuescerent oues, non usque adeo maiores oues et pinguiores uerterentur, ac transformarentur in lupos, insultantes in debile pecus negligentia pastoris. Quid iam tritius ac uerius, quam quod solet uulgo iactari, minores minusque nocentes maioribus a furibus ac improbissimis suspendi? An est qui noceat uerius, frequentius, perniciosius, quam /qui boni uiri speciem gerit et quem nullus audet proritare, ueritus ne noceat aptius et impunius desaeuiat?

B1

Cum receptum sit ad magistratus urbanos, qui praesunt iuridicendo sontiumque quaestionibus atque suppliciis praepositi sunt, non recipi, ni moribus et iuris peritia praestantes, tum ad senatorias dignitates uiros

every small detail, will not blush, then thoroughly and wholly fearing to do wrong — especially when he knows that, even if he may pay little heed to the censure of a bishop, eventually the crown, following the rec- ommendations of that bishop, will later punish him even more severely, depriving him of his goods or something worse. Wouldn't those who govern the cities, whom the Romans called senators, attend to public duties in a holier and more vigilant manner, even if they only feared some sort of scolding from their shepherd? They claim that they attend to the public good, when for the most part there is nothing they do less. Very many of them buy those positions, so that out of public remuneration they can scrape together something by being appointed to be in charge either of public buildings, or to public posts, such as the granary or the treasury. Or perhaps they are named as superintendents over public coun- cils (our people call them *curiae*, assemblies), which are often appointed by the king. They all are very inclined to this sort of management, or del- egated authority, since in it they are sure to make at one stroke more

A 8v money than / they paid out to the person who sold them their office. What's more there are many opportunities for them to deceive and claim for themselves the rights of the public. They are taking care of the city, as they want it to appear, but they also take care of their own interests. What should have been shared in common by them and everyone, through a thousand sorts of frauds they make their own by bribing judges, who consign it to them eventually on some pretext.

I am speaking of certain ones with a depraved character, not indeed of all, but sometimes just one mangy sheep infects the whole flock. But if the good shepherd would be watchful and present in all places and times, taking pains that the sheep not grow accustomed to bad habits and forbidden pastures, then the sheep would not constantly get bigger and fatter and be changed into wolves, stepping on the weaker animals through the carelessness of the shepherd. What is more of a cliché, or more true, than that which is commonly bandied about — that the smaller and less harmful are choked to death by the bigger and more perverse thieves? Is there anyone who does harm more truly, more frequently and

B 1 more perniciously / than a person who only takes on the appearance of a good man? Or one whom no one dares to provoke, afraid that he will only do harm more skillfully and ravage with greater impunity?

Still, it is an established practice that men are not appointed as city judges (who preside over the administration of justice and are put in charge of judicial investigations of criminals and their punishments)

modo nobiles et quos honestae reddunt divitiae commendabiles, solum
admitti. Qui quidem facillime reducerentur in uiam ciuiumque si non
omnino bonorum, at non penitus improborum speciem ferrent, modo fuisset eis persuasum, administrationem reipublicae praesulibus esse curae
nonnullae et quidquid ipsi patrarint, quod ciuium non sit in rem, siue
cunctorum uel cuiusque pauperculi, execraturum episcopum dirisque
manibus atque Plutoni deuoturum. Ceterum dormitant pastores, uel potius
cura seposita ouium, lucris maioribus inhiant. Interim lupi grassantur,
B 1v canes (hoc est sacri contionatores) iam his, iam illis / applaudunt, capti
lucello, capti deuia, ne dicam impia, quapiam spe. Quid superest, ni Christum obtestari, suppetias det gregi suo [*M omits* suo] destituto pastoribus,
destituto canibus, qui lupinam paene omnibus pellem induerunt?

Iam magnates, magnificis qui titulis superbiunt, quanto moderatius,
aequius, sapientius suas gererent perpetuas dictaturas, si norint episcopum
ac uerum pastorem ouium amantem, si uigilantem prorsus circa curam
gregis animaduerterent! Eo quid episcopus magnatem non adeat affec-
tuque paterno uel his admoneat uocibus? "Heus, ouis tu mea es, aber-
rantem ac deuia quaeque sectantem te conspicari non feram; reducas
gradum oportet, si tuae uitae rationem, qualem expedit et ipse percupio,
me supremum uis apud iudicem reddere. Scio, neque me putes omnino
latere, quo pacto mortales oues agas, qui tua sub ditione degunt exigis
indebita uixque toleranda uectigalia, protrudis pro tua libidine
B 2 quocumque, uel in bellum, uel in seditionem. / Trahis, distrahis, tamquam

unless they are outstanding in their knowledge of the law and in their character. And when it's a question of senatorial dignities, the only ones accepted are nobles whose honorable wealth has given them a good reputation. Indeed, men such as those could quite easily be brought back to the path again and then maintain the public appearance of being, if not of the absolutely best citizens, then at least not of being the most completely corrupt. All that is necessary is that they be persuaded that the administration of the republic has become a concern of the bishops, and that whenever they do something which is not in the interests of the citizens — either of all or only of some insignificant poor man — the bishop will curse them and consign them to the dread spirits of the dead and to Pluto.[13] But the shepherds doze, or rather, neglecting the care of their sheep, they long open-mouthed for greater gains. In the meantime, the wolves grow fatter; the dogs — that is, the preaching clergy —

B 1v applaud first one and then another faction / as they are captured by a small gain, captured by a false — or should I say immoral? — hope. What is left except to call on Christ, begging him to come to the aid of the flock? It is destitute of both shepherds and dogs, nearly all of whom have dressed themselves in wolf skins.

Now magnates, who grow proud with magnificent titles, how much more moderately, fairly, and wisely would they manage their perpetual dictatorships if they recognized that their bishop, a true shepherd and lover of the sheep, was thoroughly alert when it came to the care of the flock? Why, then, would a bishop not go to a magnate and with a father's affection admonish him with words like the following? "Listen! You are my sheep and I will not stand by and see you wandering away and chasing after everything which lies off the path. You must turn back, if you want me to defend your life before the Supreme Judge with an accounting such as I also long to find favorable to you. I know, lest you think that it has escaped my notice completely, how you drive the human sheep who live under your power. How you demand from them taxes which they do not owe and are almost unbearable; you drive people

B 2 wherever your whim dictates, as into war or sedition. / You drag and pull

---

[13] A reference to the bishop's power to excommunicate. Maldonado speaks as though that act would be followed by eternal damnation to hell of the rebellious soul, but strictly speaking its effect is on the here and now: "excommunication deprives clerics and laymen of all their rights in Christian society" and need not be permanent, as it can be removed by absolution (see *Catholic Encyclopedia* under "excommunication.")

pretio seruos emptos, imperas pecunias nouis titulis, quas tu uenatu, spec-
taculis, ludis atque immodicis conuiuiis insumas. Alis ad haec familiam
inutilem, scurras, aleones, uenatores, lusores, comessatores, ganeones,
feminas impudicas, petulantes, insanas. Num horum non putas rationem
subducendam apud deum omnium parentem, seruatorem animarum nos-
trarum qui pro nobis nostrisque maximis commissis tot pertulit cruciatus,
tot ignominias subiit? Haud utique modo ratio exigetur a te dictorum
atque factorum tuorum, sed et a me, cui grex huius prouinciae commis-
sus est. Proinde muta, obsecro, uiuendi rationem, tempera tuos affectus,
christianum esse te non obliuiscaris. Habes (ut uideo) non modo dum peragitur sacrum, sed et in mensa, et in quotidiano conuictu, theologos contionatores, habes confessores laureatos magistros: si eos audis, et sunt
illi qui uolunt uideri, / haud opinor ignorabis, quid a suis exigat Christus,
quid postulet uirtus, quid ratio humanitasque deposcant, quid denique sit,
quibus notis ac symbolis dignoscatur uerus Christianismus. Sin contem-
nis, paruis momentaneisque uoluptatibus perpetuos tibi cruciatus parabis,
cum uere nihil dulcius, nihil sit amoenius, quam sinceram gerere consci-
entiam, nullis stimulis nullisque morsibus dilaceratam, uidelicet per bona
sic externa, per diuitiarum affluentiam ita sapienter et caute pertransire,
ut summa bona non amittantur. Non enim obsunt diuitiae, bonae paran-
dae conscientiae nec uitae uere Christianae, sed prosunt maxime, dum
utaris Christiano ritu, dum mortis memineris, reddendaeque rationis. Non
desinam identidem officii te Christiani admonere; si boni tu consulueris
studium meum, sentiet anima tua propediem: instat dies ultimus et hora;
sin minus, functus fuero sollertis pastoris officio teque perditas inter oues
re/ponam. Prostant ad genua famuli, cum tibi ministrant aliquid aut
respondent rogati, quoquoue modo te adeunt. Etiam si sedeas ad aram in
templo, culturam tuam praeferunt Christi. Si more fit et recepta consue-
tudine, laudare non possum, feram tamen, dum non id exigas tu nec si
praetermittatur, facias pili. Porro adorationes has putare debitas, atque

B 2v

B 3

your people to pieces as though they were slaves bought for a price. You requisition fees with new excuses, so you can spend the money on hunting, shows, games, and extravagant parties. To this end you nourish a useless household of buffoons, gamblers, hunters, clowns, gluttons, and revelers, and women who are immodest, wanton, and mad. Can it be you don't realize you will have to render an account of all these to God, the father of all and the savior of our souls, who for us and our immense sins bore so many tortures unto death and endured so many humiliations? By no means just from you will an account be demanded of what you have said and done, but also from me, to whom the flock of this province has been entrusted. Therefore change, I beg you, your way of life, moderate your desires, and don't forget that you are a Christian. I see that you have living with you, not only while mass is being said but also at meals and in daily activities, preachers who are theologians. You have confessors who are teachers crowned with laurel wreaths. If you listen to them —

B 2v   and if they really are the persons they want to look like — / then I am entirely sure that you will discover what Christ requires of his own, what virtue requires, what reason and humanity demand. In sum, you will learn what true Christianity is and by what tokens and symbols it can be recognized. If, however, you scorn them, you will prepare for yourself perpetual tortures in exchange for small and momentary pleasures. Truly nothing is sweeter, nothing more pleasant, than to have a clear conscience, not one torn ragged by goading, biting sins, and to pass wisely and cautiously through the midst of many external goods and an abundance of riches in such a way that the highest good is not lost. For wealth is certainly no obstacle to obtaining a clear conscience or leading a truly Christian life, but it is most beneficial when you make use of the Christian liturgy, while you remember death and that you will have to render an account of yourself. I shall not cease to remind you repeatedly regarding your Christian duty. If you have a good opinion of my efforts, very soon your soul will feel the difference, for the last day and hour are at hand. But even if you do not, nonetheless I shall have performed the duty of a skillful shepherd and shall put you back among the lost sheep.

B 3   / Servants present themselves on their knees whenever they serve you something. They respond to your requests no matter how they approach you. Even if you are sitting at the altar in church, they prefer your worship to that of Christ. If it is done out of custom and by established practice, still I cannot praise it, although I will allow it, provided that you don't demand it or care in the slightest if it is overlooked. To think of this

praetermissas reposcere, paganismi cuiusdam insolentissimi plane sym-
bolum est, Christiana simplicitati pugnantis ex diametro.

Eiusmodi sunt, quae si curae medullitus esse pastoribus proceres intel-
ligerent aliquandoque fuissent experti, melius haberent uici, pagi,
oppidula, moderatiusque compilarentur a militibus et uectigalium redemp-
toribus uicani, rarius segetes ungulis equorum contererentur. Tributa census pensiones milleque molestiae non utique passim redigerent ad men-
dicitatem, nonnunquam ad laqueum miseros agricolas opificesque
B 3v   urbanos. Opulenti / mercatores, qui per maria et terras merces longinquas
in regiones transuehunt, ferunt ac referunt emolumenti gratia, praeferentes utile recto, numquam non aberrantes ab honesto (de auaris super-
stitioseque Christianis sermo nunc est, bonos ordine quocumque uolumus exceptos, nedum in hoc, ubi summae pietatis uidimus ipsi clarissima
monumenta) quanto iam in periculo uersantur, ni bonus quispiam pastor
reducat in uiam, fucatis prohibens a rapinis?
    Circuiens pastor oues, cum in harum inciderit aliquam pinguem,
rogabit, cuinam congerat tam sitienter opes; si forte retulerit, quo laute
sibi uiuat aut quo nobilitati filios ascribat, uel potius ut sacellum aut
aedem sacram magnifice construat, in qua nobilitatis insignia, qualia sibi
ipse finxerit, futuris saeculis spectentur, laudabit pastor mentis celsi-
B 4   tudinem magnificosque conatus, postea uero quaeret, num / bona fide,
sine cuiusquam incommodo diuitias parauerit; solito more dicet, sicuti
solent eiusdem paene ordinis omnes, qui nobilitant filios, qui dissimulata
tandem negotiatione, emunt praefecturas dignitatesque senatorias. Mercatores enim qui non ab omni negotiatione penitus ablegant ueritatem,
esuriant semper et algeant necesse est. Ibi pastor,

    "Errabunda quidem ouis es" inquiet, "ego uero pastor, haud certe
bonus, quando te tamdiu deuiare sum passus; reducas cum primis gradum

worship as due you, and to demand it when it is overlooked, is clearly a sign of some sort of outlandish paganism, diametrically in conflict with Christian simplicity."

Your Example Will Have a Wide Influence

These are the sort of things which, if the magnates knew to be of deep concern to the shepherds, and if they had sometimes experienced such an admonition, then the hamlets, the rural districts, and the small towns would be better off and the villagers would be more moderately plundered by soldiers and the tax farmers. Less often would the corn fields be pounded by the horses' hooves. Exactions, property taxes, and a thousand other harrassments would not so completely and so widely reduce wretched farmers and city craftsmen to poverty — and sometimes the noose. Wealthy

B 3v merchants / transport their wares through seas and lands to distant regions, taking them back and forth for the sake of profit. They prefer that which is advantageous to that which is right, never failing to wander away from that which is honest. (Here I am talking about greedy and superstitious Christians, and we want an exception made of good men of whatever rank, not to mention the man in whom we ourselves have seen shining monuments of the highest integrity). How great is the danger into which they are already getting themselves, unless some good shepherd leads them back onto the path by forbidding their disguised robbery.

As the shepherd goes about among his sheep and comes upon one of them that is quite fat, he will ask him for what purpose, pray, is he heaping up wealth so thirstily? If by chance his answer is, so that he may live for himself luxuriously, or so that he may confer nobility upon his children, or rather so that he may magnificently build a chapel or a holy building in which his noble coat of arms (which he invented for himself), can be put on display in coming ages, then the shepherd will praise the loftiness of his mind and his magnificent undertakings. However, he will

B 4 also ask him whether / in good faith, he has won his wealth without troubling anyone else. The rich man will answer in the usual way, just as do nearly all of that same class, who improve their children's rank, and finally with secret negotiation buy official offices and senatorial rank. For merchants who do not entirely cover over the truth about all of their dealings always starve and inevitably are left out in the cold. To him the shepherd will say:

Shepherd's Admonition to a Rich Man

"You are indeed a wandering sheep, and I, the shepherd, am far from being a good one, for allowing you to stray so long off the path. It is

oportet; timeo maxime tibi, timeo mihi. Deus quidem ex alto cuncta prospectans, moderans atque gubernans, patientissimus est, qui me non perdiderit pastorem, proicientem curam ouium in mercenarios, qui te nec reduxerunt, nec perditae me quidem ouis admonerunt. Non utique damno, quod opes tibi paraueris, quod orbe quocumque asportaueris, / sed quod aequi bonique metas longe praeterieris. Honestum est uitae necessaria nobis atque nostris quaerere, posteris etiam interdum cura non omnino segni prospicere, ceterum sine fraude, sine dolo malo, Christi proximique semper et ubique caritate protenta praeuiaque. Si nauigas enim ad Indos, ad insulas maris rubri, uel ad nouam Hispaniam, quae maris est Oceani limes postremus — sed longinqua praetermittamus —, si nauigas in Angliam, in Flandriam, in Germaniam, et sine Christi Christianique nominis respectu per fas et nefas lucrum sectaris, fallis, mentiris, peieras, nihil tandem omittis ad quaestum augendum, etiam si pugnet cum aequitate pietateque, fur omnium earum es rerum, quas ita parasti furtoque teneris. Vide tu quibus artibus paraueris, si fraus intercessit neglectusque diuini mandati detines alienum, dum iniuste paratis uteris. Resipisce igitur, frater in domino dilecte, tempera, reprime, moderare cupidita/tes effrenes, lucrum certius illud rere, quod recta dictat conscientia, locupletioresque fore, partisque diutius fruituros crede pie solertes quam impie dissolutos."

In hanc sententiam si pastores dissererent cum suis ouibus, melius haberent omnia, resipiscerent quamplurimae, suspicerent suum pastorem, Dei timorem prae omnibus ducerent, negotiarentur, nundinarentur, sed in Christo Iesu, lucrum sectarentur, sed honestum, inuiolato diuinae legis praecepto, quo non secus iubemur amare proximos quam nos ipsos. Veniamus tandem ad uniuersum gregem, qui constat uariis et ordinibus et hominum generibus uariis uiuendi institutis, uariis fallendi ciues ac uicinos artibus. Vendunt alii telas aureas sericas Damascenes, alii laneas, lineas diuersorum ponderum ac existimationum; mille tamen fraudibus irretiunt emptores, fallunt pretio, mensura, genere, specie, materia, colore,

B 4v

B 5

important for you to turn back immediately. I fear especially for you, but I fear also for myself. Indeed, as God from on high looks out over all things, moderating and governing, he is exceedingly patient in not having destroyed me as a shepherd, even though I foist off the care of the sheep onto hired hands, who have neither led you back nor informed me even about a lost sheep. I do not necessarily condemn your having obtained wealth, or that you have carried it off for yourself from some-
B 4v where in the world, /but that you have gone far past the boundaries of what is just and good. It is honorable to seek the necessities of life for us and ours, even with efforts not entirely sluggish to make provisions for our descendants — but without trickery, without any evil deception, and with love of Christ and our neighbor always and everywhere held out in front and leading the way. You may sail to the Indies, to the islands of the Red Sea, or to New Spain, which is the farthest limit of the Ocean Stream — but let us skip over places far distant. If you sail to England, to Flanders, to Germany, and without respect for Christ and your name as a Christian you seek profit by fair means or foul, by tricks, lies and perjury, finally omitting nothing as you seek to increase your profit even though that profit is incompatible with fairness and integrity, then you are a thief of all those things, since that is how you obtained them; you are caught in the act of theft. You must look at the devices by which you have gained wealth, if fraud has played a part, or neglect of divine command, and you hold back what belongs to someone else while enjoying what you have unjustly obtained. Therefore come to your senses, beloved brother in the Lord. Temper, control, and moderate your
B 5 unrestrained / desires. Reckon any gain to be more certain that your clear conscience recommends, and believe that those will be more enriched, and will enjoy their gains longer, who are piously resolute rather than impiously dissolute."

If shepherds would preach along these lines to their sheep, all things would be in better condition. The greatest possible number of sheep would come to their senses. They would look up to their shepherd. They would put the fear of God before all things. They would do business and conduct trade, but in Jesus Christ. They would pursue profits, but honest profits, without violating the teaching of the divine law, in which we are commanded to love our neighbors no differently than our own. Now let us, finally, consider the condition of all your flock, which is made up of various orders and sorts of people, with various regulations for living together, and various devices for deceiving fellow citizens and neighbors.

B 5v praesertim si domi *[in domo M]* uendant, ut assolent, subobscura. / Iam si mox non numeratur pecunia, distrahunt multo pluris, nec modus est impondendi nec finis ulla. Quid dicam de uestiariis, calceariis, pileariis, sutoribus, et aliis eiusmodi rerum opificibus, qui suis multifariam artibus fallunt, neque ualeas, si sis Argus aut ipse Mercurius, uitare captionem? Quid dicam de his qui uendunt obsonia? Qui panem? Qui uinum? Enimuero tam celebris est imponendi consuetudo, ut socordes, hebetes, somniculosi iam habeantur, qui mentem gerant sinceram.

    Nec facile nubunt simplices feminae; uiri difficile ducunt uxores, qui fraudes non admodum callent, qui non uulpinam quandam in uicinum uafritiem exercent. Primam iam dicunt dotem, scire uiuere, uidelicet fraude nosse duplicare rem, fallere semper emptorem, uitiare obsonia, adulterare quidquid ad manum uenerit. Haec prima ducitur ars, haec pronior uia rem ad familiarem augendam. Quid? Viuitur e rapto, uel potius

B 6 e mutuo lania/tu. Diluit hic uinum, sed calceos emit arietinos pro hircinis. Fallit alius butyro, caseo, pastillis, et fallitur carne rebusque ad uictum omnibus necessariis. Medici aggrauant morbos atque producunt, non nunquam negligentia erroreue perimunt quos nequaquam letalis morbus tenebat. Pharmacopolae uitiant medicamenta, miscent quae maxime nocent, mentiuntur longinquo catapotia, pharmaca, malagmata petita, cum sint quam uilissima. Sed par pari refertur, si cum uitae discrimine posset pecuniarum iactura conferri.

    Ad disturbandas insidias, fraude, deceptiones uendentium, commenti sunt sibi mortales nouum quendam magistratum, proxenetas scilicet, qui

Some sell cloth of gold or of silk from Damascus, while others sell woolen or linen cloth of varying weights and qualities. They tangle buyers up with a thousand sorts of cheating, deceiving them as to the price, the measure, the sort of merchandise, the appearance, the material, the color, especially if they sell, as they are accustomed to, in a dark
B 5v house.[14] / When cash is not paid immediately, they sell at a much higher price, and there is no moderation or any limit at all to cheating. What shall I say about clothing dealers, shoe salesmen, purveyors of felt caps, shoe-makers, or other craftsmen of items of this sort, who deceive in many ways with their tricks; you would not be able to avoid being caught, even if you were Argus or Mercury himself. What shall I say about those who sell victuals? Or bread? Or wine? For in fact the custom of cheating is so common that those who have moral integrity are now considered lazy and weak minded, and as if in a daze.

It is not easy for honest women to marry, and men with difficulty find brides if the men are not great experts in deceit who practice a kind of foxy cunning against their neighbor. They now claim that the primary dowry is to know how to live, that is, to know how to double your possessions by trickery, always deceive the buyer, sell tainted victuals and adulterate whatever comes to hand. This art is considered first and foremost. This is the most likely method for increasing your estate. In a
B 6 word, everyone lives by theft,[15] or rather, by mangling each other. /One man dilutes the wine he sells, but the shoes he buys are made of ram's skin in place of goats' hide. Another man fools others with the butter, the cheese, and the cakes, but he is fooled with the meat and other things that are more necessary to life. Doctors make illnesses worse and lengthen them, and sometimes by negligence and error they kill those who had shaken off the grip of a fatal disease. Pharmacists taint medicines, mix in things that do the most harm, and dream up far-fetched pills, drugs, and emollients which are as disgusting as possible. But here like is returned to like, if danger to life could be compared with loss of money.

To thwart these treacheries, fraud, and deceptions by sellers, mortals have invented for themselves a new sort of magistrate, called negotia-tors.[16] They run up and down and intervene as arbitrators between

---

[14] *domi* emended to *in domo* in M.

[15] "Lives by theft": *uiuitur ex rapto,* cf. Vergil *Aeneid* 7.749.

[16] *Proxenetai,* a word that also denotes business agents, but this word in later Latin, along with this entire passage, seems to have sexual overtones. *Proxeneta* is defined by the Dictionary of the Spanish Royal Academy as "A person who obtains benefits from the

cursitent et inter emptorem ac distractorem arbitratores intercedant et,
cum imposturas tollere aliquas adnixi sint, ingens [*M, corrected from*
ingentem] earum agmen inuexerunt. Enimuero credo legem de hoc cre-
B 6v ando magistratu tulisse feruidos quosdam impatientesque morarum,/ qui
quouis damno uolunt statim habere quod cupiunt, acceptumque proxenetis
ferant, quod ipsi dicto citius uoti fuerint compotes. Certe proxenetae, qui
mulas et equos uendunt, quali sint digni cruce, norunt illi, qui bis eorum
opera sunt usi. Quae Furia, quod sidus infestum tot mala in populum
Christianum inuexit? Somnus dormitatioque pastorum. Aliam rem agunt,
curant cutem et uentrem; de pascendis, instituendis, bonisque moribus
imbuendis ouibus nec per somnium quidem cogitant, de tondendis ipsa
uix in morte curas deponunt, si quo forte pacto ualeant prouentus relin-
quere successoribus uberiores ac pinguiores.

Qui boni officio pastoris fungi studet episcopus, lustret quotannis oues
suas, censum faciat, praesens ipse praesentes salutet uicatim ac oppida-
tim, si non uacat aut non datur alias singulatim, mores ac uitae rationes
discat, doceat quousque per instituta Christi fas sit quaerendis opibus

buyers and retailers. Although they have made an effort to stop some cheating, they have introduced a huge battle line of new frauds. I truly believe that some impetuous people, impatient of delays, passed the law to create this magistrate, / people who, at no matter what cost, wish to get immediately what they desire, and they give the credit to the negotiators, because thus they have gained what they wished faster than can be uttered. Certainly when people have [once or] twice used the service of negotiators who sell she-mules and stallions, they know what sort of torture they deserve.[17] Which Fury, or which unlucky star has brought in so many evils directed against the Christian community? It is the sleeping and the dozing of the shepherds. Their attention is focused elsewhere; they are taking care of their own skins and bellies. About feeding, teaching, and training the sheep in good habits they don't think at all, even in dreams. But they don't stop thinking about shearing them. Scarcely even at the point of death do they lay aside their thoughts of whether, by chance, in some way they can leave to their heirs a richer and juicier yield.

B 6v

Getting to Know the Sheep Personally

Any bishop who is eager to perform the duties of a good shepherd should go to look at his sheep every year; he should take a census. He should greet them in person, village by village, town by town. If he does not have the leisure for that, or he has no opportunity at another time to visit them, one by one, let him learn their character and the nature of their lives; let him instruct them how long it is permitted by the

---

prostitution of another person," and the word is similarly used in the drama *La Celestina*. This may also add point to the statement that they appeal to "people who, no matter what the cost, wish to get immediately what they desire." Finally, "she mules and stallions" may refer to female genitalia and male prostitutes.

[17] This passage about the negotiating magistrates is somewhat enigmatic, and complicated by the apparent sexual implications as suggested above, whereby the "negotiators" are actually pimps. On the surface it suggests that impatient buyers, unwilling to be delayed by the process of haggling over the price, prefer to pay the first asking price and then to file a complaint with, and perhaps offer a bribe to, the magistrate in charge of retail sales, alleging that they have been overcharged. The magistrate, it seems, would then immediately render a judgment in favor of the buyer, perhaps ordering as punishment a refund of part or all of the price paid. Historically, the existence of municipal officials – known as *corredores*, 'brokers,' — to supervise public markets in Spain began in Andalucian cities. City councils, to avoid fraudulent reselling and to insure that commercial transactions conformed to the official weights and measures, supported salaried posts. Eventually, however, these officals lived entirely off of the fines they collected and from fees for the performance of their durties. By the end of the fifteenth century cities not only no longer payed salaries, but charged these brokers a licensing fee. While figures are not available regarding the amount of money the city of Burgos collected from them in 1530, by 1649 that source of revenue represented about four percent of the city government's income. See Gutiérrez Alonso - Méndez Sáez 1997.

B 7 intendere, / quot modis quolibet in opificio et arte peccatur, quibus poenis diuina lege subiaceant qui damno alterius non omnino parcunt, qui
posthabita caritate quaestui se deuouent; et quos repererit dociles, blande
moneat atque, si sit opus, coarguat, indomitos maleque persuasos deterreat et uindictam cum praesentem, tum futuram minetur.

Non est profecto quod episcopus excuset, unum tot millibus non sufficere: habet mercenariorum ingentem turbam episcopalis functio; hos si
comperit episcopus minus studere commoditatibus ouium, ut sunt cum
conducebantur polliciti, sed uulpibus ac lupis esse nocentiores, redigat in
ordinem ut cum aliis ouibus errent aut, quod sanius est, magalibus abster-
reat, accersatque uiros aequos ac uere pios, qui onus ex parte leuent, qui
uicem praesulis cum candore gerant, qui uelint et possint praestare, quod
episcopum addecet, ipsos praestare; ii difficiles non sunt inuentu sub
B 7v bono pastore. Ta/les uidemus induere mores, studia et affectus aulicos
omnes, quales norunt principi placere. Venantur cum uenatore, ludunt
cum lusore, belligerantur, affectant stratagemata cum bellatore, amant,
ducunt choreas cum amatore. Denique certant in ea maxime re praestare,
quae principem potissimum iuuat. Idem usu uenire in episcoporum aulis
etiam animaduertimus. Si studet episcopus esse quod dicitur, conantur
idem clerici omnes, nedum domestici et familiares. Bonum agit pastorem
episcopus, gregis non amat spolium, sed profectum, tondet, sed nihil sibi
uendicat, ni quod suum est, pauperibus relinquit aequam portionem, totus
denique intendit pascendis ouibus; et ne uicina laedant contagia, idem
praestare laborant bene morati clerici: ponunt concubinas, minime ue-
xant decimarum redemptores, fugitant lites, filiorum cooptationem ad
paternum sacerdotium haud ita pecunia redimere procurant; postremo
B 8 sacrificant / sine probro, sine totius ordinis ignominia. Non dubium est
quin ualente capite cetera conualeant membra. Fontes ni sint purissimi,

B 7 teaching of Christ to devote oneself to the seeking of wealth, / in how many ways sins are committed in each kind of occupation and craft, which punishments, by divine law, are meted out to those who do not completely refrain from harming others but who put charity second and instead devote themselves to profit. Those he finds receptive he should gently warn, and if necessary he should prove their guilt. Those who are stubborn and of an evil disposition he should frighten and threaten with punishments both present and future.

When To Delegate Your Authority

A bishop certainly cannot excuse himself by the fact that one person isn't enough for so many thousands. A bishop's position calls for the use of a huge crowd of hirelings. If the bishop finds that these are not as eager for the well-being of the sheep as they promised to be when they were hired, but are in fact more harmful than foxes and wolves, he should put them back in their place, so that they can wander along with the sheep. Or he will do what is healthier: drive them away from the huts, summoning just and truly religious men who will lighten part of the burden, who will with integrity play the role of the superintendent, who will be both willing and able to give what is proper for a bishop, that is, of

B 7v themselves. They are not hard to find under a good shepherd. / They are similar to men whom we see adapt themselves to the character, interests, and manners of court, which they know will please a prince. They hunt with the hunter, play with the player, they make war and carry out strategies with the warrior, they love and lead their lover in dancing. In short, they vie with one another above all to act in a way which pleases the prince. This same behavior we observe also being acted out in episcopal courts. If the bishop strives to be what his name implies, all the clergy try to do the same, not to mention the domestics and the servants. The bishop who acts as a good shepherd does not like to see the flock plundered, but rather to increase. He shears, but claims nothing for himself but his own portion, leaving a fair portion for the poor. Thus he strives with his whole being to feed the sheep. So that contact with their neighbors will not do harm, clergy of good character strive to set the same sort of example. They put aside their concubines. In no way do they interfere with the tithe collectors. They avoid lawsuits, and by no means do they arrange with money for a priest's

B 8 son to take over his benefice. In sum, they say mass / without there being any grounds for reproach, without any dishonor to their entire office. There is no doubt that when the head is strong, so, too, the other members with it. If fountains are not completely pure, how can the rivers derived from

qui flumina eisdem deriuata clarescent? Pastoris situm in manu est bene
ualeant an male oues. In episcopi situm arbitrio est, sapientes sint, offi-
ciosi, pii, uirtutis amantes clerici, an idiotae pessimi, pecus inutile.

Sed discutiamus an monachi subsint episcopo, an sint oues, an aliud
forte genus animantum. Contendunt quidem ipsi suos habere pastores,
nec ius quidem ullum habere episcopum in ipsos. Sit uerum quod praedicant, habeant suum forum, suum tribunal, suos ariopagitas, sed sua dum
se contineant intra saepta, praescriptos dum non praeteruehantur ultra limites, dum monachi sint, hoc est uitam ducentes solitariam. Ceterum si
miscent se negotiis mundanis, si bini totum cursitant orbem, lites agitant,
uendunt, emunt, quaerunt quae sua sunt, non Dei, si dum curant igitur
B 8v mundi res, humane quid forte /designant, non coarguentur ab episcopo,
primario quidem pastore? Non protrudentur, non abigentur ab deluso
grege? Non cogentur in suum ouile, si tergiuersentur, uel fuste? Irruunt
in aliena pascua, metunt quae non seminauerunt, simulant haedos sim-
plicissimos et agunt lupos rapacissimos, fingunt se castratos ob Christum
et salacitate superant quoslibet procos et non erit quem timeant, cuius
seueritate coerciti mitigent effrenatos affectus? Non eo quidem animo
isthaec dicuntur a me, quod damnem sanctissimos monachorum ordines,
in quibus compertissimum est, quamplurimos inesse doctissimos uiros et
eminentissimos, ac ueluti uirtutum omnium clarissima lumina: per quos
quidem solos stare non dubitem, quin Deus optimus maximus iterum cata-
clysmum infundat in orbem ob nostra maxima commissa; uerum sunt
adeo quidam exorbitantes, peruicaces, indomiti, ut eorum ob insolentiam

them run clear? It lies in the shepherd's hand whether the sheep will be in good or bad health. It lies in the bishop's judgment whether the clergy are wise, hardworking, pious, lovers of virtue, or instead the worse sort of morons, useless cattle.

The Love Affairs of Monks

But let us discuss whether monks are beneath a bishop, or if they are sheep, or maybe some other sort of living creature. They themselves contend that they have their own shepherds, that the bishop has no legal control at all over them. Let what they preach be true: let them have their own court, their own tribunal, their own courts of the Areopagus,[18] but only so long as they stay within their own walls and do not wander outside of their prescribed boundaries; so long as they remain monks, that is, leading a solitary life. However, if they mix themselves into worldly matters, if two by two they run up and down the whole world stirring up lawsuits, selling, buying, looking for what is theirs, not God's — in short, while they are paying attention to things of this world — if they happen to / be guilty of something as humans often are, should they not be chided by the bishop, who is certainly their primary shepherd? Should they not be thrust and driven away from the flock they have cheated? Should they not be forced back into their own sheepfold, even with a club, if they show reluctance? They rush into another man's pastures, they harvest what they did not sow and pretend to be young and very simple-minded kids, but they act like highly rapacious wolves. They claim to have been castrated for the sake of Christ, but in their lust they outdo any suitors. Will there be no one for them to fear, whose sternness might force them to moderate their unbridled passions? I certainly do not say such things with the intention of condemning the very holy orders of monks. In them are found, as is very well known, a great many highly learned men, who are like the brightest luminaries of all virtues. Were it not for their existence alone, I don't doubt that God, the best and the greatest, would once again pour out on the world a cataclysm caused by our enormous sins. But certain of those monks are such transgressors — stubborn, disobedient and insolent — that even though they are outstanding for

B 8v

---

[18] The supreme tribunal of Athens, the Areopagus heard the gravest cases in its sessions on the hill of Ares west of the Acropolis. The place received its name, according to myth, because there the gods tried and acquitted Ares of the murder of Poseidon's son, who had raped Ares' daughter. The severity of the mortal court's verdicts and the justice of its judgments made it famous for knowledge and impartiality. See *Oxford Companion to Classical Literature*, pp. 51-52.

C 1 pietate doctrinaque praestan/tes male nonnunquam audiant. Pastores siquam suas inter oues alienam deprehendunt, ferunt, sinunt tantisper prata cum propriis tondere, dum se tenet intra peculium, dum non diuertit ad segetes; sin uero intemperans est et lasciua, funda conteritur, pedo retrahitur, pedibus nonunquam et manibus ligatis, remittitur ad herum. Similiter et episcopus ferat monachum mendicantem ostiatim, adeuntem ciuem febricitantem ac lecto decumbentem, domicilium pauperum inuisentem; at homicidam ob interceptam mulierculam, conciliatorem inhonestorum amorum, uirginis raptorem, adulterum qui feret? Nec otiantem quidem animi causa, qui mos illis solemnis est. Irrepserunt quondam monachi Romanorum pontificum indulgentia atque permissu in occultas confessiones, nec episcopos quidem aut parochos paenituit onere perquam graui ex parte fuisse leuatos; eam illi confessiones audiendi

C 1v ueniam sic postea dilatarunt/ ita deinceps ambierunt, ut nulla paene sit iam femina diues, quae non supplex ac gemebunda monachi genibus succumbat et peccata confiteatur. Exaggerant illi non infacunde quandoque se meros theologos, candidatosque magistros, clericos, si sint quantumuis eruditi, uideri plerumque parum theologiae peritos, propterea quod argutiis ex Aristotele petitis garriant moderatius, dilemmata multicornia nec ingerere quidem curent, nec regere clamorosi; proinde minus esse natura aut arte compositos, eruditione minus instructos, ad examinandum, ad excutiendum quod alieno latet arcanum in pectore. Sint tamen sane

C 1 their piety and doctrine they / some times acquire a bad name. Shepherds, if they find someone else's sheep among their own, put up with her and allow her for a while to graze with their own, provided she stays within the pastures he controls and does not go off into the corn fields. But if she cannot control herself and is mischievous, he frightens her with his sling, pulls her back with his shepherd's crook, and sometimes ties up her hands and feet and sends her back to their owner. Similarly the bishop should put up with a monk who asks for alms from door to door, who visits a citizen who is confined to bed with a fever, who visits the humble home of the poor. But who will stand for someone who murders because some woman is taken from him, for a go-between in illicit love affairs, for someone who rapes a virgin, or an adulterer? Or indeed who will stand for someone who loafs because it suits him, as is their sacred custom? Certain monks once insinuated themselves with the indulgence and permission of the Roman pontiffs into secret confessions, nor were either bishops or parish priests sorry to have been relieved in part of an exceedingly heavy burden. But later they so expanded that permission to

C 1v hear confessions, / and thereafter so extended it, that now there is scarcely a rich woman who does not fall with entreaties and moans at the knees of a monk and confesses her sins. Not without eloquence do they increase their stature whenever they can, making themselves out to be genuine theologians. They claim that magistrates dressed in white, and priests, no matter how highly educated, seem for the most part to be insufficiently skilled in theology, mainly because, when subtle arguments from Aristotle are sought, they only babble a little bit, without rushing into any of his multi-horned dilemmas or clamoring to set them straight.[19] Therefore, [these men claim] that they are less qualified by their nature and their skills, less instructed with erudition, to examine and search out what lies hidden in someone else's heart. And although certainly monks may be more expert at examining the breasts of virgins, and purifying the crimes of matrons, let them have their own shepherds; but when a lawsuit arises between them and the clergy regarding a funeral, will not the highest shepherd of any region, i.e., the bishop, hasten over, as the

---

[19] The Greek philosopher Aristotle sometimes presents two-horned dilemmas, alternatives which present a problem or seem to cancel each other out. An example sometimes cited is the following: "This also shows that one cannot both opine and know the same thing simultaneously; for then one would apprehend the same thing as both capable and incapable of being otherwise — an impossibility." Aristotle, *Posterior Analytics* 89a 38-39, trans. Richard McKeon.

monachi doctiores ad examinanda uirginum pectora, ad expianda crimina matronarum, habeant suos pastores; cum lis tamen eis est cum clericis de funere, non accurret summus pastor in regione qualibet episcopus,
sicuti Romanus pontifex in orbe, pedo percutiet utrosque, dum arma reti-
C 2 nent, uinctos denique / trahet in carcerem et uerbis inde castigatos remit-
tet ad coenobium? Quos si postmodum forte compererit a praesule coeno-
bii non impunitos modo relictos, sed etiam collaudatos, quod aduersus
hostes ad instar ueteranorum militum praetorianae cohortis rem praeclare
gesserint, num correptos iterum in simili conflictu magistratibus merito
tradet profanis, ut si leges omnino non timent, pudore saltem com-
moueantur? An potius questus apud summum pontificem, ius ac potes-
tatem impetrabit in pseudomonachos uindicandi? Bono nimirum soller-
tique pastori non deerunt artes ac occasiones percommodae ad continendas
oues intra praescriptos limites et ad communiendas, ne infestentur a lupis
captiosisque uulpeculis.

Vidimus ipsi concertationem eiusmodi monachorum cum clericis super
funere ciuis, qui cadauer suum legauerat monasterio. Cum significatum
C 2v est monachis proselytum suum animam egisse, causantes clericorum /
morulas, prodierunt crucem praeferentes, uelut in iusto funere ad deducen-
dum cadauer. Parochi, quorum erat ea praeda, crucem extulisse monachos audientes (uetitum adhuc monachis est crucem extra limen efferre)
prorumpunt irati, crucem ac monachos inuadunt; monachi nec minus
cucullorum obliti, non segniter Martem capessunt. Certatur utrimque
gnauiter, crux interim aut iacet aut uicem conti praebet. Res primo pug-
nis gerebatur, postea tandem armis, quae casus obtulerat. Eo denique
pugna prouecta est, ut frustra magistratus eam comprimere conarentur.
Praesulis uicarii, quorum fuerat auctoritas maioris momenti, continuerunt
sese, ueluti solent in eiusmodi seditionibus, intra cubiculum, siue mona-

Roman Pontiff does in the world, and with his shepherd's crook strike both of them while they are still holding on to their weapons, and then C 2 finally, having bound them, / take them to prison, verbally chastise them and send the monks back to the monastery? Afterwards, if by chance the bishop finds out that those monks were not only left unpunished by the superior of the monastery but even praised for acting with distinction against the enemy as though they were the veteran soldiers of the Praetorian guard, then if they are caught again in a similar fracas, will the bishop not be right in handing them over to the civil authorities, so that, even if they do not at all fear the laws, at least they will be disturbed by the shame. Or better, won't he make a complaint before the Highest Pontiff and obtain the legal power to punish the pseudomonks? Of course a good and skillful shepherd will not be lacking in tricks or fail to find suitable opportunities to hold the sheep within their prescribed boundaries, thus safeguarding them from being attacked by wolves and tricky little foxes.[20]

Fighting at a Funeral

We ourselves saw a contest of this sort between monks and priests over the funeral of a citizen who had left his body to a monastery. When it was made known to the monks that their proselyte had given up the C 2v ghost, taking as a pretext some little delays by the priests, / they came out carrying the cross before them, as though to take away the body in a legitimate funeral. When the parish priests, to whom that booty belonged, heard that the monks had brought out the cross (it is still forbidden for monks to take the cross out beyond the threshold [of the monastery]), they angrily burst out and attacked the cross and the monks. The monks, no less forgetting their hoods, were not slow to take up weapons. Both sides contested the field zealously, while in the meantime the cross was either lying unused or served as a pike. At first the affair was carried out with fists, then later finally with whatever weapons were at hand. At last the brawl was taken so far that in vain the magistrates tried to control it. The bishop's deputies, whose authority would have carried the most weight, stayed in their rooms, as they usually do in this sort of quarrel, either since they fear the monks, whose anger is implacable and whose

---

[20] Secular, i.e., non-monastic, priests considered as theft attempts by monks to profit from funeral fees, behests by the deceased and gifts from the dead person's family. The "prescribed boundaries" excluded monks from acting as a person's primary confessor or otherwise exerting undue influence on the dying. Today the financial development offices of American universities carry out their mission making use of similar policies, as reflected in their frequently heard motto: "Where there is death, there is hope."

chos timentes, quorum est ira implacabilis ac odium nesciens modum, siue rixis, quibus intersunt clerici, applaudentes, ueluti lucro tum uberi, tum praesentissimo.

C 3   Nemo igitur est, in quem ius aliquo modo /non habeat episcopus, certe nullus in quem fulmen non uibret trisulcum. Quapropter per eum potissimum stabit, quo minus res sint quietiores, peccata minus frequentia, minus inuerecunda, minus usitata. Verum si dormitat pastor, si conniuet ad flagitia quaeque, se in partem lucri censusque reponit, esse quotidie qui peccent, qui fisco sint commodi, causans proprias non esse oues, qui mali fuere auctores, aut occupationes minus necessarias, quis ouibus uitio uertet, si petulanter lasciuiant, si ad uetita quaeque diuertant?

Sed tandem ad clericos recurrat stilus, qui magis peculiares uidentur oues episcopi, cum in eo, quo uerus est pastor, nil minus iuris habeat in laicos quam in clericos. Ceterum quoniam in clericorum corpora saeuit nonnunquam, in loculos autem persaepe, familiariores uulgo uidentur. Certe pastores, qui solo commodo metiuntur peculium, has proprias putant
C 3v oues, quoniam tondent ac mulgent pro suo / arbitratu. Bonus autem pastor, quem animarum cura potissimum uersat, nullo discrimine clericum agit et laicum, nil referre putat, cuius sit ordinis anima, quam lucrifaciat Christo, pecunias in postremis reponit. Quod quidem si conarentur omnes episcopi, aliam sibi faciem indueret orbis Christianus, longe secus agerentur humanae res. Has tamen peculiares, ut existimat uulgus, oues episcopi, quales sint attendamus, quae quidem bonae sint an malae ab episcopis maxime pendet. Possunt praesules in quam uelint eas faciem formare, huc et illuc flectere, ius habent summum, non est quod tergiuersentur. Sunt tamen inter clericos multi gradus. Urbanum collegium canonicorum (capitulum uocant) tenet primum locum. Alia quae sunt per

hatred is boundless, or since they applaud quarrels in which priests are involved, since they produce monetary gains which are both rich and very quickly made.

Turning Sin into Monetary Profit

There is, therefore, no one over whom the bishop does not have, in some way, authority. / Certainly there is no one whom he does not threaten by brandishing the three-pointed thunderbolt [of excommunication]. Wherefore it will mostly be his responsibility if matters do not become more quiet, if sins do not become less frequent, less shameless, and less customary. If the shepherd dozes, if he winks at every sort of shameful act, if he tallies up to his monetary gain and wealth the fact that every day there are those who sin, i.e., who are advantageous to his money-bag, while giving as an excuse that those who began the evil were not his own sheep, or pleading other less necessary activities — then who will turn the sheep away from vice if they wantonly leap and gambol, if they wander toward every sort of forbidden thing? But my pen should return to the priests, who seem to be more the bishop's own sheep, even though insofar as he is a true shepherd he has no less authority over laymen than over priests. What's more, since he sometimes vents his wrath against priests' bodies, but much more frequently against their money boxes, they seem to the public more like members of the family. Certainly shepherds who judge the flock only for profit, consider these to be their own sheep since they shear and milk them as they see fit. / The good shepherd, however, whose main motivation is the care of souls, with no distinction acts as both priest and layman, nor does he think it matters to what social group a soul belongs that he can gain for Christ, and money is his last consideration. Indeed, if all bishops would try to do this, the Christian world would put on a new appearance, and human affairs would be conducted far differently. Nevertheless, as for those sheep which belong specially (as the public believes) to the bishop, let us concentrate on their condition, for indeed, whether they are good or bad depends chiefly on the bishops. Bishops are able to form them into whatever shape they want, to bend them back and forth, nor is there any reason for them to hold back, since they have the highest authority. However there are many levels among the clergy. A city college of canons (which they call a chapter)[21] holds the first place. There are other colleges of canons that

C 3

C 3v

---

[21] A cathedral chapter, or college of canons, was a group of ecclesiastics dedicated to both liturgical and administrative duties. The ancient institution came to be considered a

regionem canonicorum collegia solent ab urbanis plerumque uiuendi morem ac instituta sumere. Certe per omnia contendunt aemulari quos norunt, episcopo quandoque praescribere, / nonnunquam eius et uices agere.

C 4

Quomodo igitur canonici, abbates, archidiaconi plerumque cooptentur, dormitantibus episcopis, primum contemplemur. Non peritia quidem aut uirtus, non candidi mores commendant aut faciunt canonicum aut archidiaconum, sed pecuniae, gratia, fauor, iuris diuini contemptus, fraus, ambitio, denique quidquid opponitur iis uirtutibus, quae magis in clericis commendantur ac exiguntur. Ciuis quicumque, florens opibus, uafritiorem ex filiis Romam mittit cum auri iusto pondere. Compertissimum inter hos habetur, quot aureis sit opus uenanti canonicatum, uenanti archidiaconatum aut abbatiam. Non quod uerbis nudis et propalam ueneant eiusmodi honores, absit. Sed ita nonnunquam praescribit pater filio Romam proficiscenti: I, felix fili, munus tibi Romae aliquod eme, quo sis pontifici maximo uel a manu, uel ab aure, uel a libellis, uel ab re quapiam. Dede te nec minus alicui cardinali, circumspice tandem, / quibus artibus ditescant qui Romae diu uersantur; nos interim funera diuitum clericorum nuntiis celerrimis nuntiabimus. Tu si gratis nequeas canonicatum aut abbatiam obtinere, adi mox qui te gratia, fauore, aut forte diligentia praecesserit, tantum offer ei pensionis annuae, quantum ualet ipsum sacer-

C 4v

are regional. They usually take from the urban ones most of their way of living and their customs. Certainly they strive to emulate whom they C 4 know in all things, to prescribe to the bishop whenever possible, / and sometimes also to act in his place.

Bribing One's Way Into Office

Therefore let us first consider how canons, abbots,[22] and archdeacons,[23] are usually chosen in cases when the bishop dozes. Indeed it is not expertise or virtue, not a pure character that recommends someone or makes him a canon or an archdeacon, but rather money, service rendered, favor, contempt of divine law, fraud, extreme ambition, and finally whatever opposes those virtues that in clergymen are most to be commended and required. Any citizen who is flush with money sends the most crafty of his sons to Rome with the right price in gold. It is extremely well known among them how many gold coins are necessary for someone to buy a canon's position, to buy an archdeaconate, or an abbot's post. Such offices are not bought openly and with plain words alone; God forbid! But sometimes a father sends a son off to Rome with instructions like these:

"Go, blessed son, buy yourself some appointment in Rome where you will be at the Pope's hand, or at his ear, or at his memorandum book, or something similar. Devote yourself no less to some cardinal, and in short C 4v look around carefully / to see by what devices they who spend a long time at Rome grow rich. In the meantime we will inform you by very fast couriers of the deaths of wealthy clergymen. If you are unable to obtain for free a canon's position or an abbot's, go quickly to someone who has surpassed you due to services or favor or perhaps diligence. Offer to him

type of senate or council for the bishop of the corresponding diocese. In 1474, Pope Sixtus IV established two official canon positions for each college: one whose essential function was to preach on certain solemn dates (known in Spanish as *el magistral*) and one charged with watching over the defense of the rights of the college (known as *el doctoral*).

[22] In addition to being a monastic title, the word 'abbot' designated a secular priest that presided over a college of canons for a given period of time.

[23] In the early church, archdeacons served as the superiors of the deacons and ministers of the Church, an office of ecclesiastical dignity and government. For many centuries, archdeacons governed cathedrals, acting as judges, administrators of wealth, and visitors of the diocese, with power over the rural presbyters. The authority of archdeacons, however, was limited by many bishops when they began to function too independently. The Council of Trent further limited their jurisdiction as a result of the abuse of power which many of them displayed. The role of the archdeacon was thus reduced to a mere dignity and replaced by the vicar-general.

dotium, stipulatione quam occultissima, statim te redempturum aliquot annorum eam pensionem, quo tandem liberum maneat sacerdotium; ita locum tenebis in ecclesia, quem cupimus, talares tibi uestes non uerrent pauimentum, puer tibi pone caudam sustinebit et nobilibus adaequaberis, salutaberis canonicus et archidiachonus, sedebis in altis ac primis hemi-cyclis, nunquam sacrificabis; ad haec, si quid humane designaueris, fi-lios forte procreaueris, nullum in te ius habebit episcopus, libere uiues et laute. Tum cum uita functus fueris, magnae campanae boabunt funus tuum,
C 5 denuntiabunt canonicum interiisse, ne mali genii /praedam quamlibet exis-timent. Cauebis igitur ne socors aut superstitiose religiosus habearis; nam si ceterae non successerint artes, nosti solemnissimam capturam, quae puppis et prora dormitantibus est. Litem intendes diemque dices quo-cunque simulato praetextu clericis longaeuis, qui phaleratis mulis uehuntur et dum cursitant Romam ex ultimis terrarum aut procuratores mittunt, forsan morientur: tuque surrogaberis in eorum locum, certe diu non possint uiuere et lis intentata te faciet iure successorem, cetera tem-pus, locus aulaeque ministri subministrabunt."

Hic tritus mos est uenandi maiora sacerdotia. Atque utinam non diuer-teretur ad pacta foediora. Nullum apud collegium urbanum sedentem in altis hemicyclis propemodum uideas, qui arte consimili non conscenderit, nisi perpaucos sane nobiles aut litteratos et quibus uel a parentibus per manus traditi sunt honores, uel ab episcopis et ipso collegio ob merita
C 5v nescio quae, frequen/tius tamen commutatione commissi.

Nil mirum est si rari sunt inter hos sapientes, nulli qui bonas litteras calleant: non uacat bonis disciplinis intendere; uix adolescentia totaque iuuentus sufficit ad ecclesiasticos ambiendos honores. Qui possunt horum studiosi litteris uacare? Sed neque datur in his collegiis honori peritia

an annual pension in the same amount as is generated by the priestly position you seek, but with the very secret provision that you will promptly
pay him that pension over the course of a specific number of years, so
that the position in the clergy will remain free for you. Thus you will
have the place in the church which we want. Your ankle-length robes
will not sweep the pavement, as a boy will hold up your train behind
you. You will be considered the equal of nobles, greeted as a canon and
archdeacon, sit in high and prominent circular chairs, and never have to
say mass. Add to all this the advantage that if you should commit some
sin in a human way, if you should by chance father some children, the
bishop will have no legal power over you, and you will live freely and
splendidly. Then when you will have come to the end of your life, huge
bells will boom out your death, announcing that a canon has died, lest
anyone should think / that a demon in some way might have carried off
your soul. You will, therefore, take care not to be considered either lazy
or superstitiously religious, and if other tactics should fail, you know a
very well established trick for taking prey. It's a complete package for
fooling those who are dozing. You will institute a legal action and set a
date on some false pretext with aged clergymen who ride caparisoned
mules. While they are traveling to Rome from the ends of the earth, or
sending agents, by chance they may die. Then you will be substituted for
one of them in the following way: they certainly can't live long, and as
the case will have remained untried, that will make you the successor by
law. All the rest will be conveniently supplied by the time, the place and
the officials at court."

C 5

   This is the old and common way of hunting for the bigger positions
among the clergy, and I wish it didn't degenerate into deals that smell
worse. You will see almost no one sitting in the city college in circular
seats who has not risen through similar tactics, except, of course a very
few nobles or learned men, and those whose honors were passed down
to them in succession by their parents or by the bishops and the college
itself due to I-don't-know-what merits. / More often, however, they got
the title by barter.

C 5v

   Insufficient Education of Clergy
   So it is not at all surprising if wise men are rare among these and if there
are none who have a thorough knowledge of good literature. There isn't
time to master good disciplines. Indeed, scarcely have their adolescence
and all of their youth been sufficient to allow them to pursue
honors in the church. How can the studious among these have time for

litterarumque cognitio propterea, quod ambitionem congerendique sacerdotia impium studium non probant eruditi. Veluti hostes arcentur doctrina praestantes ab collegio, ne uel imprudentes exigant aliquando rationem caerimoniarum, aut euangelicum sensum exquirant, coganturque proxime sedentes imperitiam suam fateri. Videre licet aliquos in subselliis litteratos bonisque disciplinis non infeliciter institutos, sed sacrificant quotidie, seruiunt iugiter choro uel altari, ne quaestiunculas ex euangelio Latino sermone per otium ingerant. "Satis uiderunt maiores," aiunt idiotae, "qui C 6 nobis instituta con/diderunt, leges sanxerunt, libros conscripserunt. Quid sciolis nunc opus grammaticis, qui nouos accentus inducunt, qui libros tot annos et a tot ingeniis conprobatos, emendant, radunt et interscribunt? Itaque siqui sunt eruditi, seruiunt ministeriisque sanctioribus quidem illis adhibentur, sed emolumento perquam tenui. Idiotae complent alta pleraque sedilia, praeterea nihil agunt in choro, foris strenui sunt negotiatores. Sane nil minus in eis reperias, quam quod Christi ministros decet. Cur hoc? Dormit episcopus aut abest plerumque. Eius uicarii, qui sunt nonnunquam ex eodem collegio, mutuo scabunt, muttiunt ad turpia fratrum, quo uicissim ipsi tolerent turpiora. Nam quod canonici iactant, unum habere se iudicem Romanum pontificem, surdo canerent fabulam, si uir dignus ea persona, quam sustinet, episcopus esset. Obiurgaret dictis paternis, castigaret supercilio uerbisque seueris, tentaret quae sui sunt C 6v muneris exequi. Et quem / insanabilem cognosceret, fultum patrocinio libertatis sublimem, correptum Romam suum ad iudicem transmitteret. Profecto submitterent caput reliqui nec auderent episcopum negare pastorem. Bonus pastor nihil intentatum relinquit, quo prosit ouibus, cum ueritas dicat, animam esse deuouendam pro eis, nedum curam omnemque laborem subeundum et impensam. Negligentia quidem episcopi non ipsi

literature? But in these schools one doesn't find expert knowledge to be regarded as an honor, and especially not knowledge of literature, for learned men do not approve of ambition and of immoral eagerness to accumulate benefices. As though they were enemy soldiers, those who are outstanding for their learning are expelled from school, lest they either imprudently ask at some point for the rationale for the ceremonies, or inquire into the meaning of the gospels, and those who are sitting next to them may be obliged to confess their ignorance. It's possible to see some well-read men on the benches, who have been educated not too badly in the good disciplines, but they say mass every day, serve constantly in the choir or at the altar, so they don't have leisure to introduce small points from the Latin Gospel in their conversation. Those who are ignorant say: "Our C 6 ancestors saw enough, they who founded our institutions, / enacted our laws, who composed our books. So what need now is there for people with a smattering of grammar who introduce new accents, who emend, erase, and write in the margins of books that have been sanctioned for so many years, and by so many great talents?" So as for those few educated men who exist, they act as servants, and they are employed, it is true, in the more holy ministries, but are paid exceedingly little. The ignorant fill most of the high seats, and do little else as a group, though out of church they are hard businessmen. You can be sure that what you will find in them is nothing less than what suits ministers of Christ! Why is this? The bishop is asleep or very often absent. His deputies, who are sometimes from the same college, scratch each others' backs, lower their voices about the foul acts of the brothers, so that in turn those same brothers may tolerate even fouler deeds. For while the canons brag that they have only one judge, the Roman Pontiff, that song would fall on deaf ears if the bishop were worthy of the role which he is filling. He would scold with fatherly advice, he would punish with a frown and harsh words, and would attempt to carry out the actions which fall within his charge. Whomever C 6v he should recognize as being incurable, / someone who has been relying on the protection of freedom, he would snatch him up in his high position and send him to his judge in Rome. Then indeed the others would submit their necks, and they would not dare to deny that the bishop is their shepherd. The good shepherd does not leave anything untried by which he may be useful to his sheep, since the truth tells him that his soul must be offered up on their behalf, not to mention his care, and every labor and expense must be undergone for them. A bishop's negligence does not injure only himself and his sheep, but even provides a handle for archdeacons and

solum et ouibus suis officit, sed ansam etiam dat archidiaconis et abba-
tibus, qui contendunt certis limitibus esse pastores, ad compilandas oues
et deglubendas. In summa, officium suum exequi se putant sanctissime,
si per singula conentur episcopum et eius uicarios aemulari, tam in iuredi-
cendo, quam in decimis et aliis tributis exigendis.

Est ingens aliorum clericorum turba, qui non sunt maioribus honoribus
ascripti, est frequentissimum utique peculium, in hoc tuo praesertim epis-
C 7 copatu. Tot enim iniciuntur quot ali te/nuiter possunt redditibus ac decimis paupercularum etiam ecclesiarum, adeo quidem ut in uico uiginti
circiter incolarum quattuor nonnunquam clerici beneficiarii sint. Tres episcopatus Hispaniae uel maximi non aequant frequentiam clericorum Burgensis. Haec tamen tanta sacrificulorum turba pastorum incuria liberius
errat ad hanc diem, uel potius aberrat, quam par est. Castigantur identidem atque multantur, non ut rectius uiuant affectusque parum honestos
temperent, sed ut aerario subinde sint commodi. Inter hos, praeter agmen
turpitudinum ac uitiorum, summa litterarum Latinarum regnat ignorantia.
Preculas, quae uulgari paene sermoni sunt affines, nec per somnium quidem callent plurimi, tantum abest, ut teneant quae faciunt ad enarrationem
euangeliorum aut epistolarum apostolicarum. Vix quidam tria uerba

abbots, who strive within fixed boundaries to be shepherds, to rob from the sheep and strip them of their hide. In short, they think that they are carrying out their duties very religiously if in one thing after another they try to ape the bishop and his vicars, as much in administering the law as in demanding tithes and other taxes.

Too Many People Ordained

There is a huge crowd of other clergy, who do not hold positions of greater honor, and certainly there is an exceedingly numerous flock particularly in your diocese. As many people jump in as can be precariously C 7 supported / by the income and tithes of even extremely poor churches, and to such an extent that in a village of about twenty inhabitants, sometimes there are four clergy who receive a benefice.[24] Three of Spain's dioceses, even the largest ones, do not together equal the great number of clergy that are in the Burgos diocese.[25] Nevertheless this crowd of so many little celebrants of the mass to this day wander in neglect, or rather wander astray, more freely than is appropriate. Over and over again they are reprimanded and fined, but not so that they may live more in the straight and narrow and moderate their improper passions, but rather so that from then on they may be profitable for the treasury. In addition to their array of moral defects and vices, there reigns among them the deepest ignorance of Latin letters.[26] Most of them cannot even dream of understanding their little prayers which are almost next-door to the vulgar language, so far are they from grasping what they need to go into, the exegesis of the gospels, or of the letters of the apostles. They can scarcely read three words without uttering a solecism, and oh shame! —

[24] A benefice is a determined salary or property attached to an ecclesiastical post or office.

[25] An idea can be obtained of the high numbers in Spain of those in holy orders through the demograhic study cited by Azcona 1980. For 1531 it shows a total of 4,485,389 inhabitants of Castile, and of these 23,171 were secular priests while 28,054 more were in monastic orders. The number of priests or benefices in the diocese of Burgos at the time is not known but does appear to have been very great, to judge by the fact that in 1534 it had many more baptismal fonts, 1,673, than surrounding dioceses. See Azcona 1980, p. 188. In 1591, according to the ecclesiastical census of Castile, the district of Burgos was home to 4,957 members of the clergy, both secular and monastic. The commerical power achieved by Burgos throughout the fifteenth and sixteenth centuries, the progressive growth of its population and its preeminent political positon made it one of the principal cities of Castile and led to its designation by the church as a metropolis on October 22, 1574. See *Diccionario de Historia* "demografia eclesiástica", vol. 2, p. 695, and "geografía eclesiástica", vol. 2, p. 1008.

[26] Here Maldonado speaks from experience as an official examiner of candidates for the priesthood in Burgos; one of his duties was clearly to test their competency in Latin.

legunt, quin pronuncient soloecismum; et — o pudor! — uident pastores
C 7v et tolerant ueluti comprobantes. Nam quos idiotas / reperiunt, si sunt idem
laniferi, non arcent quidem a colloquio, non utique sacris interdicunt.
Nescio quo res prolapsura sit, diuino tamen, ni tu commodum inter-
cesseris, qui rebus in cunctis, quas administrasti, semper integerrimus ac
summus fuisti, futurum ut hebetiores ac indoctiores sint uiri sacrorum
ministri, quam profani, quandoquidem inutiles et inepti plerumque deuo-
uentur a parentibus sacerdotio, certe minores natu et quos non adeo placet
fuisse procreatos. Qui si rudes et parum eruditi cooptentur ad sacerdotia
sacrisque initientur, fore quis dubitet, quin a laicis aliquando leges accipi-
ant, quo pacto se gerant in diuinis, quam multam irrogent commissis?
Mercenarii quidem pastores, quorum non sunt oues propriae, diligentissime profecto censuram exercent in clericos parum pudicos, uel alias
flagitiosos ac facinorosos, seuerissimeque castigant, non ut flagitia tol-
C 8   lantur /ac extinguantur, sed ut quam saepissime redimantur. Si clericus
uicanus sedit obiter ad oenopolium, si collusit aut perpotauit in eo, trahi-
tur ad tribunal tamquam facinorosus, si piscaturam exercuit, si uisus est
arcitenens, ut auiculis insidiaretur, criminis agitur reus. Si concubinam ac
filios domi alit, accersitur ueluti capitis, sed persoluta multa redit auda-
cior. Non enim prohibitus est filiis gignendis operam dare, sed quantum
constatura sit amica biennio quoquo doctus, si perpetuo uelit habere.
Verum si fornicatur, si meretricatur, si peierat et blasphemat, si ludit
aleam, unaque hora diffundit totas Croesi diuitias, si lenonem agit, si
faeneratur, si sacrilegus, si prorsus est indoctus, unde manant clericorum
omnia mala, uix male audit, dum modo non inutilis sit delatoribus et fisco.
Bonus ac uerus pastor aliter multo consulit, ac medetur his morbis. Aut
C 8v enim penitus tollendos curat, a/ut ita obruendos, ut nunquam suppullulent.
Quod foret admodum cuique praesuli perfacile, si qui sacris initiantur,

shepherds see, and tolerate, them as though they approved. For when they
C 7v find ignorant men, / so long as they are wool-bearers, they do not exclude
them from the conversation, and they certainly do not forbid them to enter
holy orders. I don't know how far this situation will slide, but still I fore-
see that unless you intervene appropriately (you who in all things which
you administered have always shown the highest integrity) it will get to
the point where men in the holy ministry will be more dull-witted and less
educated than laymen, due to the fact that the useless and foolish are, for
the most part, dedicated to the priesthood by their parents, at least the
younger ones, and those whom they are not so happy to have begotten.
If indeed those who are unskilled and very little educated are chosen for
priesthoods, and admitted to holy orders, who would doubt but that they
will sooner or later accept rules from laymen about how to conduct themselves in holy offices and what penalty to impose for sins? Indeed,
mercenary shepherds, whose sheep are not their own, very zealously
censure clergy who act immodestly, and most severely punish those who
are disgraceful or wicked in some other way, but not so that the shame-
C 8 ful actions be corrected / and snuffed out, but rather so that they may be
paid for as often as possible. If a village clergyman happens to sit in a
wineshop, if he gambles or drinks heavily there, he is hauled into court
as though he were a felon. If he goes fishing, if he is seen pulling a bow
to ambush little birds, he is charged with a crime. If he supports a
concubine and children at home, it is looked upon as though it were a
capital offense. But after he has paid a fine, he becomes more daring. In
fact he is not forbidden to devote his time to fathering children, but rather
he learns how much his girlfriend is going to cost him every two years
should he wish to keep her permanently. But if he fornicates, if he visits
whores, if he perjures himself and blasphemes, if he gambles with dice and
in a single hour wastes all the wealth of Croesus,[27] if he pimps, if he lends
money at interest, if he is sacrilegious, if he is completely uneducated —
which is the source of all evils of the clergy — he hardly hears anything
bad about it provided he is not useless to the informers and the exchequer.
   The good and true shepherd takes a very different approach, and heals
these diseases. In fact he sees to it either that they are entirely removed,
C 8v / or so uprooted that they never sprout again. That would be very easy
for every bishop if those who are ordained had an expertise which was
appropriate and suitable, specifically, so that every improper way might

[27] The last king of ancient Lydia (560-546 BC), famed for his immense wealth.

peritiam haberent accommodam et adaptam, uidelicet ut uia omnis improba clauderetur ad ineunda sacerdotia, lege lata atque in aere incisa, neminem sacris ordinibus aut sacerdotio prorsus admouendum, quem non mores et litterarum maxime peritia commendaret. Atqui cum sint tenuissima nimiam ob frequentiam hoc in episcopatu sacerdotia numerusque quotidie crescat, minus curantibus praesulibus clerici mendicent necne, crescit nec minus frequentia clericorum.

Qui non suppeditantibus ecclesiis uictui necessaria, diuertunt ad artes seruiles, nonnunquam ad impias, emptitando, quod carius uendant, commodando quod cum faenore recipiant, quae nimirum mercatura iam inter laicos solemnis est, nuper in perniciem pauperum ab inferis excitata. D 1 Sepulta credebatur uel exterminata cum Iudaeis, sed postea quam / merces non tuto tranant, nec feruntur ac referuntur sine iactura propter bella continua, non equidem [*M deletes* equidem] modo christianis est usurpata, sed et ab infamia uindicata. In laicis uideri poterat turpe lucrum ac inhumanum, at in clericis execrandum et impium merito censeatur. Non enim intra pauperum limites turpis haec actio continetur, ut praetextu ualeat aliquo excusari. Diuites corripuerunt eam nec iudicant inhonestam, quam lauti sacrorum ministri, quoties datur, non erubescunt amplecti. Certe tu,

be closed against entering the priesthood by passing a law and then engraving it in bronze, a law that in no case should anyone be advanced to holy orders or the priesthood unless recommended by his character and especially by his expertise in letters. But since the positions for clergymen in this diocese are very precarious financially because there are too many of them, and their numbers increase daily as the bishops don't care whether or not the clergy become beggars, the clerical population grows none the less.

Clerics as Loan Sharks

There are those who, since their churches do not supply what is necessary to live, turn to devices typical of slaves, sometimes to immoral ones, by buying what they can resell at a higher price, or making loans and collecting interest. This sort of commerce, of course, is already common among the laity, a practice recently called forth from hell to ruin the poor. It was believed to have been buried, or wiped out, along with the D 1 Jews,[28] but now that / merchandise does not get through safely, nor is it transmitted back and forth without loss because of the constant wars, not only indeed[29] has this business been taken over by Christians, but defended against the charge of infamy. Among the laity it might seem shameful and inhumane profiteering, but among clerics it would rightly be judged as execrable and immoral. In fact the commission of this shameful act is not limited to the purview of the poor, among whom it might be in some way excused. The rich have snatched it up and do not judge wrong an action that even elegant ministers of holy rites do not blush to embrace, whenever the opportunity is offered. Certainly you, who now act in the service of the supreme pontiff and the emperor — who is favorably beginning his command over the world — would be able very easily to provide support for poor clergymen,[30] lest by hunger they be driven to

---

[28] Ostensibly in order to prevent the spread of heresy, the Catholic Kings Fernando and Isabel decreed the expulsion of Jews not baptized as Christians. Proclaimed on March 31, 1492, in Granada, the decree caused 150,000 to 200,000 Jews to flee Spain under the threat of death, with confiscation of all their possessions.

[29] Reading *equidem* with Z; M deletes.

[30] Bishop Ampudia had deplored the gap between the wealth of the upper clergy and the poverty of village priests: "a las ripas del río quedan los pobres clérigos letrados y de buena vida defraudados, y no les queda sino arar y cabar como labradores o ir a pedir por Dios como romeros." Priests often worked at other jobs, from doctors and lawyers to innkeepers, butchers and beggars. They had to be prohibited from working as judges in the civil courts, as notaries or estate managers. See Azcona 1980, p. 170.

qui summum nunc apud pontificem et Caesarem auspicantem orbis imperium agis, perfacile posses clericis pauperculis subuenire, ne fame cogerentur ad quaestus minus idoneos, ne dicam impios, confugere, si tuo uetuisset rogatu pontifex summus sacerdotia, quae uocantur in hac tua dicione patrimonialia, diuidi tot in portiunculas, uel potius si redditus assignarentur cuilibet uicano sacerdotio sufficientes alendo sacerdoti.

D 1v Tum enim clerici essent pauciores, / honestiores ac peritiores, denique tolerabiles.

Verum in iugulum iam tandem propositae quaestionis incurrit oratio, nimirum ut qualem tuam esse familiam expediat decensque sit ac pium, qualemque pertulerimus proximorum episcoporum, edisseramus. Non de domesticis famulis loquor, qui tuo quotidiano sunt cultui dedicati, quos nondum nouimus et habere te domi uirtutum omnium exemplar certo scimus, sed de iis, publicis qui sunt muneribus a te praeficiendi uel iam praefecti, in quibus sane tota de qua nunc agimus res sine controuersia uertitur. Nimirum in illis ex parte situm est, bonus tu censearis pastor an secus; illi possunt praestare, ut praesul tu sis idem, qui fueris priuatus, integer, incorruptus, pie doctus, atque doctissime quidem pius, sanctus, innocens, minime auarus, quae profecto uirtus in episcopo quoniam rara, admirabilis quidem est et illustris, sed adeo necessaria, ut ea si careat,

D 2 quamuis ceteras omnes habeat, bonus dici pastor / non possit.

Vide, sapientissime praesul, diuque tecum uolue, quos rebus agendis et administrandis adhibeas, quos causarum atque litium cognitores denique des. Maximae res tuo deciduntur tribunali, multum boni malique pendet a tuo ariopago. Contemne paruulam pecuniam, et eos mercenarios pascendis, reficiendis et intra septa continendis ouibus conduc, qui summum ante tribunal audeant intrepidi gestorum rationem reddere bonumque te pastorem constanter asserere, qui per te quae nequiueris obire,

take refuge in sources of gain that are less suitable, not to say immoral, if, at your request, the supreme pontiff should forbid that those benefices that in this demain of yours are called patrimonies be divided into so many small portions,[31] or alternatively the income could be assigned to any one of the village benefices in sufficient quantities to feed the priest.

D 1v   Then certainly there would be fewer clergymen, / and they would be more honorable, more competent and, finally, bearable.

Keep Your Own House in Order: The Choice of Vicars

But now at last my discourse is going for the jugular of the topic it has set for itself to investigate, namely, to lay out what would be useful, proper, and pious for your household to be like, and the kind of household we have endured under recent bishops. I'm not speaking here about your domestic servants, whose position is to wait on you on a daily basis and whom we haven't met, and we know certainly that those you maintain at home are a model of all virtues. Rather I am speaking of those whom you are to appoint to public positions, or have already appointed. On them, indeed, as no one will dispute, turns the whole situation which we are discussing. Without doubt, it depends in part on them whether or not you will be judged a good shepherd. They will be able to help you to be the same as a bishop as you are in private life, a person of integrity, uncorrupted, devoutly learned, and most learnedly devout, holy, innocent, lacking in all avarice. In fact, since this last virtue is rare in a bishop, it is indeed admirable and outstanding, but so necessary that if he should lack it, even if he might have all the other virtues, a shepherd could not

D 2   be called good. /

Look carefully, oh most wise superintendent, and ponder with yourself for a long time about which men you should employ in carrying out and administering matters, which men you will present as your representatives in legal cases and suits. Things of the greatest importance are decided in your court. Much for good or for evil depends on your areopagus. Reject a small amount of money, and guide those hired hands in feeding, restoring, and containing the sheep within the fold, so that they may boldly dare before the highest court to give an accounting of their deeds, and to proclaim you as the good shepherd, as one who, for those matters which he cannot undertake himself, delegates them to men who do not swell with pride or with any untoward opinion of their own worth — men in

---

[31] As Maldonado explains below, these benefices were reserved by tradition for men from the specific village where the church was located.

uiris delegaueris nulla superbia, nulla plus aequo existimationis suae opin-
ione insolescentibus, nulla denique turpi auaritia, quae seruitus est diaboli,
contaminatis. Primum in tuo foro locum tenent, immo soli, dum tu praesertim abes, possunt, quod uolunt primores uicarii, qui uulgo prouisores
appellantur. His grex uniuersus concreditur, ab his pendet episcopi salus

D 2v uel interitus. Quapropter / indagine multa sunt inuestigandi, quorum est
arbitrio salus permittenda. Si leuiter aegrotat episcopus, undecumque con-
uocantur medici clarissimi, praemiis non uulgaribus inuitantur, ut uel
tantillum melius corpus habeat. Ubi uero negotium agitur animae, ubi
supplicium manet aeternum, si uolens ac prudens offenderit, gloriaque
perennis, si recte collimauerit, socors aut parum uigilans erit antistes?
Solent plerumque uicarii non infeliciter ab scholis peti, si quadragesimo
sunt anno proximiores quam tricesimo, quandoquidem retinent aliquamdiu,
qui uigilantem fuerint episcopum nacti, candorem illum iuuentutis, quae
nullis adhuc auaritiae laqueis est irretita, uafritiae nullis fluctibus agitata,
durat in eis amor uirtutis in gymnasiis tantopere praedicatae. Quamquam
et hic opus est odore peracri iudicioque non leui. Qui enim famelici diu
per academias praelectiunculas uenditarunt, nunquam satis explent aui-

D 3 ditatem, habendi sitim uix umquam extingunt. Sunt qui iam / dudum
munera obierunt, ius non uno loco dixerunt, quos quidem callos duxisse
frequenter uidimus tum in bonum, tum etiam in malum. Si uiros agere
bonos instituerunt, ab eo raro deducuntur, si possidentur ab auaritia, muta-
bunt pilum quidem illi, animum nunquam, ni numen aliquod forte propitium affulserit, quod esse Christianos amittendamque proxime pellem
cum nummis et latifundiis admoneat. Sed ex ante acta uita, ex sodalitate,
ex rumore, qui solet celare plerumque nihil, perfacile dignoscuntur utrique;

short who are not corrupted by foul avarice, which is servitude to the devil. They have the first place in your court, and indeed they are the only ones, especially while you are gone, who are able to do what they want. They are the most eminent vicars, commonly called vicars-general.[32] To these the entire flock is given for safekeeping, and on them D 2v depends the health or the ruin of a bishop. For this reason / there should be a careful tracking down and beating of the bushes for those into whose judgment his health is to be entrusted. If a bishop develops a slight illness, the most famous doctors are summoned from every direction. They are tempted with promises of extraordinary rewards, so that his body may improve even a little bit. So then when it is a question of the soul, where eternal punishment awaits if the bishop willingly and with full-knowledge stumbles in some way, or perpetual glory if he aims his gaze straight, will the bishop be lazy or inattentive? Often many vicars are sought with some success from schools, if they are closer to forty years of age than to thirty, since those who have acquired a diligent bishop keep for some time that bloom of youth, which thus far has not been snared in the traps of avarice, nor shaken by any of the waves of craftiness, and that love of virtue that is so vigorously preached in secondary schools, is still alive in them. Nevertheless, even here there is a need for a keen sense of smell, and for a judgment that is not too capricious. Indeed, those who have been starving for a long time and promote themselves through academic lecturing, never completely fill up their D 3 greed and hardly ever satisfy their thirst for possessions. / Indeed there are those who long since have filled posts, who have administered the law in more than one place, whom we actually often see to have developed an insensitivity toward both good and evil. If they have started out by acting like good men, they rarely turn away from that. If they are possessed by avarice, they might indeed change one hair, but never their soul, unless by chance some good spirit shine favorably upon them and warn them to be Christians and quickly to get rid of their outer coverings along with their coins and big estates. But from the life they have led before, from their friendships, from rumor, which usually hides practically nothing, it is very easy to find out both kinds of men. If the bishop has eyes to see and ears to hear, certainly he can't be deceived for long. Those who after being lawyers become judges can rarely be commended. They are

---

[32] Vicars-general exercised the authority and jurisdiction of the bishop, legal cases included.

sit oculatus episcopus, sit auritus, falli certe diu non potest. Iam qui ex aduocatis fiunt iudices, raro probantur, uersipelles sunt, fraudulenti: sane uulgo dici solet, ueridicum aduocatum semper egere, bilinguem et mendacem bonis omnibus diffluere. Quot eorum reperias, qui quamlibet iniquam causam non probent, si consultor adeas cum pecuniis? Applaudunt iam reo, iam arrident actori, uictoriam utrique pollicentur nec faciunt teruncii, quod summus / sit pronuntiaturus iudex de pessimis aduocatis ac iniquis iudiciis. Si quis bonus ex his iudex euaserit, bono genio ascribendum est, qui ab ea eum uitae ratione deduxerit, in qua non ex animi sui sententia tenebatur. Deliguntur nonnunquam ex urbano collegio uicarii, ius eadem in urbe dicturi, quod si semel forte cedat ex uoto, bis equidem raro. Qui fiet, quin canonicus studeat placere canonico, frater fratri, amicus amico, ciuis ciui? Plurimum canonici ualent tum gratia et auctoritate, tum propinquis et amicis; sunt enim quamplurimi ex urbis ditioribus. Qui ius igitur dicetur ex aequo, si reus habet canonicum intercessorem et fautorem apud canonicum, ciuem apud ciuem? Permultos habet canonicus propinquos, affines, necessarios, clientes, amicos; perraro ueniet usu, propensior ne sit alterutram in partem. Vidimus hisce annis eiusmodi quaedam miseranda magis ac deflenda, quam suppressis nominibus referenda: pudet meminisse. / Ex collegiis externis non improbauerim electionem, si uir reperiatur bonus ac doctus. Magni refert, sacerdotium habere suppeditans [*corrected in M and Z from* suppeditante] uel ex parte necessaria, qui sit futurus iudex in tanta dicione, ne cogat egestas habendique sacerdotium immensa cupido ius peruertere mune-ribusque corrumpi. Persuasissimum uulgo est malos ob mores nunquam defutura sacerdotia, cui non desint pecuniae. Proinde uigilantissimus sit oportet episcopus in deligendis ac subrogandis uicariis. Qui si auaritia forte capti eum honorem ambierunt, nihil auidius conabuntur, quam ut expleant illam inexplebilem auiditatem uoraginemque immensam. Vidimus nonnulla, timemus permulta, res ut quotidie labuntur in deterius. Tu qui pastor es, si cupis uideri bonus, fac sis, eos conducendo mercenarios, qui boni uicem pastoris agant, qui iudices se praebeant incorruptos, qui tuam

D 3v

D 4

turncoats and full of deception. As the popular saying goes, a lawyer who speaks the truth is always poor, while one who lies with a forked tongue is swimming in all good things. How many of them will you find who won't lend their approval to a case, no matter how evil it may be, if you go to consult them with sufficient funds? First they applaud the defendant, then they smile on the plaintiff, promising victory to both sides, nor D 3v do they care a farthing for what / sentence the high judge will pass on very bad lawyers and unfair decisions. If any of these should turn out to be a good judge, it should be ascribed to a good guardian spirit, who has led him away from that sort of living in which he was not restrained by the dictates of his conscience. Sometimes vicars are chosen from the city college to administer the law in that same city, but if that, perhaps, turns out once as desired, it hardly ever does twice. How can it not turn out that a canon will try to please a canon, a brother his brother, a friend his friend, and one resident of the town another? For the most part, canons do well on the strength of their grace and authority, then due to their relatives and friends, for a great many of those are among the wealthier residents of their city. How then will the law be administered fairly, if the accused has a canon to intercede for him, and a protector in a canon, or a neighbor to back him? A canon has a great many neighbors, in-laws, kinsmen, clients, and friends, so very rarely will it happen that he isn't predisposed in favor of one side or the other. We have seen in recent years certain things of a sort that are more to be pitied and lamented than to be D 4 recounted with the names deleted. The recollection makes me feel ashamed. / I would not disapprove of choosing them from external colleges, if one finds a good man who is also learned. It is of great importance for him who will be a judge with so much authority to have a benefice that will supply his basic needs, at least in part, so that poverty, and the immense desire to have a benefice, will not drive him to pervert the law or be corrupted by bribes. The common people because of their bad character are completely convinced that someone who has plenty of money will never go without benefices. Therefore it is important that the bishop be highly vigilant in choosing and introducing vicars. If those who solicit that honor are perhaps slaves of greed, there is nothing they will attempt more eagerly than to fill up that unfillable eagerness, that huge chasm. Some things we have seen; many things we fear, while the situation deteriorates every day. You who are the shepherd, if you wish to be seen as good, make it happen, I beg you, by hiring assistants who can act in the place of a good shepherd, and offer themselves as incorrupt judges. In

D 4v non spontaneam absentiam aliquo pacto leuent ac / dissimulent, qui
quando 'prouisores' uulgo dicuntur, prouideant, sed non sibi, sacerdotia
mandent, quibus iure debentur. Denuntient sine fuco tibi, sine commen-
datione sui, denique sine adulatione quaslibet res. Iactant nonnunquam
pinguiores ditioresque reddere se census et uectigalia prouinciae, minu-
endo eorum salaria, qui muneris partem gerunt, quo sit episcopus in eos
ipsos munificentior, illectus commodis sapienter, ut ipsis uidetur, excog-
itatis, cum uere commoditas, si qua paratur ex imminutis salariis, in eos
ipsos auctores rationibus improbis refundatur, atque episcopus ipse praeter
suspicionem auaritiae pudendam ferat profecto nihil.

Post uicarios sequuntur expensores exploratoresque tironum (uulgus
'examinatores' uocat), quorum muneris est expendere qui sint idonei ad
sacram initiationem, qui satis sint periti ad auspicandos ineundosque
sacros, quos uocant, ordines; tum etiam ex candidatis sacerdotiorum, qui
D 5 praestent eruditione, quae sane functio non / est cuilibet apta: uirum
desiderat cum grauem ac fidum, tum eruditione doctrinaque praestantem.
Huius enim episcopatus sacerdotia paene omnia, quae diximus patrimonialia uocitata, incolis oppidorum ac uicorum iure quodam ueteri deman-
dantur, ita quod ubiuis ciuium ratio solum habeatur et ex his peritior semper praeferatur, censentibus id expensoribus. Quapropter magnum hoc
nimirum munus atque sanctissimum est iudicandum, si pie sincereque
[*MSS* sinceque] geratur. Pendet ab eo potissimum fides, bonitas et integritas episcopi. Vertitur siquidem in eo uelut regionis totius harmonia, docti

D 4v   that way they to some extent can lighten and disguise your involuntary absences. / Since vicars-general are commonly called *provisores*, i.e., providers, let them provide, but not to themselves. They should deliver benefices over not to themselves, but to those to whom they are lawfully due. They should report to you every sort of thing, without deceit, without self-praise, and finally, without adulation. Sometimes they brag that they make the tax rolls — and the tax revenues of the province — fatter and richer by reducing the salaries of those who carry out the duties of an office. By doing this they hope the bishop will be more generous to them, seduced by the profits that they have thought out so wisely (in their own opinion). The truth is that the profit (if any is actually obtained) from the decrease in salaries is transferred over, by crooked accounting, to the same men who have ordered the decrease, and the bishop himself gains absolutely nothing except for the shameful suspicion of avarice!

The Role of Examiners

After the vicars come the *expensores*, and the testers of beginners, which the common people call examiners, whose office it is to evaluate candidates for sacred ordination, to decide which know enough to begin and undergo what they call sacred orders. Then also from among the candidates for the priestly positions who are outstanding for their learning —

D 5   and the position certainly isn't suited / to just anybody — he looks for a man who is not only dignified and faithful, but also outstanding in learning and knowledge of doctrine. Almost all the priestly positions in this diocese which (as we said) are called patrimonies, are entrusted, by some ancient right, to the inhabitants of the towns and villages. Thus in every place it is only the local citizens who are taken into account, and of these the most knowledgeable one is always preferred, based on the judgement of the examiners. For this reason there is no doubt that this office must be judged as great and most holy if it is carried out devoutly and properly. On it in particular depend a bishop's fidelity, goodness and integrity. Indeed the harmony of the whole region turns on this, whether or not the clergy is educated, whether or not the priestly positions are entrusted to worthy people, whether everything will be turned upside down[33] by avarice, whether the untaught, and virtually unteachable that is, those

---

[33] Cf. "The world's a stage that's topsy-turvey now, as you can see," in Erasmus' *Abbatis et eruditae*. See Erasmus 1997 (the *Colloquies*), p. 505. As Craig Thompson, the editor, points out (p. 519), the "idea that the world seems upside down nowadays is found in two other colloquies, 'the New Mother' 592:17-35 and 'Cyclops' 869:32-870:4."

sint clerici necne, sacerdotia committantur dignis, an per auaritiam
sursum omnia deorsumque ferantur, indocti prorsusque indociles, turpi
scilicet negotiationi aut stiuae nati praeferantur, esuriant docti bonaque
mente praediti. Vicarii solent interdum (quantum mali uidimus!) precibus
D 5v expugnati, sententiis examinatorum intercedere uel potius ita uel/le tem-
perare, ut qui sunt minus idonei, atque sacram ad initiationem aut ad
gerendum sacerdotium minus eruditi, sacerdotio fungantur aut initientur,
proposita non leui multa ad praetexendam culpam, si post adeptum mox
honorem scholas non repetierint et tantum litteris uacauerint, quoad ordini
atque functioni respondeat peritia. Quod utique sicut nemini uidetur non
intempestiuum, ita succedit nunquam nec in aliud sane proficit, quam ut
multam annumerent et alteram mox et alteram subeant, donec uir bonus
aliquis intercedat, qui tandem precibus obtineat ut multis finis imponatur,
multatique frustra initiatione, uel sacerdotio fungantur analphabeti paene.
Cauendum igitur est episcopo maxime, tales ut huic muneri praeficiantur,
qui norint inter optime institutum et inauspicatissimum blateronem dis-
cernere, qui precibus omnino nesciant flecti, qui gratia non ducantur, qui
D 6 muneribus non capiantur, / alioqui scaena penitus inuersa est sacrorum
ordinum ac sacerdotiorum, corruit omnis aequitas et iustitia, quae suum
cuique tribuit. Sed facillime fugitat episcopus hunc scopulum, si deligendis in examinatoribus famae constans praeiudicium perpetuosque
rumores prorsus non neglexerit. Fallit persaepe fama, fateor, in rebus
quamplurimis, at diuturna raro suis non depingit coloribus mores et eorum
naturam, qui publicum munus obeunt. Aperit sese quantumuis simulator
ac dissimulator, qui diu rempublicam tractat, qui munus negotiosum
exercet, qui omnium in oculis et in media luce uersatur. Prima tamen erit
cautio, ne sit ille, qui praeficitur delectui clericorum habendo, ciuis, aut
ita multum uersatur in eo munere, ut prae se cunctos faciat nihili, aditu
sit difficilis, uultuque deterreat, et spem protinus adimat mediocritatem
praeferentibus, quam ipse uix forte prostitit initiandus. Aegre manebit
D 6v aequitas inconcussa, ubi propinqui, necessarii, et affines urgent, repetunt
merita, /con-iunctionem sanguinis et officia exaggerant. Multis necessitu-

who were born for immoral dealings or the shaft of a plow handle —
will be given preference, whether the learned and those gifted with a good
mind will go hungry. Meanwhile, won over by entreaties, vicars are accustomed (how great is the evil we have seen!), to veto the decisions of the
D 5v examiners, or rather / to want to modify them in such a way that those
who are least suited and least educated to perform holy mass or carry out
the duties of a priest will carry out the office or be ordained. To cover
over their guilt, they propose a stiff fine if, soon after receiving the honor,
the candidates do not go back to school and make enough time for literary studies to bring their expert knowledge into line with their position
and their duties. There is no one who doesn't think that is unreasonable,
and it never happens that way, nor is anything at all accomplished, except
that they pay a fine, and then undergo another and yet another, until at
last some good man intercedes and finally by his prayers succeeds in
obtaining an end to the fines, so that nearly illiterate men, having been
fined in vain, may undergo ordination or perform the duties of priests.
Therefore the bishop must be extremely careful to appoint to this office
the kind of men who can tell the difference between an excellent candi-
date and a worthless windbag. They must refuse entirely to bend to
D 6 entreaties, be unmoved by favors, and not be susceptible to bribes. / Otherwise the whole system of holy orders and priests is turned upside down.
All fairness and justice, which allots to everyone what is theirs, collapses.
But a bishop very easily navigates around this rock if in choosing the
examiners he doesn't entirely neglect the unwavering advance report of
reputation and persistent rumors. I will admit that reputation is often mistaken in very many matters, but when it is long-lasting it rarely fails to
depict in their own colors the character, and the nature, of those who hold
public offices. No matter how much a charlatan and pretender he may be,
he reveals himself immeasurably who for long manages public affairs,
who has a busy post, who is engaged in things done in everyone's
sight and in broad daylight. In the beginning, though, caution should
be exercised, lest he who is in charge of conducting the choice of
clergymen be from the same city or is so deeply involved in that office
that he cares nothing for anyone except himself. Let him be hard to
approach, scare people away with his expression, and quickly take away
any hope from those who promote mediocrity, [a level of accomplish-
ment] which he himself, perhaps, could scarcely offer when he was going
to be ordained. Fairness can scarcely remain unshaken where relatives,
D 6v in-laws, and neighbors apply pressure, ask for favors, / and exaggerate the

dinibus tenetur, multis nominibus huic et illi obnoxius est qui uiuit inter suos. Iam qui diu munus exercuit, audet quae non auderet, libenter accipit, magna sui fiducia munitus est. Paedotriba ludique magister procul erat nimirum arcendus ab hoc munere, periclitatur fides, iustitiae candor denigratur, inficitur denique tribunal, ubi cognitor manifesto tenetur alterutri parti. Frequentissime uenit usu, ut idem sacerdotium petant, diuersis qui sub magistris merent, qui non eadem gymnasia frequentant. An non applaudet suis magister discipulis? Non praeferendos curabit? Sollemne quidem paedotribis est, ut odio maximo prosequantur alterius scholae proselytos. Et est cui ueniat in mentem, urbanum praeceptorem manibus pedibusque non conaturum, uertere sese prius in omnia non tentaturum, quam rumores ferat spargi, quem ipse erudiuit, ab alio fuisse superatum?

D 7   De parocho curione non audeo / pronuntiare; certe uidebitur suis ouibus plus aequo studere. Praeter tot offendicula, quae sinceritatem examinatorum obturbant, candorem obnubilant, hoc est nocentius, quod acerrimo quodam olfactu nunc peruestigatum est ab iis, qui blandiuntur episcopis, fierique posse redditus magis in dies uberiores ad aurem ogganniunt. Existimarunt uidelicet operae pretium, examinatoribus imminui salarium, immo prosus negari, scilicet ut ab iis ipsi discerent utilitatem capere, quorum eruditionem expendunt, quando fisco praesulis essent parum utiles et aerario decederet nihil, si munus eiusmodi tolleretur aut ita negligenter ageretur; ut nemo illud optaret nec oblatum quidem accipere uellet, ni referre qui parui putaret, bonaene indolis adolescens institutusque optime sacris initietur aut ad sacerdotium cooptetur, an idiota potius et cuiuis opificio quam sacrorum ministerio magis natus. Enimuero possunt examina-

D 7v tores, si uolunt, stipendium / habere sat pingue, solutis modo Christianae bonaeque mentis repagulis, ueniam cuilibet dando emendi sibi ius sacerdotii initiationemue sacram. Vidimus ipsi praeclarum Fonsecae praesulis

ties of blood and their services. Anyone who lives among his own people is bound by many close friendships, and on many accounts is obliged to this person and that. Anyone who long holds an office dares what he ought not to and takes freely, is bolstered by his great confidence in himself. He who was a *paedotriba* or a schoolmaster must of course be entirely excluded from this office, as his integrity would be in danger, the purity of justice would be stained, and in short the court would be contaminated when he is caught acting as an attorney for one side or the other. It very frequently happens that those who do not frequent the same schools, who have studied under various teachers, seek the same benefice. But won't a teacher applaud his own students? Will he not take care to give them preference? Indeed it is usual for *paedotribae* to pursue with great hatred the graduates of another school. And is there anyone who thinks for a moment that a teacher living in the city will not make an all-out effort with all his might? That he will not attempt to turn himself inside out, rather than let rumors be spread that someone he himself educated was defeated by another? Regarding a parish priest who

D 7   presides over a curia I do not dare / to make a statement, but certainly he will appear to root for his own sheep more than is just. But more than all the other stumbling blocks which compromise the sincerity of the examiners, which cloud their honesty, the most harmful one, which ought now to be tracked down with a very keen sense of smell, is this. There are those who flatter bishops and who whisper in their ear that their income could be increased on a daily basis. For example they have judged it worthwhile to decrease the salary of the examiners, or eliminate it altogether. Clearly they said this so that they themselves could learn how to make a profit off those whose knowledge they were to test. They argued that the current examiners were insufficiently useful to the bishop's exchequer, and there would be no loss to the treasury if an office of this kind were eliminated or provided for so negligently that no one would desire it or want to accept it even if it were offered — unless he should suppose that it does make some slight difference whether a young man of good lineage and excellent education undergo holy orders, or rather an uneducated man born more for some trade rather than the ministry of the

D 7v sacraments. In fact examiners are able, if they want, / to get pretty fat pay, provided they undo the restraints of a good and Christian mind by giving anyone at all permission to buy for himself the right to a benefice or to ordination in holy orders. We ourselves saw the very famous

iudicium ac pronuntiatum, qui peculatus conuictos examinatores, maxime quos ipse probabat carosque habebat, quod litterarum Latinarum rudes prorsus et ignaros quosdam adolescentes, eruditos sacraque perunctione dignos ob pessimum lucellum pronuntiassent, ignominia notatos perpetuum in exilium egit. Maxima turba quidem est in hac regione, ingens concursus ingerere sese uolentium ad clericatum et sacerdotia; si praebita sit causa iudicibus ac censoribus auferendi sibi ab initiandis, quae non ipsi grauate quidem reddent, maior profecto numerus initiatorum quam profanorum erit. Conantur toto pectore quam plurimi sine sacerdotio, iure quamuis sit interdictum, sacris initiari, certi scilicet non defuturum sacerdotium, uel iisdem artibus / partum, quibus initiati sunt. Proinde non usque adeo ualeat oeconomorum aut uicariorum uel immensa quorumcunque palponum cupiditas obsequendique praeposterum studium, ut munus, quo nullum oportet ad commune bonum incorruptius esse, paruulam ob retentam pecuniam, lapsui non minus foedissimo quam perniciosissimo sit expositum et episcopi candor ac integritas prauis iudiciis pateat traducenda.

D 8

Putabis, optime praesul, negotium me agere meum, cum prorsus habueris conpertum, functionem me hanc aliquot annos gessisse paeneque nunc gerere; sed cum rem penitus noris, intelliges tandem (opinor) me cum candore gessisse, nunc uero sic gerere, quasi non geram, propterea quod mihi nondum est persuasum tui ex animi sententia pleraque decernenda, quae tuo iam nomine constituenda denuntiantur, et sunt, me quidem cessante, qui munus exerceant uigilantissime. Fuit nimirum in hoc sollers eorum parsimonia, qui antiquandi salarii fuerunt auctores, quod nulli munus petenti denegatur, dum modo non sit / importunus petitor, qui

D 8v

judgment and sentence of Bishop Fonseca,[34] who singled out for disgrace and sent into perpetual exile some examiners who were convicted of embezzlement, even though he liked them and thought very highly of them. He did so because for a wretched little bribe they had pronounced some candidates who were ignorant of and unfamiliar with Latin letters to be well educated and worthy of ordination. Indeed there is in this region a huge crowd, an immense throng of people who want to intrude themselves into the clergy and hold benefices, so if a way were available to judges and censors to steal something for themselves from the candidates which in fact the candidates on their own would pay over to them without reluctance — there would doubtless be a bigger number of ordained people than of laity. A great many people with no benefice try with their whole heart to be admitted to holy orders, though it is forbid-

D 8 den by law, and they are no doubt certain that a benefice will not fail them, since they will get hold of it through the same tricks / by which they get ordination. Thus the greed of financial managers and vicars, or the immeasurable greed of certain flatterers and their perverse efforts at flattery, should not have so much power that an office, which, for the common good, ought to remain more free of corruption than any other, should, for the sake of holding on to a little money, be exposed to a lapse of morality as foul as it is harmful, and the honesty and integrity of the bishop be open to betrayal by depraved judges.

Maldonado's Own Frustrations in Service

You will think, most excellent superintendent, that I do my job when you have thoroughly verified that I have carried out this duty for several years, and almost up to now have still done so. When you have become thoroughly informed about the subject, I think you will conclude that I have done it honestly. But now I do it in such a way that I might as well not be doing it, particularly because I am not yet convinced that most things will be decided as you would like, regarding matters which are announced as needing to be determined in your name, and there are those who, at least if I stop performing the duties, will carry them out most vigilantly. The thriftiness, no doubt, was adroit of those who supported making the salary obsolete, because to no one seeking the office is it

D 8v denied, unless he is / rude in his request or is unwilling to arrange his salary from what he himself will obtain, or rather extort, from those who wish to be ordained or receive a benefice, if I can put it that way. What's more, while under those shepherds Lodovicus and Pascual, who were

---

[34] On Fonseca see below, note 49.

procuret salarium, ni sibi quod ipse parauerit uel potius extorserit ex initiandis ac beneficiandis, ut ita dicam. Itaque cum sub Lodouico et Paschali bonis, ut creditum est, pastoribus unus sufficeret expensor, cui salarium adnumerabatur honorarium et accommodum, nunc cum ingerunt sese quicumque sine mercede, duo etiam pauci uidentur, trium numerus censetur iustus, quattuor certe iam uidimus. Quis hoc induxit? Quis persuasit? Auaritia quidem, male suada pestis, ambitio, sed magis adulatio. Quidam mediocriter instituti sacerdotes putant non infrugiferum munus cum sit honorarium, in quo tot examina clericorum tribus uerbis censentur uel apta uel inepta sacerdotio, docta satis an mediocriter, uel prorsus imperita. Proinde cum ambiant multi albo scribi, locum occupare festinant uel sine mercede. Praesules ad haec persuasi perperam ab iis, qui semper ogganniunt ad aurem redditus augendi turpes occasiones, / ex hoc quidem munere nihil in aerarium inferri, seponunt curas disquirendi quam ex hac parte pendeat salus animae. Per interuallum, quo praesule caruimus a morte Fonsecae, multi uehementer conati sunt examinatores fieri uotisque sunt quidam potiti, quibus successurum audio neminem ante tuum aduentum.

Laudo tuum equidem consilium; rem haud ita sinunt, quibus plurima permittis. Sum ego tibi quidem iam unus (ut audio) ab hoc munere laborioso magis quam utili, nescio quidem an casu, quod fracta sim in nauicula repertus, an forte quod clarissimus frater tuus Franciscus Stunica Comes Mirandae locum, quem tenebam, deferendum mihi tuis in aedibus edixerit. Nam cum hos ante annos ferme duos, quattuor in hac urbe menses Caesar egisset, postremis tandem diebus, euocari me iussit comes illustrissimus et ut ei filio Guterio Cardenati, bonae nimirum indolis

E 1

believed to be good,[35] just one examiner was needed, to whom an appropriate and honorable salary was paid. Now, when practically everybody jumps in without payment, even two seem like only a few, three is thought the right number, and in fact we have already seen four. Who introduced this? Who argued for it? Avarice, indeed, that wickedly persuasive plague, along with ambition, but even more so adulation. Certain priests with a mediocre education think that this is not an unfruitful office, in that it is offered voluntarily and since so many crowds of clergy are judged by three words that decide whether or not they are suited for the priesthood, whether they are educated sufficiently or in a mediocre way, or whether they are completely ignorant. Therefore, since many seek to be included on the list, they make haste to step into the post even without salary. Bishops are wrongly persuaded to this by those who are always whispering in their ear the shameful opportunities to increase income and the fact / that from this office nothing is actually paid into the treasury. So they banish all concern about thinking through the fact that the health of their souls depends on this matter. During the interval in which we lacked a bishop after the death of Fonseca, many tried avidly to become examiners. Some found their prayers answered, and I have not heard that any replacement for them will be made before your arrival.

E 1

Tutoring the Count's Son

I certainly praise your plan, but those whom you permit to do many things are not leaving it that way. I am now the only one left to you, as I hear, in this office, which, rather than being useful, multiplies [my] work. I don't know whether it is by chance, because I was found in a broken little boat,[36] or perhaps because your very distinguished brother Francisco Zúñiga, Count of Miranda,[37] has proclaimed that the post I used to hold in your house is to be conferred on me. Now when almost two years ago the emperor[38] passed four months in this city, finally, in the last days, the most illustrious count had me called and very politely persuaded

---

[35] Lodovicus: Luis de Alcuña, Bishop of Burgos 1456-1495; Pascual: Pascual de Ampudia, Bishop 1496-1512. For Pascual, see the full study by Ortega Martín 1973.

[36] Maldonado seems to compare the neglected office of examiner to a broken boat, and perhaps suggests that he fears the bishop will do away with it, at least as a paid position.

[37] Brother of Iñigo López de Mendoza, Francisco Zúñiga, the third count of Miranda, served as master of horses for the household of Empress Isabella of Portugal (1503-1539) She married Carlos V, her cousin, in 1526. See Bietenholz and Deutscher 1985-1987, vol. 3, pp. 479-480.

[38] The Emperor is Carlos V (1500-1558), to whose court Erasmus was closely connected and to whom he dedicated the *Institutio principis Christiani* in 1516.

adolescenti, Ciceronem aut classicum quempiam alium enarrarem auc-
E 1v torem et in dicen/do scribendoque Latine quoad fieri posset et tempus
pateretur, instruerem, humanissime persuasit. Conatus sum pro uirili nec
docilitas quidem ac ingenium peracre deerat adolescenti, temporis tamen
angustia non passa est uoti nos omnino compotes esse: discessit Caesar
celerius quam fuerat creditum. Atqui cum aegre diuelleretur a me
Guterius, tandem efflagitauit uerbis quam humanissimis, ut compendi-
ariam aliquam uiam praestruerem ac designarem, qua certissime posset
ad eloquentiam bonasque litteras peruenire. Gessi tum morem adolescenti
litterarum amore flagranti, quantum licuit, dum scilicet sternitur mula.
Postea uero scripto rem ipsam longius pertractaui uerbosiusque multo
rationem studii prosequutus sum, cupiens Guterio placere proque uirili
felicitatem indolis iuuare. Certe formulam illam ad Guterium de ratione
studii, quam Paraenesim inscripsi, typographi corripuere, et quamuis non
omnino feliciter, typis quidem scissere; si uacauerit uel subsiciuis
E 2 aliquando tempori/bus inspicere, meum quidem propensum tuam in familiam olim studium cognosces. Non equidem multo post clarissimus
Comes frater tuus suam in familiam et domesticum contubernium per
quosdam amicos accersit, quo Guterio ceterisque filiis domesticus prae-
ceptor adessem. Distuli tum rem in tuum aduentum (eras enim praesul
designatus), ut tibi, qui clares sapientia doctrinaque uere christiana, quod
magis exoptabam, adiungerer uel ex tuo arbitrio fratri nepotibusque.

Interim cum sum rebus praepeditus eiusmodi, ut me facile non queam
euoluere, tenebo locum inter tuos non omnino postremum, si res ueris

me to interpret Cicero or some other Classical author for his son Gutierre
E 1v de Cárdenas,[39] a young man who is of course of a good innate character,
/ and to instruct him to speak and write Latin as far as might be possible
and time would allow. I tried earnestly, and certainly neither ability to
learn nor a sharp intelligence were lacking in the young man, but the
shortness of the time did not permit us to accomplish our goal completely,
[and] the emperor left sooner than had been anticipated. But when they
finally succeeded in dragging Gutierre away from me, he asked earnestly
in very polite words that I should prepare and design a short method by
which he could with certainty attain to eloquence and good letters. So
then, as time permitted, in fact while the mule was being saddled, I prepared some precepts for the young man so on fire with love of literature.
But then later I finished writing the piece in a longer form, and with many
more words I developed the plan of study, wanting to please Gutierre
and as much as possible help along the happiness of his natural character. The fact is that the typesetters seized that guide for Gutierre on a plan
E 2 of study, which I entitled *Paraenesis,* and they printed it, though not completely happily. You will learn, if you / have the leisure someday in your
free time to look through it again, of my longstanding and carefully considered devotion to your family.[40] It wasn't at all much later when that
most illustrious Count, your brother, summoned me into his household
and domestic companions, acting through certain friends, so that I would
be present to act as the teacher for Gutierre and other children of the
household. I deferred the matter until your coming (as you were already
appointed bishop) so that I might join myself to you, who are famous for
your wisdom and truly Christian doctrine — which is what I most eagerly
desired — or, in accordance with your opinion, to your brother or
nephews.

In the meantime, although I am so tied up with matters of such a kind
that I can't easily extricate myself, I will hold not the lowest position
among your people if things should be weighed according to their true
value and persons were to be adjusted to positions and not positions to

---

[39] On Gutierre de Cárdenas, son of don Francisco de Zúñiga, Count of Miranda, see
Bataillion-Devoto-Amiel 1991, 1, 356-357.
[40] The little manual which he wrote for Gutierre, published in 1529, has now been
republished by Juan Alcina Rovira (1980). Alcina Rovira (p. 96) testifies to the faulty condition of the original published manuscript and its numerous typographical errors (hence
Maldonado's reference to its being printed "not completely happily.")

ualoribus pensarentur et personae muneribus adaptarentur, non munera
personis. Tamdiu tum tenebo quoad uicarios mei officii non paenitebit.
Plenum habere se ius uolunt uideri, tam redigendi, qui muneribus praesunt, in ordinem, quam alios subrogandi, nec satis mihi uidentur expendere, quod cuique sit muneri magis accommodum, quod prorsus repugnet.

E 2v   Post examinatores sequuntur ordine scribae, / quos uocant notarios et
secretarios. Ii praescribunt nonnunquam uicariis et ceteris officialibus,
nonnunquam ita iacent, ut fides eorum, quae nunquam deberet non esse
sanctissima, periclitetur. Sunt causae, quae sacro tractantur in foro tot,
tam uariae, multiplices et ambiguae propter improbitatem hominum, ut
quattuor uix iam sufficiant scribae, cum ante praesulem Fonsecam unus,
ad summum duo plus satis essent. Stipulantur singuli, cum ambiunt
ascribi numero (nouum est commentum) ut quadripartito suo dimenso,
quod unciatim (ut ait Terentius) ex uitilitigatoribus et commissis clericorum collegunt [*M emends to* colligerunt], partes tres fisco praesulis
annume-rent. Viderint ipsi quid muneris ambient; hoc certe uelint nolint,
exsol-uendum est. Ita coguntur multis extorsionibus uexare tum reos, tum
actores, ne prius lites finem inueniant, quam quid extra sortem eis clanculum porrigatur. Et si quando forte deprehenduntur in furto, clamitant
E 3   non posse tantum pensionis solue/re ni furtim bonam partem corradant.

Lis mihi erat quondam de sacerdotio non admodum certe pingui; euice-
ram manifesto cunctorum iudicio, fatente propemodum etiam quicum

persons. I shall have it at least as long as the vicars are not displeased with my office. They want to seem to have full power, both of restoring to rank those who are in charge of positions, and of replacing others. They do not seem to me to give sufficient weight to the fact that a person is more suited to a position if he wholeheartedly resists it.

The Role of Scribes

E 2v Next in line after the examiners are the scribes, / whom they call notaries and secretaries. They sometimes direct the vicars and other officials. Sometimes they lie so prostrate that their faithfulness, which should never be less than sacrosanct, is endangered. There are so many cases handled in the episcopal court — so varied, multi-faceted, and ambiguous due to human dishonesty — that four scribes are now hardly enough, when before under bishop Fonseca, only one, or at the most two, were more than enough. One after another they promise, when trying to get themselves added to the number (and this is a new scheme), that they will pay to the bishop's exchequer three fourths of the money that comes to them ounce by ounce (as Terence[41] says) from troublemakers and that they obtain from the crimes of clergymen. Which position they are seeking is up to them; this is surely the sum which must be paid, whether they like it or not. Thus they are driven to harass with many forms of extortion not only the accused, but also the plaintiffs, to prevent the cases from coming to an end before something is offered to them secretly beyond what they have been allotted. And if by chance they are eventually caught in their theft, they cry out that they are not able to make such a big

E 3 payment / unless they furtively rip off a good part of it.

Maldonado's Personal Experience in a Law Court

A lawsuit was once brought against me over a benefice that certainly wasn't very rich, and everyone's opinion was that I had obviously won, as was virtually admitted even by he who was in disagreement with me. But even by pleading and begging I was unable to get the scribe to hand over the written accusation to the judge so that the sentence could be pronounced, while the scribe made first one excuse and then another, always in a haughty manner and looking at me out of the corner of his eye. Then I began lodging my complaints to the judge, but he was always disparaging the matter, giving as an excuse that the scribe was busy with

---

[41] Widely read by sixteenth-century academics, Terence was admired for the exceptional purity of his Latin and for his dramatic realism. Brought to Rome from Carthage as a slave and educated by his master, he wrote six comedies before his death in 159 BC. Maldonado quotes the word *unciatim* from Terence's *Phormio* 43.

mihi non conueniebat. Precibus ac obtestationibus obtinere non poteram
ab scriba, ut libellos iudici traderet ad pronuntiandam sententiam, iam
hoc iam illud causante, supercilioso semper et ex transuerso me prospec-
tante. Denuntiabam interdum iudici meas querellas, ille maximas scribae
praetexens occupationes rem diluebat. Tandem amicus summus meus
amici miseratus angores, litium et ipse non alias imperitus, "Nescis"
inquit "tu lites tractare. Dum sic fueris animatus, operam ludis. Mitte uel
meo periculo, si tui ex animi sententia res non successerit, munus aliquod
ad scribam, nec minus, si celerem percupis uictoriam, ad cognitorem; et
negotium confecisti, aliter quidem ambis." Ego uero litteris perperam
E 3v intermissis, cupiens iam tandem uacare, litium mirandum in / modum
osor, aggredior exequi consilium amici, minimeque ausus de sanctitate
iudicis temere iudicare, secretarii manibus furtim, quasi aliud agens,
nescio quot nummos argenteos indidi, "Cape munusculum" inquiens
"quo scribendi molestiam leues; cum sententia dicta sit, persoluam magnifice, quod litis eiusmodi causaeque uictoriae praescriptum est." Accepit
subinuitus, ut uoluit uideri, castigatoque me blandissimis uerbis, quod
eius de fide dubitarim, rem meam acturum diligentius nullo praemio,
quam alterius cuiusque emolumento quammaximo promisit. Tum laetus
admodum, cum euentilasset digitis argenteos, domum abiit et ante tres
non plenas horas rem meam confectam retulit meque ad praefectum sigilli transmisit, ut impressis episcopalibus insignibus, summam totius litis
adnumerarem diplomaque tandem mecum ferrem. Ita muneribus expug-
naui quod aequitate aut gratia quidem non ualueram.
     Ego tunc familiaris episcopo: quid pati tu coniectabis externos? Non
E 4 equidem multos ante hos dies, / ante tum quam tu designareris episcopus,
clericus quidam montanus, posteaquam menses aliquot causam suam egit
ad sacrum tribunal, ut sacerdotii iure sibi debiti compos euaderet, uictoria tandem parta, cum ratio subduceretur ab scribis nummorum, quos erat
adnumeraturus, priusquam iudicis obsignatum decretum acciperet, summae magnitudinem admiratus quam quidem post tot expensas pecunias
apud eosdem scribas, procuratores, aduocatos, soluendo non erat:

many other cases. Finally a very close friend of mine, pitying his friend's anxieties, and as he was not inexperienced with law suits, said to me, "You don't know how to manage these cases. As long as you approach it this way, you are laboring in vain. Take my word for it, and send something to the scribe as a gift, if the matter has not turned out as you would like it. Send the same, if you want very much to achieve a rapid victory, to the lawyer and you have settled your business; otherwise you are really going in circles." Since the indictment had been wrongly delayed, I very much wanted to be finally free of the matter. Since I hate lawsuits to an

E 3v extraordinary degree, / I undertook to follow my friend's advice. Since I didn't dare at all rashly to reach conclusions about the sanctity of the judge, I placed in the hands of the secretary — secretly, almost as though I were doing something else — I don't know how many silver coins, saying, "Take a little gift, with which you may relieve the burden of writing. When the sentence is pronounced, I shall generously pay in full the fee that is set down for a case of this sort and for the victory in the suit." He accepted reluctantly, as he wished it to seem, then after reproving me with very gentle words because I doubted his faithfulness, he promised that for no reward he would take care of my matter more carefully than he would for anyone else, even for a huge fee. Then surpassingly happy, tossing the coins with his fingers, he went home, and in less than three hours he brought back my paperwork all finished up, sent me over to the prefect of the seal so that, after it was sealed with the bishop's insignia I might pay for the whole cost of the lawsuit, and finally take away with me the magistrate's document. Thus with bribes I was able to take by storm that which I had been unable to through either justice or favor.

Then, considering that I am part of the bishop's household, what will you guess that those suffer who are not so positioned? Not many days,

E 4 in fact, before this, / before you had been appointed bishop, a certain clergyman from the mountains spent some months pleading his own case before the ecclesiastical court so that he might come out in possession of a benefice that he was legally entitled to. After he finally obtained the victory, when the scribes added up the total of the coins he would have to pay before receiving the judge's signed decree, he was amazed at the size of the sum. After so much money spent on those same scribes, agents, lawyers, he was not able to pay.

"Me miserum" inquit, "patrimonium omne libellis ac subscriptionibus consumpsi et nunc denique cogor etiam sanguinem reddere? Plus aeris a me repetitur, quam ipsum est pensurum sacerdotium annos multos? Valeat sacerdotium, ualeat clericatus, ualeant raptores isti, detestor pacem tam iniquam, bello quouis sanguinario certe atrociorem. Crastino, Deum testor, exortu proficiscar in Italiam, et auctoratus militiae iugulandisque hominibus deuotus, strenuum militem agam. Malo quidem inter ferratas

E 4v   acies et fulgura bombardarum uersari, mori denique, quam tanti / emere sacerdotium aegre uictui suffecturum. Pereat male quod expensum est temporis et pecuniae, sero uel cum Phrygibus sapiamus." Ita furibundus sese proripuit e medio.

Delatores, quos uocant fiscales, aut sequuntur post scribas aut forte praecedunt. Gerunt illi quidem munus saeuum, inhumanum, Christianae caritatis in perniciem excogitatum. Traducunt persaepe famam ho- nestissimorum clericorum et flagitiosissimis nonnunquam parcunt. Neque solum quidem ipsi per se, quod est calamitosius, calumnias praestruunt, habent singulis in oppidis et uicis suos uicarios conductos, qui noctu diuque seruent uestigia sacrificulorum, sermones progressusque notent, qualibet ex re nectant calumniam. Parum hoc lege nuper sancitum est, ut qui clerico dixerit diem et criminis arcesserit, tertiam multae portionem ferat. Quamobrem est factum, ut pagis in rusticanis et ubiuis, laboribus ingratissimis qui uiuunt in diem, perfacile sese uertant ad calumnias cleri-

E 5   corum, partim / iam inimici, partim inuidi, nihil non siue dictum siue fac- tum calumnientur. Fiscales postea quam clericum praetextu quocumque

A Clergyman's Lament

"Poor me," he said. "I have used up all of my fortune in memoranda and documents. Am I now obliged to give even my blood, as I am asked to pay more money than the benefice itself will pay after many years? To hell with the benefice, to hell with the priesthood, and to hell with these bandits of yours. I hate such an unjust peace, which is unquestionably more atrocious than any bloody war. As God is my witness, tomorrow at dawn I will set out for Italy and hire myself out in the wars, committed to butchering people, and act the part of a vigorous soldier. I actually prefer to busy myself in the armored ranks and the glare of the E 4v bombs, and so finally to die, rather than at such a price / to buy a benefice that will scarcely be sufficient for food. Damn the time and the money spent, and let's join the Phrygians in growing wise, even though late.[42]" In this rage he tore himself away from the presence of all.

The Role of Informers

Informers, whom they call prosecutors, either come after the scribes, or perhaps before. They fill a post that is certainly savage, inhumane, and thought up to harm Christian charity. They very frequently besmirch the reputations of the most honest clergymen, while sometimes sparing the most shameful. Nor is it, indeed, only by themselves (which is very destructive) that they prepare false accusations. In individual towns and villages they have their hired deputies who day and night follow the footsteps of the clergy who say mass, mark down the directions of the sermons, and can patch together a false accusation out of anything. And as if this weren't enough, a new law has been enacted that anyone who makes an accusation against a clergyman and indicts him of a crime, may receive a third of the fine. For this reason it has come about that in rural districts, or wherever the people are obliged to earn a living, day after day, by very unpleasant work, most willingly they turn to making false accu- E 5 sations against the clergy. Partly they are / already enemies of the priests and partly they are envious, so there is nothing said or done that they would not misrepresent. The prosecutors, after they have with whatever pretext dragged in the clergyman in chains, not only exaggerate the charges, but heap them up along with anything else that can be, and often is, twisted into crimes of corrupt clergymen, and leads to their

---

[42] The Phrygians were a people of Asia Minor, identified with the Trojans, who were said to "grow wise too late" because of the stubborn refusal of the Trojans to give up Helen. Cicero in *Fam.* 7.16.1 quotes this proverb from a lost play, "The Trojan Horse."

traxerunt in uincula, non exaggerant modo quod est datum crimini, uerum omnia quae possunt et solent quandoque flagitiosis clericis uitio uerti ignominiaeque dari congerunt, ut si se testibus idoneis de quibusdam expurgauerit, de aliis poenas det non capitis, sed pecuniae. Sapientissime quidem in foro sacro seruantur rei, quamuis sicarii, quo fiant nimirum subinde rei. Fiscales tamen ii, qui pacem ecclesiae plerumque turbant, qui clericos cum laicis committunt, qui sacra clericis secure peragere non sinunt, cum sint hostes humanae concordiae, tamen habentur in aliquo pretio primumque fere tenent locum apud uicarios et oeconomos episcopales. Quid? Sunt sacerdotes et quotidie sacrificant, quasi nullius criminis sibi conscii, ueluti quae faciant, studio pietatis faciant, quo clerici sacrificent sanctius et uiuant honestius, non autem quo loculos eorum extenuent et / suas ipsi peras dilatent. Honestam aliquam praetexuisse causam primos huius muneris auctores non equidem dubitarim. Ceterum cum mala omnia bonis ex principiis frequentius orta sint, boni pastoris fuerit praeposteris hominum moribus obsistere cauereque ne canes uertantur in lupos, opiliones in saeuos latrones, et si quos semel offenderit, oues hostiliter insectantes, ferro candenti inustos, ab ouium caula longissime disturbare. Melius est lupis oues nonnunquam expositas errare, quam a canibus et mercenariis custodiam simulantibus passim trucidari. Vigilantia nimirum pastoris canes atque mercenarii non discedunt ab officio nec pecudes ipsae diuertunt ad negata penitus et interdicta pascua.

Salus et interitus ouium a pastore plane dependent; si prohibentur discurrere ad infectas pestilentesque lacunas, ad noxias herbas, ad loca lupis habitata, uulpibus frequentata, pardis ac leonibus non inaccessa, si non tondentur/ praeter tempus et modum, extra commoda loca, si non mulgentur extra mensuram, si commodum arcentur a contagiis uicinarum, equidem durabunt ad senectam, reddent annuum prouentum in dies uberiorem, et cum sint tandem effectae senio gignendoque fetui minus

disgrace. Thus, even if he should clear himself by means of excellent witnesses of some of the charges, he would still be punished for others — not with a death sentence but with a fine. It is the wisest plan to keep the accused, even though they may be assassins, under guard in the church court — so that they can be put on trial repeatedly, of course. Nevertheless those financiers, who, for the most part, are disrupting the peace of the church, who set the laity against the clergy, who do not allow the clergy peacefully to perform their sacraments, although they are enemies of human concord, they are nonetheless held in some esteem, and hold almost the first place among the bishop's vicars and financial managers. What? Aren't they priests and don't they daily say mass, as though feeling guilty for no crime, as though what they are doing were done out of eagerness for piety so that the clergy may say mass in a more holy manner and live more honorably, and not in order to deplete the clergy's mon-

E 5v eyboxes while / stuffing their own wallets? The first authors of this office must have justified it with some honest pretext; I don't doubt it at all; and yet, since all evils very frequently spring from good beginnings, it should be the role of the good shepherd to oppose people's perverted character and to be careful lest the dogs turn into wolves, the shepherds into cruel thieves. And if he once encounters any group who chase the sheep with a hostile intent, it is his role to burn them with hot iron and chase them at a great distance away from the sheepfold. It is better for the sheep sometimes to wander exposed to the wolves than to be slaughtered left and right by dogs and hired hands that only pretend to care for them. But of course with vigilance by the shepherd the dogs and the hired hands don't abandon their duties, nor do the flocks themselves turn aside into pastures that are entirely forbidden and prohibited.

The health or destruction of the sheep depends entirely on the shepherd. All is well if they are forbidden to go off the track into contaminated and pestilent hollows, or go after poisonous plants, or to places where wolves live and foxes are common, and even leopards and lions are found; if

E 6 they are not sheared / at the wrong time, or to the wrong degree, outside of appropriate places; if they are not overmilked; if they are properly protected from contagious diseases of their neighbors, then indeed they will live all the way to old age, and they will produce offspring every year which will continually grow more fruitful. And when finally they are affected[43] by old age and become less apt for breeding, they will bring

---

[43] The text reads *effectae* here, which perhaps should be emended to *effetae*, "weakened."

idoneae, carne proderunt et pelle. Sin curam earum neglexerit pastor, neque lana utiles erunt neque caseo, fetus distrahent uulpes, ipsae denique incautius agentes, morbos contrahent et a lupis denique deuorabuntur. Nec eleuat quidem culpam pastoris quod mercenarios conduxerit ad pascendas oues; fugiunt ueniente lupo mercenarii, immo sunt ipsi plerumque rabiosi lupi cum maius illis accrescat lucrum ex dilaceratis quam ex integris pecudibus. Diuexant ipsi nonnunquam oues, quo pereant ipsique pelle potiantur et lana. "Pasce oues meas" Petro dixit Christus optimus maximus, et cum se bonum praedicasset pastorem, quod pro suis ouibus animam libenter impenderet, a mercenariis bonos pastores deterruit. / Sunt diuersorum munerum alii in foro sacro ministri, sed procuratores qui uocantur, potissimum eminent, qui tum reo, tum actori uelut aduocati patrocinantur, crimina libellis intendunt, litem contestantur, ex nihilo magna iurgia suscitant atque producunt. Proximis annis lex lata est, ut nemo suam per se causam agat, sed per procuratorem, quo nobilitetur ordo tum procuratorum tum aduocatorum, et sit tribunal frequentius. Norunt probe cognitores alere suos fastus et uix ferendam impotentiam, sua norunt commoda reddere magis in dies pinguiora, norunt nec minus, quid ouibus conducat et prosit; uerum cum ex earum damno ditescant uberius ipsi, pastoris absentia, dum licet, largissime fruuntur. Olim leges rogabantur, ferebantur, in aes incidebantur ad communem omnium utilitatem, ad contrahendas comprimendasque lites, ad sedanda iurgia, ad quietem et pacem inter ciues constituendam, ad subleuandam plebeculam; in summa nullum uel plebiscitum ferebatur, quod non euidentem / aliquam uiderent utilitatem afferre. Nunc ob nostra maxima commissa nihil sancitur, nihil a magistratibus sacrosanctis statuitur, quod non uergat in

E 6v

E 7

profit with their meat and hides. But if the shepherd neglects their care, they will not be useful for wool or cheese, the foxes will tear away their lambs, and finally they themselves, acting without caution, will contract diseases and finally be eaten by wolves. Nor does it lessen the guilt of the shepherd that he has hired others to pasture the sheep. When the wolf comes the hired hands run away; rather, I should say that mostly they are themselves rabid wolves, since there is more profit for them when the livestock are torn to pieces rather than left untouched. They themselves sometimes harass the sheep, causing their death, and so they take possession of the hide and the wool. "Feed my sheep," Christ, the best and the greatest shepherd, said to Peter.[44] So when he proclaimed himself a good shepherd by freely giving his life for his sheep, he deterred good

E 6v   shepherds from relying on hired hands. / There are other ministers of various offices in the ecclesiastical court, but *procuratores*, i.e., 'agents', as they are called, are especially prominent. Acting like attorneys, they defend sometimes the accused and sometimes the plaintiff, they lay out the charges in indictments, they call witnesses in the case, and out of nothing they stir up and develop big quarrels. In recent years a law has been passed that no one on his own can handle his own case, that it must be done by an agent, in order to ennoble the rank of agents as well as that of attorneys, and make the court busier. Lawyers know very well how to nourish their own haughtiness and their outrageous, intolerable behavior. They know how to cultivate their interests and make them more profitable daily. They also know just as well what helps and brings advantage to the sheep. But when they themselves can get richer and fatter by harming the sheep, they fully exploit and enjoy the shepherd's absence while they can. Formerly, laws were requested, passed, and engraved in bronze for the common good of all, for diminishing and suppressing lawsuits, for calming quarrels, for establishing peace and quiet among citizens, and for raising up the poor. In short, no law, even a decree of

E 7   the people,[45] was passed, that did not clearly / bring some evident benefit. Now, due to our very great sins, nothing is sanctioned, nothing is decided by the most holy magistrates that does not aim at the destruction

---

[44] In John 21.15-17, Christ asks Peter three times if he loves him, and after getting affirmative answers each time adds, "Feed my sheep." The triple question may be intended to correspond to Peter's triple denial of Christ in John 18. 18-27.

[45] A plebiscite. Perhaps Maldonado is referring to an act passed by the Spanish parliament.

perniciem miserae plebis, quod non tendat potissimum ad contrahendas pecunias, ad id denique, ut facile quis multam incurrat.

Retuli, praesul amplissime, quae nulli clam est tuum ante praesulatum fieri frequentissime, quae cuncti damnant mortales in sacris magistratibus, et in clericis plerisque, quae malorum omnium semina sunt et scelerum quasi uelamenta. Diues enim mercator si forte fidei ius iurandique sit contemptor audacissimus ob lucellum quodcumque, ita secum ratiocinatur, cum sibi conscius timet aliquando supremum iudicium:

"Quid hebes ego lepore sum timidior? Sacrosancti sacerdotes, qui nobis in exemplum uitae traditi sunt, quibus instituto Christi iubemur nostra fateri commissa, fraudibus ditescunt, interdum et periuriis, uolitant per maria et terras, ut amicum et uicinum sacerdotio spolient. Pecu/nia persaepe ius sibi uendicant rei numquam uenalis et ne causa quidem cadant, solum Acheronta non mouent. Famelicis alii ciuibus et agricolis triticum decimae iure sacrum faenori dant, milleque modis imponunt, quibus oportuisset ex officio consulere. Sed nec in monachis paene quicquam inuenio sanctius, imo pleraque tanto foediora, quanto generosius est fateri crimen, quam per turpem hypocrisim dissimulare. Leuiora sint igitur minusque proritantia Deum oportet facinora turpiaque commissa, leuius etiam iis supplicium deberi, quam isti iactitant suggestu; alioqui non ipsi, qui ea traducunt, ferrentur tam praecipites ad semel et iterum perpetrandum quod supplicio decantant dignum aeterno. Nimirum ea propter, opinor, insectantur in pulpitis et occultis confessionibus uitia ipsis solemnia, quo bonae mentis uiri securiores sint monstroque simile iudicent, imo numquam inducant animum fieri posse, ut a quibus male tam frequenter au/diunt flagitia, uitiis uel leuioribus inuoluantur. An mihi felicitatis aditus occludent quae patefit his? Praesertim cum occlament ipsi subinde, maius quodcumque censeri flagitium, quod admiserit uir sacris initiatus, quam quod profanus quicumque? Soluamus tandem

E 7v

E 8

of the wretched poor, that does not tend as much as possible to diminishing their money, that, in short, does not aim at making it easy for someone to incur a fine.

I have reported, distinguished superintendent, things that — and it's no secret to anyone — were very commonly done before your supervision began, things which all mortals [find and] condemn in holy magistrates and in most of the clergy. They are the seeds of all evils, and like veils that cover crimes. Indeed, if by chance a rich merchant should be contemptuous of his faithfulness and oath, growing very bold for the sake of making some little profit, this is how he reasons with himself when, aware of his guilt, eventually he fears the final judgment:

Laymen Excuse Their Own Crimes by Pointing to Example of Priests

"Why am I so sluggish and more fearful than a rabbit? The most holy priests, who are held up to us as examples of how to live, to whom by the direction of Christ we are commanded to confess our sins, are all the while becoming rich through deceits and sometimes also by perjury. They fly about the seas and lands to strip both friend and neighbor of their E 7v benefices. Very often by money / they claim for themselves the rights to something which was never for sale, and lest they fail in the lawsuit, they stir up everything but hell itself. Others loan out at interest to starving farmers and townspeople the wheat which has been hallowed by the law of the tithe, then impose in a thousand ways on the same people whose interests they should have consulted as part of their duties. But even among the monks can I scarcely find anything at all more holy, or rather, usually more shameful, so much so as it is more honest to confess a crime than cover it over through shameful hypocrisy. Thus, let them be lesser sins — their shameful deeds must outrage God less, and a lesser punishment is due them than those [priests] claim from the pulpit. Otherwise the men who denounce them would not be driven headlong to commit over and over again the very sin that they claim is deserving of eternal punishment. For this reason, I believe, sins customary among them are denounced in the pulpits and in private confessions — so that well intentioned men may be more worry-free and judge it to be a monstrosity. No, I should say it would never occur to them as possible that the very men E 8 who so frequently denounce vices / could be involved in even the smallest sins. Will the path to happiness be closed to me when it lies open to them? Especially when they themselves repeatedly cry out that any shameful act is judged worse if it is committed by a man in holy orders rather than some layperson? So let us finally give free rein to our desires,

igitur affectibus habenas, a quibus sacerdotes infrenes aguntur, truduntur, raptantur; illi nobis uiae duces traditi sunt, illos aequis passibus subsequamur. Si nobis imponunt, nostri miserebitur Christus, quod sumus ab his seducti, quibus nos uoluit ille parere parentumque loco reuereri, aut certe nostra in eis culpa cudetur."

Perperam ac impie cogitat, qui sic cogitat. Ceterum mirandum non est si profani blatiunt interdum crepantque blasphemias, quas ipsis sacerdotum uita moresque ministrant, ingerunt, obtrudunt. Nobiles ac magnates quid suis sceleribus obtexunt? Quomodo sua eleuant commissa nulliusque prope momenti ducunt? Superbia et cunctorum hominum per se despici- entia contemptusque grauat potissimum hos, solis sibi rentur / cuncta cre- asse Deum, fastidiunt mortales cunctos, uolunt ubique suspici flexisque genibus adorari. Quid tamen mirum? Vident idem cupere seniores, quibus prostrati commissa fatentur, sacrificulos, monachos, theologos, magistros. Reputant nimirum secum:

"Si canonicus et archidiaconus, qui cum Deo dicati, decimas frugum nobis extorquent, phaleratis mulis uehuntur, satellitio incedunt comitati, contemnunt uilem plebeculam, uiam non cedentes protrudunt et cum plerumque infimo sint loco nati nullaque doctrina praediti, sanctissimo- rum sacerdotum sibi uendicant honorem, triticum sacrum pluris uendunt, quam impii faeneratores, bonas collocant horas in defraudandis pauper- culis, laute scilicet ut ipsi uiuant et amplissimum haeredibus relinquant patrimonium…"

Nam execrandam quibusdam in rebus eorum superbiam quis audeat profanus imitari? Qui cum supellectilia, uasa instrumentaque omnia tem- plorum ex oblationibus et eleemosynis populi piis parata sint, suo / nescio quo iure sibi uendicant. Campanas habent selectas eximiae magnitudinis, quas mouere aut pulsare, ni cum est funerandus abbas, canonicus aut archidiaconus, religionem uolunt uideri. Certe senatusconsultum profe- runt ea de re siquando nobilis quispiam summoque loco natus effertur, ne frustra precibus sollicitentur ad soluendas uastissimas illas campanas, quasi sit eis persuasam, ualere solum eas ad expiandam simoniam quam

E 8v

F 1

the desires by which priests are driven unbridled — indeed, not driven but thrust forward, pushed at full gallop! They have been handed over to us as pathfinders; let us follow them and match their pace. If they deceive us, Christ will take pity on us, who have been seduced by them, whom he wanted us to obey and honor in the place of our parents, or certainly they will smart for any guilt we incur."

Anyone who thinks this way thinks wrongly and irreligiously, but of course it is not surprising if sometimes laymen talk foolishly and babble blasphemies that the lives and character of the priests serve up to them, heap up, and force upon them. What pretext do nobles and magnates offer for their crimes? How do they make light of their sins and consider them of almost no importance? The arrogance, the obvious contempt, and scorn E 8v   of all men for them weighs heavily on them especially. They think that / God created all things for them alone, they care nothing for any mortals, they wish to be looked up to everywhere and worshipped on bent knees. But why is this surprising? They see that the same thing is desired by the older men before whom they prostrate themselves and confess their sins: priests who say mass, monks, theologians, teachers. Doubtless they think to themselves:

"If a canon and an archdeacon, who certainly are dedicated to God, extort from us one tenth of our income, are carried along by caparisoned mules, walk accompanied by an entourage, despise the lowly poor and push them off the road without yielding, and though for the most part they were born in the lowest place, have received no education, yet claim for themselves the honors due to very holy priests, sell the holy wheat for more than the unscrupulous usurers charge, spend good hours cheating the little guy who has no money, and all so that, of course, they themselves may live elegantly and leave a huge legacy to their heirs...".

What layman would dare to imitate their execrable arrogance in some matters? When the furniture, utensils, and all the equipment of the churches have been purchased from the offerings and devout alms of the F 1   people, / I don't know with what right they can claim them as their own. They have some special bells that are of remarkable size, but they seem to have superstitious scruples about tolling or striking them, unless an abbot, a canon or an archdeacon is to be buried. In fact they produce a decree about this matter: If any nobleman born in the highest place is being buried, they must not in vain be entreated to loosen those immense bells. It is almost as though they were convinced that only these bells can expiate what they call simony and keeping a concubine, two of the

uocant et concubinatum, duo sacrificulis solemnissima uitia. Cruces etiam
serico uestiunt tumulandis sacerdotibus, ceteris ciuibus contemptim nudas
proferunt et ut existimant ipsi, inhonoras.

"Quinam igitur nos uiri profani, nobiles, regia stirpe prognati, qui
rex si iubeat aut hostis immineat, arma sunt induenda, expendendae
multae pecuniae, frequentissima alenda familia, cura praeterea filiorum et
uxoris habenda, prospiciendum ne filii natu minores, quos Hispaniae mos
in claris familiis reddit haereditatis propemodum expertes, egeant,
F 1v uidean/turque degeneres, quoquo modo nitemur, ut explendeat familia,
niteant equi, mulae coruscent, filii luxurient illustriumque puellarum fiant
proci, uxor monilibus et splendido famulitio diuitique mundo abundet?
Nobisne uitio uertetur aut summum ante iudicem crimini dabitur, sacrosanctos sacerdotes imitari studuisse, qui nobis in exemplum praepositi
sunt et tamquam scopus praefixi, in quem actiones nostras dirigamus?"
    Magistratibus equidem urbanis non deerit quod causent, quo sua flagi-
tia obuelent:

"Sacrosancti iudices leges ac iura peruertunt et in suum emolumentum callide nonnunquam interpretantur, lege sanciunt, ut quodlibet ministri sacrorum commissum pecunia expendatur, nulli pauperculo parcunt, quin si non multam annumeret, in uinculis pereat, nullum denique
uirtutis aut pietatis respectum habent, sed cupiditatibus obcaecati, ruunt
in omnium perniciem, quos nacti sunt semel intra nassam. Cur nobis,
F 2 quibus praeter manubias, uidelicet litigantium spolia, suppetit quo / uiua-
mus, nihil non condonabitur, si uictum nostris paremus et causas nonnunquam protrahamus, commissa quaeque pecunia redimamus? Quin
faciunt idem praesides ecclesiarum, quibus sacerdotia sunt pinguissima,
possuntque lautissime sine magistratu quidem uiuere? 'Praefectus urbis',
inquiunt minores praetores, 'qui nobilis ac ditissimus plerumque est, sit

most common vices of priests who say mass. They even dress crosses in silk when priests are to be buried, but when it comes to other townspeople's funerals, out of contempt they carry them bare at the head of the procession, a sign of dishonor, in their opinion.

The Laymen's Lament

"Who then are we laymen, nobles, sprung from royal lineage, who, if the king commands or the enemy becomes an immediate threat, must[46] arm ourselves, spend a great deal of money, and support a very large household, in addition to caring for our children and wife, seeing to it that our younger sons (whom our Spanish custom, in illustrious families, F 1v leaves virtually destitute of any inheritance) not be needy and / not seem degenerate? How, pray tell, will we strive to make our family stand out, the horses shine, the mules flash, our sons live in luxury and become suitors of honorable girls, and our wife enjoy abundant necklaces, elegant servants, and rich adornments? Will it be construed as a sin, or be denounced as crime before the highest judge, that we have striven to imitate the most holy priests, who have been held up to us as examples and set before us like a target toward which we should aim our own actions?"

Certainly city judges won't lack excuses with which they can hide their shameful deeds:

The City Magistrates' Lament

"The church judges pervert the law and people's rights, sometimes cunningly interpret them to their own advantage, and sanction by the law that a minister of the church must come up with cash for any crime whatsoever. They don't spare the most insignificant pauper; in fact if he doesn't pay in full the fine, they let him die in chains. Finally, they have no respect for virtue or piety, and blinded by their greed they rush to destroy everyone once they have found him in the trap. Why not then in our case, for whom the profits from booty, that is, the spoils of litigants, F 2 supply us enough / to live on, anything will be condoned if we are earning a living for our families, and sometimes drag out cases, allowing each and every sin to be paid for with cash? Why, the guardians of the churches do the same thing, and they have very fat benefices, so that they could certainly live splendidly without a judgeship. The lesser shepherds say that the *corregidor* of the city, who is usually a nobleman and very wealthy, should be uncorrupted and a man of great integrity. But for us

---

[46] The grammar is marked here by an apparent anacoluthon; *qui* "who" is used in the nominative where a dative seems needed for the upcoming gerundive construction.

integerrimus ac incorruptus; nobis iureperitis, quos scholae tot annos exercuerunt et paternis paene bonis omnino nudauerunt, sit satis, bone Deus! nos eos praestare, quos censores morum ac uitae sacerdotes probent: probabunt certe necessario, ne sua uideantur opera damnare, qui nunquam ita commissa grauia puniunt, ut penitus sublata uelint, sed ut perpetua maneant, uelut in explebilium cupiditatum alimentum.'"

Iam promiscua populi turba, omne genus opifices, tabernarii, quicunque denique uiuunt in diem aut manuariis opellis aluntur, a uulgo clericorum F 2v et monachorum audaciam sumunt ad perpetranda quaeque flagi/tia. Quod genus est fraudis aut periurii faenorisque, quod inter sacerdotes peculiariter non obuersetur? Locant redditus decimarum adeo seuere propeque dixerim inhumane, nummis aureis illicientes licitatores ac redemptores, ut, ni faenori dent ipsi locatum, reddere non modo creditum non possint, sed et solum non uertere, si uel dimidium persoluant, ad inopiam redacti. Qui centum aureis decimas redemit unius uici, pertinentes ad episcopum uel collegium canonicorum, quae minus quinquaginta ualebant, nonne triticum mutuare cogitur ad menses aliquot ea lege, ut duplicatum pretium accipiat, cum sit ei certius nihil, si pecunias ad diem praestitutam non adnumerauerit, quam fano sacrisque disturbandum et in uincula eundem coniiciendum spoliandumque bonis? Sunt tunc inter canonicos unus interdum aut alter theologus aut iurisperitus, qui probant turpes has licitationes lucroque applaudunt. Si episcopis cura quidem esset ouium, prohiberent F 3   uel inter clericos impia saltem lucra, persua/derentque magistratibus etiam profanis, ut idem conarentur inter laicos. Ita tollerentur e ciuitate Christiana imposturae nec uitia uenirent tantum in praecipitium, pauperes non tractarentur inhumane, quibus nimirum subtrahitur faenerationibus eiusmodi uictus, cum licet annus abundet, modii tritici quattuor nequeant emi

— we who are experts in the law, whom the schools trained for so many years and stripped of almost all our parents' property — let it be enough, good God! for us to be better than the kind of people whom the priests approve as censors of life and character. They will approve them out of necessity, lest they seem to condemn their own works, since they never punish serious sins in such a way that they want them entirely to disappear, but rather so that they will remain forever as a fuel to satisfy their greed."

Exploitation of the Poor

Already the common crowd of the people, workmen of every sort, shopkeepers, or in short, anyone who lives for the day, or those who feed themselves with small manual jobs, acquire boldness from the common F 2v sort of priests and monks, and commit all sorts of shameful / acts. What kind of fraud or perjury or usury exists which is not especially prevalent among priests? They loan out the return on the tithes so severely, and I would almost say inhumanely, enticing bidders and tax farmers with gold coins, that unless they themselves lend it out at interest, they are not only unable to pay back the loan but are even forced to move to another country if they pay only half, being reduced to poverty. Whoever buys the tithes of a single village for a hundred gold coins, tithes that belong to the bishop or the college of canons, when they were worth less than fifty, is he not driven to lend the wheat for some months under an agreement that he will get twice the price? After all, nothing is more certain for him than that if he does not pay back the money on the stipulated day, he will be cast out from his altar and sacraments and finally thrown into chains and stripped of his goods. There are in the meantime one or two theologians or legal experts among the canons who approve of this shameful taking of bids, and applaud the profit. If the bishops' concern were for the sheep, they would prohibit, surely among F 3 the clergy, immoral profiteering, at least, / and they would persuade the judges even in the secular courts to attempt the same thing among laymen. In this way deception would be removed from a Christian city, vices would not come to such a dizzying height,[47] the poor would not be treated inhumanely. From these, of course, their living is taken away by such usury, for even if the year yields abundantly, four measures of wheat

---

[47] See Juvenal *Sat.* 1.149: *omne in praecipiti vitium stetit,* "all uice has reached a dizzing height."

toto pauperculi patrimonio. Cuius esse causam quis manifesto non uidet, quod redemptores, ut fugiant famem et laqueum, uilius uendere non possunt, quam emerunt et faeneratores (quorum heu quis numeret turbam?) claudunt ad mensem Maium horrea, pluuiarum, tempestiuique cuiuspiam nubili, aut opportunae serenitatis acerrimi hostes. Et si respondet annus contra sua uota, negant uenditionem, pauperculis mutuant stipulatione non quidem [*Z reads* equidem] aequa, nimirum ut post aestatem cum faenore reddant. Pudet eiusmodi me referre, quae si nobis inter ethnicos fuisset aliquando fieri significatum, exhorrescere deberemus. Verum cum F 3v adeo solemne sit regionibus nostris, ferant tuae/ patienter aures relatum, quod uel dum sit plurimorum quidem arrigit, nedum non offendit. Omnes aberrant oues, et quae maxime uideri uolunt officiosae, multo magis interdum aberrant, imposturis plena sunt omnia, messes alienae depascuntur, non est qui prohibeat. Conniuent pastores ad damna uicinorum, sinunt undecumque oues pinguescere, quo largius lana, fetu, caseoque prosint, uolunt eas haurire succum quibuslibet ex herbis etiam religiose uetitis, ut habeant ipsi quod exprimant. Multi sunt pastores, mercenarii quam plurimi; pascunt utrique non equidem oues, sed suos affectus, uota, studia, cupiditates, trahunt oues et retrahunt, ducunt atque reducunt, earum ut ex pinguedine pinguescant uel potius turgeant ipsi. De mercenariis minus mirandum, quorum in id modo plerique locant suas operas, ut sibi prosint, non ouibus, quas quidem non secus amant quam piscator flumina, quae iam cupit exhausta, quo facilior sit et uberior captura, iam F 4 exundantia et turbulenta, si piscandi commoditas id / exposcat.

Pascua scribit Plinius sola diu Romanis uectigalia fuisse; nunc uero unde non uectigal exigitur? Nam ut missas faciamus principum profano-

cannot be purchased with the entire patrimony of a poor man. Who does-n't see clearly whose responsibility this is, that the tax farmers, to avoid hunger and hanging, are not able to sell cheaper than they buy? The usurers (alas, who could count how big the crowd of them is?) close the granaries up until the month of May, and are bitter enemies of rains, any stormy cloud, or timely fair weather. And if the year answers in a way contrary to their wishes, they refuse to sell, and instead loan to the poor with a condition which is certainly not fair, namely, that they pay it back with interest after the summer. I feel ashamed to recount events of a kind which, if it had been indicated to us that they happened occasionally among pagans, we should find horrifying. But, when it is so common in

F 3v our regions, would your ears bear patiently an account / that, even while it happens makes many perk up and take notice, so far is it from failing to offend them. All the sheep are wandering, and those who want to seem the most dutiful are in fact wandering the most in the meantime. They are all full of deceit; the grain belonging to others gets eaten, and there is no one who forbids it. The shepherds wink at the losses of their neighbors and everywhere they let the sheep grow fat that they may profit more bountifully in wool, offspring, and cheese. They want them to suck the juice from all sorts of plants, even those religiously forbidden, so they themselves may have something to squeeze out. There are many shep-herds and a very great number of mercenary shepherds, and in both cat-egories they pasture not, indeed, the sheep, but their own passions, wishes, pursuits, and desires, taking them, like sheep, first here and then there, leading them places and then back, so that from the fatness of these they themselves may grow fat, or rather bloated. This is less to be won-dered at in the hired hands, many of whom now contract out their work for this purpose, that it may be useful not to the sheep but to themselves. Indeed they love the sheep no differently than a fisherman loves the rivers, which sometimes he wants nearly dried up, so that the catch will be easier to take and more abundant, and sometimes he wants them over-

F 4 flowing and turbulent, if that is what the best fishing / demands.

Pliny writes that among the Romans for a long time only the pastures were taxed, but now, what is not taxed? Now, not to mention the immod-erate taxes of secular princes, which a burning desire for making never-end-ing wars creates and compels[48] as though the taxes were necessary, where

---

[48] So M; Z adds, "and commands." Pliny the Elder writes in *Natural History* 18.3.3 that pastures were once the only source of tax revenue for the Romans.

rum exactiones immodicas, quas bellorum numquam finiendorum ardor
ac incendium suscitat et uelut necessarias cogit [*Z adds* ac imperat], quo
non protrusit praesules ecclesiarum uaesana dominandi cupido, diuitiarum
sitis inexplebilis? Clericos putabis solos habere uectigales: habent hos
quidem episcopi magis peculiares, ceterum multis etiam praetextibus arro-
dunt et laicos. Omnia nimirum crimina atque flagitia, quae uiri profani
perpetrant in ecclesiae sacramenta, placita atque decreta, punit et damnat
episcopus non capite aut scapulis, ut solent Caesaris magistratus, sed
pecuniis ac fundis. Porro crimina sceleraque sacerdotum et omnium clericorum, nonnullaque laicorum uectigalia sunt pinguissima praelatorum.
Hoc est certum peculium certaque seges nunquam non cum faenore repul-
F 4v lulans. Crimina si tollas malaque cuncta reseces e populo Christiano, /
multum aeris decedet episcoporum aerario, cessabunt non parum multi
magistratus et praefecturae proxime repertae, quae malis aluntur alienis,
quae sanguine pascuntur humano. Familia quidem episcoporum nihil
cupit minus, quam ut occasiones praecidantur peccandi, mores emenden-
tur, profectus fiat ad meliora. Quamobrem summopere curant, ut ita puni-
antur flagitiosi, ita coarguantur indocti clerici, sic blande multis paula-
timque assuescant, ut non tam detestentur uitia, quam inuigilent quo pacto
pecuniis subinde redimant, munera mittant, sintque parati, cum dies
iterum dicatur, secum efferre quod diluit crimina quaeque, quod nobilem
aequat plebeio, quod flagitiosum ac impium reddit persaepe innocentis-
simum.

Bonus episcopus, bonus pastor, incidet omnium malorum occasiones,
non deglubet pecus, sed frugalissime tondet. Sunt bonis episcopis ho-
nestissima uectigalia et amplissima ex decimis, et ex propriis fundis, etiam
F 5 si cessent delatores, sigilli quaestores, notarii, uiatores, et qui prae/terea
uiuunt ex molestis exactionibus. Te quidem adhuc nulla fama praestrinxit
nec (certo scimus) perstringet: retines perpetuoque retinebis candorem

has the insane desire for domination, the unquenchable thirst for riches, not thrust the leaders of the church? You would think that only the clergy have people paying taxes to them, but bishops certainly have those that are more peculiar to them. What's more, with many additional pretexts they gnaw also at the laity: in particular, the bishop punishes and condemns all crimes and shameful acts that laymen perpetrate against the sacraments, teachings and decrees of the church — not with capital punishment or flogging, as the emperor's judges usually do, but by requiring payments of money and land. Moreover, the crimes and shameful acts of the priests and all the clergy, and of a number of the laity, are very fat sources of income for prelates. This is their certain property and their certain crop, which never stops sprouting and adding interest. If you should take away the crimes and cut out the whole set of evils from the Christian people, /that would withdraw much money from the bishop's treasury. Many judges, and offices of *corregidores* which are found close to them, would be greatly cut back, since they are nourished by others' troubles and feed on human blood. The bishop's household certainly wants nothing less than it wants opportunities for sinning be cut short, character be corrected, or there be progress toward something better. Wherefore they take great care that those who act shamefully are so punished, that ignorant clergy are so reprimanded, and that they become accustomed to fines so mildly and gradually, that they do not so much hate crimes as they are on the watch for how they can redeem them repeatedly with cash or send gifts, and how to be prepared, when they are again given a court date, to take with them something which washes away any sort of crimes, which makes the nobleman equal to the commoner, and that very frequently turns someone shameful and irreligious into a perfectly innocent man.

F 4v

 A good bishop, that is a good shepherd, will attack the opportunities for all evils. He doesn't flay the herd, but with great restraint shears it. For good bishops there are very honest and ample sources of income in tithes and their own lands, even if an end were put to informers, signet rings, treasurers, notaries, summoners, and / all the others who live from troublesome exactions. Thus far no rumor has compromised you, and we know it never will. You have kept and will perpetually keep that native openness of yours, from your first days in the cradle up until this very day conducting yourself with great innocence. Your way of life, your progress and your habits have all been praised. You have always been considered and proclaimed a good man. Although the splendor of your ancestors makes you illustrious, more of glory and renown are won for you by your exceptional virtues and Christian character than the pedigree of your parents or a long

F 5

illum natiuum, primis ab incunabulis ad hanc diem innocentissime duc-
tum. Laudatae sunt omnes tuae uitae rationes, progressus ac instituta.
Vir bonus es semper habitus et praedicatus, cumque maiorum tuorum
splendor te reddat illustrem, plus nominis tunc et gloriae tibi conciliant
uirtutes eximiae Christianique mores, quam parentum stemmata longaque
series imaginum ac triumphorum. Non te rapiant igitur mores corrupti,
decedat aliquid domestico sumptui, ualeat cura posteritatis, plus est anima,
quam quidquid est usquam mundanae gloriae, quam fastus aulici super-
baque supellex. Occlude malis consultoribus aures, non audias quos es
muneribus praefecturus aut iam praefeceris. Lucrum amant atque magnam
se putabunt a te gratiam inituros, si censum ad augendum te protrudant.
Nec attendas, obsecro, quod episcopi priores egerunt, sed agere quod
F 5v   de/buerunt, nec quot equites alebant, sed quot uiduas, quot inopes
uirgines ab iniuria famis et famae uindicabant, quot pauperes alebant,
quot egentibus opitulabantur. Haec est uera materia nominis, sed animae
potius illustrandae bono pastori; hac uia proceres iere Christiani.

Ioannes Fonseca, quem optime tu quidem nosti, Burgensem episcopatum iniit, annum agens uitae plus minus quinquagesimum quintum,
prouectus aetate sane, sed adeo nimio Ferdinandi regis fauore propemodum occaecatus, ut primis nimirum annis dynastam magis egerit quam
episcopum. Totus erat intentus ampliandae rei familiari, construendis
superbissimis aedibus, constipandae pecuniae; fastus non modo deponere
non cogitabat aulicos, sed solus ipse curabat constituere aulam. Quare
exactiones nunnullas excogitauit, omnium tandem inuidiam ordinum sibi
conflauit. In haec detrudebant eum ingentes familiarium cupiditates et
auaritia, quorum ille plerosque solo extulerat et cupere magna docuerat.

series of statues and triumphs. Therefore a corrupt character could not carry you away; let there be some reduction in household expenses, and good-bye to worry about posterity. The soul is worth more than any worldly glory anywhere, more than the pride of court, more than the arrogance of ornamentation! Close your ears to bad counselors. You should not listen to those whom you are about to appoint to office, or have already appointed. They love gain, and they will think that they will enter into your great favor if they can thrust you into increasing your wealth. And I beg of you, pay

F 5v no heed to what prior bishops did, but do what / they should have done. Pay heed not to how many knights they fed, but how many widows, how many destitute maidens they saved from the injury of famine and ill-fame. Notice how many poor they fed, and to how many of the needy did they bring relief. This is the real opportunity for reknown; rather, this is what gives glory to the soul of a good shepherd. This is the path which Christian leaders have trod.

The Example of Juan Fonseca

Juan Fonseca,[49] whom you certainly knew very well, became bishop of Burgos when he was more or less fifty-five years old — advanced in age, certainly, but also pretty much blinded by the excessive favor of King Fernando,[50] so that actually in his first years he acted more like a prince than a bishop. He concentrated totally on enlarging the household budget, on constructing a very proud dwelling, seeking to pack in money. Not only did he give no thought to laying aside his courtly arrogance, but he alone supervised the establishment of a court. Therefore he thought up some new exactions, and finally stirred up great resentment of every rank against himself. But he was forced into these taxes by the huge greed and avarice of his household, many of whom he had lifted out of the gutter and had taught to have large desires.

---

[49] Juan Rodríguez de Fonseca (1451-1524), was one of Maldonado's patrons, who appointed him examiner of candidates for the priesthood in the diocese of Burgos. Fonseca had an illustrious public career. As chaplain to Queen Isabella and counsellor to Ferdinand and Isabel, he governed the *consejo de Indias* which controlled all contact with Spanish dominions overseas. He was Bishop in turn of Badajoz, Córdoba, Palencia, Burgos, and finally Archbishop of Rossano in Italy. He was also a well-known patron of the arts and commissioned Juan de Flandes to decorate the Cathedral of Palencia (on this see Brown 1998, pp. 19-20.) The *Diccionario de historia eclesiástica de España* says of him: "El arte del Renacimiento debe a este gran mecenas y a la familia Fonseca obras de la mejor calidad: Palencia, Burgos, y Salamanca son sus principales centros" (vol 2, p. 952).

[50] Fernando of Aragon (1452-1516) was at first the royal consort of Isabel of Castille (1451-1504), and after her death the sole regent. A genius at strong and effective government, he was much admired by the Italian theorist Niccolo Machiavelli.

F 6   / Annis tamen uitae supremis, cum se tandem agnouit episcopum, cum quid oneris sustineret pensiculatius animaduertit, pertaesus exactiones indebitas, cum denuntiasset publice repensurum quod perperam et non more maiorum fuisset extortum, comperit ingentes a suis per occasionem corrosas pecunias, quarum decima uix pars peruenisset ad fiscum. Coepit ex eo suam detestari socordiam omnemque uitae rationem, quod mortis oblitus et quam exacte ratio subducenda gestorum omnium esset ante tribunal Christi, animam suam famulis auarissimis permisisset et affectibus plus aequo tribuisset.

Omnium denique pauperum, uiduarum ac indotatarum uirginum censum facit, omnibus ex aequo congestum quod erat auri, distribuit, ac diffundit, horrea tota pandit. Distulerat ille quidem munificentiam in egenos episcopo dignam, aulicis occupatus negotiis, uel potius, quod degentibus in aula plerisque uenit usu, extra se positus; ceterum tarditatem benefa-

F 6v ciendi multiiuga quidem et opportuna largi/tate compensauit. Plus enim distribuit opum anno uitae postremo, ut proximos duos sileam, plures pauperes satiauit, uiduas expleuit, uirgines collocauit, quam toto praesulatu frugi quiuis alius ex prioribus.

Pauperum parens morti proximus atque post funera compellatus est, quod uitae prioris homines obliti, ex gestis unius anni, qui fuit ultimus uitae, clarissimis illis quidem, illum expendebant. Sed cur non? Toto illo anno sic sua deplanxit commissa, sic suam infelicitatem, quod non prius resipuisset, quod se Christianum et antistitem haud prius agnouisset, detestabatur ac deplorabat, riuulis lacrimarum sese frequenter umectans, ut si praeteritorum fuisset prorsus obliuio, referendum inter caelites nullus non censeret; et nihilominus sani cerebri quidam sane censebant. Gratias agebat Deo postremo illo anno, quod mentem dedisset ac tempus, antequam mors occuparet, ad resarcienda incommoda uitae, ad dispar-

F 7   tiendas opes male congestas, ad reddendum depositum, quod pau/peres si

F 6   / However, in the final years of his life, when he finally came to realize that he was a bishop, when, after more careful deliberation, he became
aware of what a burden a bishop bears, he came to despise the improper
taxes, and when he had announced publicly that he was going to repay
what had been extorted wrongly and not according to the custom of his
ancestors, he discovered that his people had taken the opportunity to gnaw
away huge amounts of money, money of which scarcely a tenth had
reached the exchequer. From that time he began to hate his own
sluggishness and his whole way of life, because forgetful of death and of
what an accurate account would have to be rendered before the judgment
seat of Christ of all his actions, he had entrusted his own soul to the most
greedy of servants, and had given more credit to his passions than was
proper.

Finally he made a census of all the poor, widows and virgins lacking
a dowry, and distributed to all of them equally what had been accumulated in gold, and opened up his entire granaries. He had certainly
diverted, to the disadvantage of the needy, a bounty worthy of a bishop
when occupied in court business (or rather, as tends to happen to most
men involved in court, he was not situated in harmony with his real self),
but he made up for his tardiness in doing good by a very manifold and
F 6v well-timed generosity. / For he distributed more wealth in the last year of
his life (not to mention the previous two years), he met the needs of more
of the poor, he filled the needs of more widows, he placed more virgins in
marriages, than any one of his honest predecessors in the whole bishopric.

When he was close to death, and after death, he was addressed as father
of the poor, for people forgot his prior life and judged him on those very
glorious actions of just one year, which was the last of his life. And why
not? That whole year he much lamented his sins and his unhappiness
because he had not come to his senses sooner. He hated and deplored the
fact that he had not sooner recognized what it was to be a Christian and
a bishop, frequently drenching himself with streams of tears, so that if
there had been a complete loss of memory of the past, everyone thought
that he should be counted as an angel, yet they also did not doubt that he
was of sound mind. He gave thanks to God for that last year of his life,
because he had given him the sense and the time before death seized him
to patch up what was wrong in his life, to share his ill-accumulated
wealth, and to hand over the deposit that the poor, although they had not
F 7   demanded it, / could have rightly demanded. The fortunate bishop kept
thinking about his lavish court expenditures and arrogance. He silently

non reposcebant, potuissent merito reposcere. Recolebat secum felix antistes aulicos sumptus et fastus, mente uersabat tacita tot annos sine cura
gregis peractos, quam fuisset ab episcopi munere semper alienus, quam
sui penitus oblitus gloriae mundanae seruierit. Saepissime sum hominem
contemplatus annis illis duobus qui fuerunt uitae supremi (nihil equidem
[*M reads* quidem] me [*M deletes* me] celabat piorum affectuum), cum fortuna et genio suo expostulantem.

   "Me miserum" aiebat, "ubi mea mens erat? Ubi iudicium? Ubi ratio?
Cum Ferdinando regi paene solus, certe primus eram a consiliis, qui de
rebus magnis consultus, de commodis reipublicae rogatus, maius prope
semper studium habui regis placitis et affectibus blandiendi, quam reipublicae commoditatibus obsequendi, magis eram attentus, quo pacto rex
meis captus officiis, seruiendique nimis anxia uoluntate pinguiori me
aliquo praesulatu clariorique donaret, quam ut rebus publicis esset bene.

F 7v Qua tandem insolentia, quo fastu, quo / mortalium omnium prae me con-
temptu adeuntibus ex negotiis respondebam? Quo supercilio salutantes
uix nutu resalutabam? Iam episcopatus mei quam nullus respectus, nulla
cura, nulla plane memoria, nisi quod me cura non leuis interdum
angebat, ne quid census ac redituum meo fisco decederet, immo ut uiae
reperirentur ad imperandas praetextu quocunque clericis pecunias, ad
conduplicanda uectigalia. Poenis, quae legibus sunt criminibus decretae,
semper addebam aliquid, seueritatem iurisque rigorem simulans, cum uere
magis me moueret studium locupletandi meum aerarium, quam ut poe-
narum metu deterrerentur a flagitiis curiones aut sacrificuli. Quo (bone
Deus!) demigrasset animula mea, si mors mihi tum contigisset? Hem,
quibus periculis ereptus sum, quae uincula rupi! Utinam tamdiu mihi uita
supersit meque a morte uindicet Christus, quamdiu sit satis ad deflenda
commissa, ad diluenda flagitia, ad tantundem bonorum operum repen-
dendum, quantum improbitatis admisi!"

went over in his mind all the years spent with no concern for the flock, how far he had always been a stranger to the duties of a bishop, how far he had entirely forgotten himself and served worldly glory instead. I very frequently watched the man in those two years which were the greatest of his life (and he hid nothing[51] of his pious emotions) expostulating with his fortune and his own inner self:

The Lament of Bishop Fonseca

"Wretched me!", he used to say. "Where was my mind? Where my good judgment? Where was my reason? When I was almost the only counselor to King Fernando, or at least the foremost of them to be consulted about important matters, when asked about what was most useful for the republic, I nearly always was more eager to flatter the king's pleasures and passions than to submit to the advantages of the republic. Was I more focused on how the king, won over by my services and by my too-eager desire to serve him, might give me some fatter and more prominent bishopric, instead of what would be good for the republic? And finally F 7v with what insolence, / with what arrogance, and with what contempt for all mortals did I answer those who came before me on business? With what a frown did I grudgingly nod to return the greeting of those who greeted me? I had no respect for my own bishopric, no concern for it, in fact no memory of it, except sometimes when worry was making me anxious that there might be a loss from the tax rolls and the income to my exchequer, or rather, when I sought to find some ways to requisition monies, with some pretext or other, from the clergy, in order to double the revenues. To the punishments decreed by the law for crimes I always added something, using as a pretext the severity and rigor of the law, when in fact I was more moved by my eagerness to fill up my treasury than, by fear of punishments, to deter from shameful acts parish priests and those who say mass. Good God! To where would my poor little soul have departed[52] if death had stolen upon me at that time? Oh! From what dangers was I rescued, what chains did I break free of! I hope that a long enough life is left to me, and Christ preserves me from death, that there may be enough time to wail over my offenses, to erase my shameful acts, to compensate with just as many good deeds all the wickedness that I permitted myself."

---

[51] Z adds "from me;" M omits.

[52] Reading *demigrasset*. The phrase used by Fonseca a few lines above, *cura non leuis*, which we translate "worry was making me anxious," seems borrowed from Horace's "Ship of State" poem, *Carm.* 1.14.18.

F 8   /Haud equidem dici potest aut credi, quam felicem exitum fuerit Deus optimus maximus Fonsecae, perpenso uitae prioris fastu feruentique congerendarum pecuniarum studio, largitus. Non enim solum eleemosynarum uix credendarum fuit postremo studiosissimus, librum etiam condidit uitae uere Christianae praeclarissimum quidem, quamuis lingua uernacula. Quem qui legerit, non utique ibit infitias me uera locutum. Asseruatur in eius scriniis, quoniam eum non absoluit nec memoriam eius moriens fecit; mihi certe curam delegauerat, ut cum ultima fuisset ei manus imposita, typographis traderem. Ceterum cum iam festinaret ad calcem eius libri bonus antistes, febre, quae illum confecit, correptus, omnium est rerum oblitus, praeterquam animae. Liber itaque, ut erat solutus, ab haeredibus est arculis cum aliis inditus; qui eius inuestigandi curam adhibuerit, me non quidem fuisse mentitum comperiet. At uero fiduciam non addat exitus Fonsecae cuicumque bene moriendi. Rari sunt eiusmodi successus.

F 8v   In primor/diis nascentis ecclesiae mutatus est repente latro, suffixus in crucem, mutatus est et Paulus, cum maxime hostis esset ecclesiae, mutata est Magdalena mediis in mundi deliciis ac oblectamentis. Sed hos transformabat ipse, qui condiderat altissimo quodam consilio, uolens ab his prodigiis stupendisque miraculis nouam persuasionem auspicari. Iam dudum desiuimus tale quicquam uidere: ad extremam auarus senectam mordicus tenet congestas utcunque diuitias. Simoniacus (ut uerbis loquar praesentibus) animam agens legat filio sacerdotium, impia forte cautione partum in adolescentia. Libidinosus foedisque amoribus deditus, quamuis

F 8   / In no way can it even be expressed or believed what a fortunate death God, in his supreme goodness and power, granted to Fonseca, who had paid for the arrogance of his past life and burning eagerness for heaping up money. At the end he was not only most eager to give alms that could hardly be believed, but he even wrote a book about the truly Christian life— a very outstanding book, albeit in the vernacular. Whoever reads it, in any case, will not deny that I have told the truth. It is preserved in his book-boxes, since he did not publish it. He made no mention of it on his deathbed, but he had actually already put me in charge of handing it over to the printers upon receiving the final touches. However, when the good bishop was already hurrying to the conclusion of his book, he was snatched away by a fever that did him in, and he forgot everything except his soul. Then the book, as it was unbound, was placed by his heirs in boxes along with other [papers]. Anyone who will take the trouble to investigate the matter will discover that I haven't lied about it. And yet, let Fonseca's death not give confidence to anyone of dying well, as such successful outcomes are rare.

F 8v   / In the first beginnings of the birth of the church the thief suddenly changed while nailed to the cross.[53] Paul also changed, while formerly the church's worst enemy.[54] Mary Magdalene changed in the midst of worldly pleasures and delights.[55] But these were transformed by the very one who had built with a kind of master plan, wishing from these prodigies and stupendous miracles to inaugurate a new way of believing. But now long ago we stopped seeing anything like that: to the very end of his old age, a miser holds on doggedly to wealth which he has heaped up on all sides. A simoniac (to use current words) when breathing his last, may leave a benefice to his son, perhaps one which he obtained by an unholy obligation in his youth. A lecher, and addicted to filthy love affairs, even though every year at the parish priest's he may call curses down on vices, he doesn't fail every so often to return to his natural character and his habits, so that when his strength is weakened by pleasures,

---

[53] The repentant thief on the cross comes from Matth. 23. 39-43.

[54] Paul's early persecution of the church is described in Acts 8.3; Gal. 1.13.

[55] Mary Magdelene, frequently confused with the repentant sinner of Luke 7.36-50, is thus described in the 13th century *Golden Legend*: "Magdelene, then, was very rich, and sensuous pleasure keeps company with great wealth. Renowned as she was for her beauty and her riches, she was no less known for the way that she gave her body to pleasure — so much so that her proper name was forgotten and she was commonly called 'the sinner.'" (Ryan 1993, vol. 1, pp. 375-376).

apud curionem parochum quotannis uitia detestetur, non cessat per interualla ad ingenium atque ad assueta recurrere et uiribus effetis cum oblec-
tamento quae olim admisit tacita secum mente uersare. Nullum denique
uitium momento insperatoque relinquitur, ni paulatim turpitudinem quis

G 1 agnoscens, aut a uiro pio sapienter admonitus, / pedem ipse referat, uel
ictus (quod aiunt) cum piscatore sapiat. A pubertate impietas est omnis
dediscenda, boni mores imbuendi, Christianus candor imbibendus, caritas in genus omne mortalium exprimenda, tum annis accedentibus
solidanda. Cum uero functio aliqua siue sacra siue profana obuenerit,
conandum pectore toto, ut ex Christi dogmate geratur, administretur,
obeatur. Nec existimandum Christiano quidem est, demandatum fuisse
honorem, magistratum aut episcopatum, quo lautius uiuat, sumptuosius et
apparatius cenet, mollius cubet, splendidius ac magnificentius uenetur,
equitet, conuiuia paret, sed quo uigilantius ardentiusque laboret, bona,
quae sunt pauperum, dispenset, lites dirimat, male ac iniuste patientibus
opituletur. Denique uitam suam ita temperet, ut exemplar esse norit ac
specimen reliquis propositum mortalibus recte beateque uiuendi.

Sed de pascendis ouibus commonefecimus hactenus praestantiam ac
G 1v celsitudinem tuam; nunc tandem quid po/tissimum constituat bonum pastorem, immo quae sit origo uera uel potius fons unicus, ex quo uirtutes
manent et affectus, soli qui constituunt bonum pastorem, ex Christi uerbis eisdem, quibus cetera confirmauimus, paucis delibemus. Traditurus
Christus Iesus summum apostolatum Petro, sic inquit: "Diligis me plus
his, Simon?" Cumque respondisset Petrus, "Etiam, Domine, tu scis quod
amo te", Christus intulit "Pasce oues meas." Et hoc quo magis fixum

he turns over in his mind in silence the sins he once committed. What's more, no vice is given up in a sudden moment unless someone, gradually recognizing his moral degradation or, wisely admonished by a religious

G1 man, / himself takes a step back, as though, like a fisherman, he feels the strike [coming], as the saying goes.[56] From childhood on all immorality must be unlearned, good character must be impressed on him, Christian purity must be absorbed, brotherly love expressed toward every sort of mortal and, as one is getting older, strengthened. And when some position, whether sacred or profane, falls to his lot, he must try with his whole heart to see to it that it will be managed, administered and performed in accordance with the teaching of Christ. Nor should a Christian think that a public honor — a judgeship or bishopric — has been entrusted to him so that he may live more elegantly, dine more sumptuously and elaborately, go to bed in greater softness, more splendidly and magnificently hunt, ride, and give parties. Rather, it is so that he may work harder and more vigilantly, dispense to the poor what is theirs, break up lawsuits, be of benefit to those who suffer wrongly and unjustly. And finally he should so temper his life that he learn how to be an exemplar and model on display to the rest of mortals, a model of just and happy living.

Final Reminder: What is a Good Shepherd?

We have reminded you up to now of your outstanding excellence in

G 1v pasturing the sheep. Now finally to know what / constitutes a good shepherd, indeed what its true origin is, or rather its unique source, from which the virtues and affections flow that alone make up a good shepherd, let us pick a few of those very words of Christ with which we have supported everything else. When Jesus Christ was about to hand over to Peter the highest apostolate, he said this: "Do you love me more than them, Simon?" And then when Peter had responded, "Yes, Lord, you know that I love you," Christ replied, "Pasture my sheep." And to make this remain fixed forever in the minds of those whom he was preparing for

---

[56] The reference to "wealth heaped on all sides" alludes to Horace, *Serm.* 1.1.70. The allusion to the fisherman makes a play on the word *ictus*, which means both a 'bite' and a 'blow.' Just as a fisherman may feel (*sapio*) an impending strike on the bait by a fish, so a hardened sinner, feeling that God is about to strike him down, may repent before his death. Similarly, at the conclusion of the first chapter of the *Lazarillo*, the protagonist mocks his blind master for having smelled (*saber*) the filched sausage in the boy's stomach but not sensed the coming blow against a stone post later inflicted on him as revenge for harsh punishments. In a larger sense, Lazarillo, unlike Fonseca here, is an unrepentant sinner who, ironically, shows no sign of realizing that God will eventually strike him down.

illis, quos ad tantam legationem praeparabat, perpetuo maneret, iterum ac tertio repetiuit. Quid, obsecro, dici potuit apertius? Quid euidentius? Num satis non explicuit, fundamentum boni uerique pastoris in amore Dei oportere primum esse fixum atque locatum, qui si uere teneatur, ne- cessario caritas in omnes consequitur? Ait enim, "Amas me?" cumque Petrus annuisset, subiunxit "Pasce agnos meos," manifesto quidem innu- ens, "si me uere diligis, quod trina responsio satis indicat, diliges oues meas et ex animo pasces."

G 2   Quam / uero Dei nunc amor rebus sit omnibus posthabitus cum apud omnes magnates, tum apud ipsos nimirum episcopos, ex ipsorum operibus manifesto dignoscitur. Surgunt multa die lecto, statim accedunt confa- bulatores, adulatores, scurrae, tum oeconomi, scribae, delatores, garriunt ac insusurrant, iam de producendis poenis commissorum, iam de locan- dis multo carius eius anni prouentibus et decimis, de caritate annonae, de pluris addicendis uectigalibus, qua ratione possint augeri. Cum horum est satietas, uel potius cum cogit instans meridies, sacrum peragitur raptim et cum instare dicatur meridies, horis interdictis plerumque sacrificatur. Post haec prandium apponitur lautissimum, in quo si quid forte non- numquam desideratur, structor, oeconomus ac dispensator traducuntur, male quidem audiunt et, ne talia rursus designent, domini colloquio dies aliquot arcentur. A prandio lusus et facetiae morionum ineptorumque pa- G 2v rasitorum, quod genus /hominum in aulis episcoporum saginari, satis arguit numinis amor quam sit in postremis, quam ouium cura posthabita.

such a great mission, he said it again and a third time.[57] What, I ask you, could be spoken more directly? What more obvious? Is it possible that he did not sufficiently explain that the foundation of a good and true shepherd ought to be first placed and fixed in the love of God, that if someone truly possesses it, then brotherly love for everyone necessarily comes with it? For he said, "Do you love me?" When Peter assented, he added, "Pasture my sheep," thereby clearly declaring, "If you truly love me, as your answering three times shows clearly enough, then you will love my sheep, and will pasture them from the bottom of your heart."

Satirical Account of a Bishop's Typical Day

G 2 But / how the love of God is now put second to all things, not only among all the magnates but actually among the bishops themselves, can be clearly perceived from their own actions. They get out of bed far into the day. Immediately they are approached by gossipers, flatterers, and parasites. Then financial managers, scribes, and informers babble on, whispering now about drawing out the penalties for offenses, now about renting out at a much higher rate the crops and tithes produced that year, about the high price of wheat, and about adding more taxes and how they might be increased. When they have had enough of this, or rather when midday is fast approaching, mass is said hurriedly, and when it is observed that midday is already at hand, then mass is usually said during forbidden hours.[58] Afterwards a very splendid meal is set before them, in which if something, perhaps, is occasionally lacking, the one who spreads the table and carves, the financial manager, and the steward are disgraced, receive all the blame, and, to keep them from serving such a dinner again, are shut out from the master's conversation for a few days. After the meal follow the games and humorous remarks of fools and silly parasites. That

G 2v such a kind / of men are fattened up in bishops' courts is sufficient proof that the love of God is in last place and what a low priority is given to the care of the sheep. Repeated yawns finally turn away this vile mob. Then after sleeping he rides, strolls, and goes to visit celebrated ladies, where in an eagerness for telling stories everyone's character and way of life are torn apart[59] and immodest remarks sometimes thrown in. Night finally

[57] Again Maldonado quotes from the exchange of Christ and Peter at John 10 (see above note 44).

[58] "Forbidden hours": Mass "may be celebrated on any day of the year except Good Friday... at any time between dawn an midday" (*Catholic Encyclopedia* 2/8/2009 under "Liturgy of the Mass: the Present Roman Mass"). Midday in Spain might refer to any time between noon and 2 p.m.

[59] Literally 'flogged,' that is, harshly criticized. This use of the Latin verb *flagello* represents the influence of the Spanish verb *flagelar*.

Oscitationes tandem crebrae pessimam turbam auertunt. A somno equi-
tatur, deambulatur, adeuntur clarae matronae, ubi fabulandi quidem ardore
mores ac omnium uitae rationes flagellantur, interdum parum pudici
sermones inferuntur; nox denique multum prouecta domum cogit redire
et eodem paene pacto cena peragitur, quo prandium, atque utinam non
diuerteretur ad turpiora. Quaeret tum aliquis, quidnam obstet, quominus
inter oblectamenta quaedam humana, Christus Deus optimus maximus
ametur? Non equidem damno rerum seriarum moderatas intermissions et
gaudiorum tempestiuas nonnumquam aduocationes; ceterum utrumque
uelim salua pietate, salua quoad fieri potest, Dei hominumque caritate
fieri: si mercenarios cognitores, quos conduxit, episcopus non leuibus
ipse explorauit argumentis, immo didicit experientia teste fideli, esse non
G 3   omnino auaros, quaerere non tam / sua commoda, quam summe cupere
totoque nixu laborare, suum ut cuique tribuatur; si oeconomus qui curat
aerarium et uectigalia, non admodum utique filiorum suorum satagit, nec
maxime studet secretarius, ut cum detrimento iuris etiam alieni benefi-
ciarius ipse sit; si delatores fiscales minime ruunt in perniciem cunctorum ob pessimum lucrum; si non ducuntur examinatores muneribus aut
aliquorum gratia.

Posteaquam interuallum illud, quod inter lectum et aram intercessit,
uinctis, qui sunt in carcere, est accommodatum, et ne quisquam patiatur
iniuste, maxima est cura prouisum atque optime cautum; horam praeterea,
aut sesquihoram est inuigilatum, ut intelligant officiales cuncti, nihil esse
in munere quocunque uel pie iusteque decretum uel perperam admissum,
quod effugere possit episcopum, haud omnino quidem uetarim, quin spati-
etur episcopus et colloquia misceat animi causa, denique hypocrisis uitet
suspicionem, fugiet uideri tetricus et inhumanus, inciuilitatem ac morosi-
G 3v   tatem procul ab-/legatam studeat, sit affabilis et gratiosus.

Voluptates ingenuas, quae magis faciunt ad demulcendas uitae huius
molestias et mitigandas, quam ad deuinciendos obcaecandosque semel
quos illexerint mortales, non interdicat sibi plane bonus antistes, dummodo

being well advanced, he is forced to go home. Then dinner is conducted in much the same manner as the midday meal, and would that it didn't degenerate into something more shameful. Still someone will ask: What is there, even in the midst of some human delights, to prevent Christ, the God of all goodness and power, from being loved? Indeed I do not condemn moderate interruptions of serious matters and occasional timely adjournments for pleasures, but I would like to see both of them happen without a loss of piety and without the loss of divine and human love, as far as possible. Even if the bishop has not personally tested the legal experts whom he has hired with simple proofs, still it is important that experience itself should have convinced him by its faithful witness that the individuals that he intends to appoint are not completely greedy, that G 3 they do not so much seek / their own advantage, but rather greatly desire and strenuously labor to assign to each his own; that the financial manager who oversees the treasury and the taxes does not overly bustle about on behalf of his sons, nor is the secretary's greatest desire to become the beneficiary of someone else, even if he violates the law; that the fiscal informers never rush to ruin everyone for the sake of vile gain; that the examiners are not influenced by bribes, or others' favors.

After that comes the interval that falls between bed and altar and is set aside for those who are bound in prison. He should make sure with the utmost care — being on the alert in the best way — that no one suffer unjustly; and in addition he should stay awake for an hour, or a half hour, when he supervises directly, so that all on his staff know that there is no decision made in any area of service, whether morally and justly or whether wrongly permitted, that can escape the bishop's notice. I certainly would not at all forbid a bishop to walk about, to engage in conversation for the sake of diversion. Finally he should avoid the suspicion of hypocrisy, avoid seeming gloomy and unfeeling. He should G 3v strive to banish far from himself rudeness or petulance, / showing himself to be affable and gracious.

A good bishop should not entirely forbid himself those innocent pleasures which are more conducive to softening and mitigating the annoyances of this life than they are to seducing mortals in order to overpower and blind them, and provided, too, that step by step his brotherly love for any sort of people becomes so apparent in him that it cannot be unknown to anyone. Let all the people of the province know, brag and proclaim that they have a good shepherd, a very watchful bishop, and in short a spiritual father, and then I won't dwell on these minor matters. What will

hominum quoruncunque gradatim caritas in ipso sic euidens appareat, ut
esse possit nullis ignota. Norint, iactent, praedicent prouinciales omnes
bonum habere se pastorem, uigilantissimum antistitem, parentem denique
spiritalem; et isthaec tum leuia nihil moror. Quid non faciet optime, quam
non functionem administrabit sanctissime, quam non sustinebit personam
accommode, quod non decorum praestabit aptissime, qui uere Deum
hominesque amauerit? Nec obscurum esse cuique potest, num amet episcopus Christum: "A fructibus eorum," dixit ueritas, "cognoscetis eos."
Si homines amat, quod indicabunt statim opera, nimirum et amat ex
animo Christum.

G 4   Verum de dispensandis bonis ecclesiae, decimis uidelicet et / redditibus
quoquomodo pastoris nomine [*M reads* pastori *and deletes* nomine] per-
uenientibus ex ara et sacro, paulisper disseramus, quandoquidem manant
inde potissimum opera, quae hominum caritatem arguunt minimeque latere sinunt. Haud equidem uidebuntur praesules sua extorsisse uectigalia,
nec omnino iudicabit quisquam indebita, si ad Christi hominumque caritatem maxime referantur, si pie et frugaliter expendantur. Alat episcopus familiam quantumlibet amplam et lautam, quam tum cum iudicio legerit, cuiusque merita singulatim pensitarit, eruditionem piamque mentem
explorauerit. Gratia, genus, diuitiae magis officiant quam commendent
quem suum in contubernium episcopus accersat, et eiusmodi quod
praestabitur famulis ac familiaribus, etiam si modum ex affectu nonnunquam excedat, neutiquam iudicabit male locatum Christus summus maximus et summe bonus. Si iuuat uiros aliquot militares annuo donare
salario, tam in urbe quam in agris, qui nostris mos est solemnis pro-
ceribus, pie quidem id facere licebit. Sunt ordinis equestris uiri quam-
G 4v   plurimi, / tacita penuria laborantes, quos paupertas magis protrudit in bellum, quam efferatur animus aut impius: horum cordatiores, saniores ac
magis egentes si uictu iuuare constituerit episcopus, non equidem omnino

he not do in an excellent way? Which of his functions will he not carry out in the holiest manner? What role will he not play perfectly? What bit of decorum will he not maintain in the most appropriate manner, when he is one who truly loves God and men? Nor can it be doubtful to anyone whether a bishop loves Christ. By their fruits, truth said, you will know them.[60] If he loves men, something that his works will immediately show, no doubt he also loves Christ from the heart.

But concerning the dispensing of the goods of the church, such as tithes G 4 / and the income which, in one way or another, comes first to the shepherd from the altar and the holy rites, let us go into them a little. From them especially flow good works, which give clear evidence of the brotherly love of men, and in no way allow that charity to be hidden. It certainly won't seem that bishops have extorted their tax revenues, nor will anyone judge at all that he does not owe them, if they are associated especially with the love of Christ and men, if they are spent in a pious and frugal way. Let the bishop nourish as big and as elegant a household as he wishes, picked out with good judgment after having thought over the merits of each member individually and tested their learning and pious way of thinking. Influence, birth, and wealth should block the path rather than clearing it for those whom the bishop summons into his brotherhood. Anything he provides of this sort to his servants and household members, even if out of affection it may sometimes exceed the norm, by no means will Christ, the greatest, highest and supremely good, judge to have been wrongly placed. If it pleases him to give an annual salary to some military men, both in the city and in the country, as is the common custom among our leading men, it will certainly be permissible, and pious, to do so. There are a great many men who belong to the order of G 4v knights and / who suffer from indigence in silence, who go to war more pushed by poverty than by a wild or unholy spirit. In the case of these men, if the bishop should decide to help some of the more sensible, sane and needy of these with their living expenses, I would certainly not altogether disapprove. For by doing so he would not only alleviate poverty, which is the proper function of a bishop, but he would actually prevent men who are not completely bad from monstrous and shameful acts which they are required to carry out while at war.

---

[60] Matthew 7.16.

improbarim. Alleuatur enim non modo paupertas, quod est proprium episcopi munus, sed arcentur etiam uiri prorsus non improbi ab immensis
flagitiis, quae dum militant designent necessarium est. Iuuat equos atque
canes alere ad uenandum, ut animus, dum taedium ceperit urbis et umbrae,
relaxetur; alat sane: sicuti non omnino probo, ita plane non damnarim,
si, dum cursitat per montes et agros uenator praesul, pastoris personam
non etiam tunc segnem ageret; quos summa uexat pauperies in uicis paganis, solaretur ac cibaret; uiduarum ac uirginum, quibus ob penuriam mar-
itus non contigit, rationem aliquam subduceret, bonam habere mentem et
spem interdum iuberet; tum eam familiam, quam pascit ob uenatum,
pietatem uerumque Christianismum doceret, sine cuiusquam ut maleficio
G 5   feras appe/terent, messes agricolarum parcius contererent, sic denique
saltus et inuia sectarentur, ut ad neminem quicquam perueniret incom-
modi. Oeconomos habeat episcopus, si placet, sericatos, dum uita sit illis
modo sincera, saltem non admodum anxia, quo pacto ualeant filios locu-
pletare et summos ad honores euehere. Amittunt quamplurimi ius suum,
ubi oeconomus aut secretarius episcopi, qui praescribunt plerumque
uicariis, ardet immensa cupiditate sibi suisque quoquo iure perspiciendi,
adeo quidem ut ad sacerdotia quaeque tenuia demittat animum. Theologos ac iurisperitos magnis, si nequeat aliter, salariis apud se praesul
retineat, qui norint euangelium et leges sacrorum sapienter annuntiare,
sed dictis magis faciant fidem morum ac uitae candore, quam argumen-
tosa quapiam alia probatione, rebus uidelicet ac exitu praestent, quod persuasione conantur aliis ingerere. Circumeant isti quotannis prouinciam,
uisitent ecclesias, clericorum et laicorum agant censuram, ita tamen ut
G 5v   omnes iam deinde pie magis et /Christiane uiuant. Non inuestigent solum,
cunctane sint intra sacras aedes pure suis decenterque constituta locis, linteamina tersa, uasa pura nitidaque, sed an sit in sacerdotibus integritas
uitae, morum sinceritas, eruditio tandem congruens professioni; et quod
animaduersione dignum offenderint, haud ita puniant, ut commodum ex

It is pleasant to raise horses and dogs for hunting, so that one's spirit, when it grows tired of the city and the shade, may relax. Yes, let him raise them, and although I don't altogether approve, I would not altogether condemn the practice if, while racing about through the woods and the fields as a hunting bishop, not even then would he act the part of a sluggish shepherd. Those whom poverty weighs on most heavily in the peasant villages he should console and feed, and he should take into account widows and virgins who have not obtained a husband, due to their poverty. He should command them to be of good cheer and good hope in the meantime. Then he would teach true Christian morality to the family that he supports for the sake of hunting, that they should eagerly
G 5 pursue the wild animals without doing harm to anyone, / trampling the farmers' grain only very sparingly, and in general following the pastures and trackless areas so that no inconvenience may come to anyone. Let the bishop have financial managers who are dressed in silks, if they wish, provided their way of life is pure and if they are not, at least, too anxious about how they might be able to enrich their sons and promote them to high honors. A great many lose their rights when the financial manager or secretary of a bishop who delegates much to his vicars burns with immense desire to provide for himself and his own people by any means possible, so that he lets his expectations sink to any benefice, no matter how slight. Let the bishop keep theologians and legal experts by his side — by means of big salaries if he has to — who know how wisely to declare the Gospel and sacramental laws, but also by their words and the openness of their lives bear witness to their character, rather than with some other kind of long-winded proof. I mean that what they try by persuasion to impose on others they should display in person and by what they have done. Let this sort go around the province for a few years, let them visit the churches. Let them make a judgment about the clergy and the laity, but in such a way that all may in consequence live more piously
G 5v and / in a more Christian manner. Have them investigate not only whether all things in the holy buildings are cleanly and appropriately stored in their proper places, the linen cloths neat, the vessels shining clean, but rather whether there is in the priests an integrity of life, a purity of character, and finally, a learning which is appropriate to their profession. And when they find something which deserves censure, they should not punish them in such a way that they seem to have sought only profit from the sins, but they should use that kind of fatherly scolding that seems to have wished to correct character and habits, not the kind which virtually

admissis quaesisse solum uideantur, sed eam paternam adhibeant obiurgationem, quae mores ac instituta uiuendi uoluisse uideatur emendare,
non quae fami prorsus ac mendicitati perpetuo miseros alliget. Aut si
fuerint eiusmodi commissa, talis quorundam uiuendi ratio, ut sine pecuniaria poena non uideatur in melius commutanda, sic ea tandem irroge-
tur, ut studium fuisse morum magistro sentiant omnes reducendi ad
caulam errabundam ouem, non autem deglubendi. In summa, nulli sunt
episcopo sumptus improbandi, nullum famulitium iudicandum inutile, si
spiritu ipse Christi ducatur, si mentem gerat piam Christique uicario dig-
G 6   nam, si / pauperes, sua qui sunt ipsius in ditione, sentiunt munificentiam
aemulatricem eius, quam Christus indixit suo primario legato, "Pasce,"
inquiens, "oues meas." Sin aliter est episcopus animatus, suoque iure
putat in quoscunque profanos usus redditus ecclesiae se posse conuer-
tere, meo quidem errat iudicio, nec puto fore perfacile aduocatorum tur-
bae, quam alit ad ecclesiae iura tuenda, causam sustinere, quae cum prae-
ceptis ex diametro pugnat diuinis. Ex dilectione quidem Dei et hominum
pendet salus animae. Quis autem Deum uere diligat, unum hoc potissimum arguit, nempe dilectio proximorum; dilectionem uero cunctorum
obseruatio Dei mandatorum constanter affirmat. Quinam (obsecro)
mandatorum erit Dei uigilantissimus obseruator episcopus, qui seruit
auaritiae, libidini et omnibus humanis affectibus, qui maxime ambit episcopatum, ut lautius uiuat et splendidius epuletur?

Sed satis et etiam forte plus satis offendimus tuas patientissimas aures,
G 6v   /dum bonum et malum pastorem conamur exprimere. Experti sumus
utrumque, et nescio quo malo mortalium fato plerumque fit ut frequentiora sint exempla nequitiae, quam alicuius eximiae uirtutis. Verum ut ad
id recurrat oratio, unde primo ducta est et fiduciae, quae nos primo protrusit, obliti non esse uideamur, tu plurimam utique facis spem corrup-
tissima tandem tempora in melius esse uertenda. Primus tibi gradus honorum opulentissimus fuit episcopatus, quod illustri loco natis raro uenit
usu monachis ob rerum omnium contemptum, quem boni uidentur eorum
prae se ferre, semel aut iterum, Isabella regnante, successit. Tu tam claris
gestis excellens, nobilitate sublimis, Christiana pietate conspicuus, nullis
cupiditatibus inquinatus, nullis ambitionibus inuolutus, ob merita solum

binds the miserable culprits to hunger and perpetual begging. But if the sins of some people seem to correspond to their way of living, so that it does not seem possible to change them for the better without a monetary fine, let it finally be imposed in such a way that everyone will feel that it was due to his character — the teacher's eagerness for bringing the wandering sheep back to the flock, certainly not for skinning it. In short, none of the bishop's expenses should be criticized, none of his servants should be judged unnecessary, if he himself is led by the spirit of Christ, G 6 if his mind is pious and worthy of Christ's vicar, if / the poor, who are under his own authority, feel his generosity striving to be like that which Christ proclaimed to his first deputy, when he said, "Feed my sheep." If, however, the bishop is motivated otherwise, and he thinks that by his authority he can turn the income of the church to whatever secular uses he chooses, in my opinion he makes a big mistake. Nor do I think that it will be very easy for the crowd of lawyers that he supports to protect the rights of the church, to uphold a cause which is diametrically opposed to divine precepts. The health of the soul depends on love of God and man. Moreover when anyone truly loves God, one thing above all proves this, namely, his love for his neighbors. But the observation of all God's commandments is a continual affirmation of that love. Now I ask you, what kind of wide-awake observer of God's commands will a bishop be if he serves greed, lust and all the human passions? If his main reason for seeking the episcopate is to live more elegantly and dine more splendidly?

But enough, and even perhaps more than enough, we have offended G 6v your very patient ears, / while we have tried to present what is a good and a bad shepherd. We have experienced both, and by some evil destiny of mortals, it usually happens that examples of iniquity are more frequently encountered than of any outstanding virtue. But now so that my discourse may return to the point from which it started, and so that we may not seem to have lost sight of the courage that first made us step forward, you indeed give us great hope of seeing these very corrupt times finally changed for the better. A very wealthy episcopate has been for you a first step on the path of honors, a thing which is rarely conferred on those born into the aristocracy. When Isabel was queen it did happen once or twice to monks due to that contempt of all [worldly] things that the good men among them seem to display. You, excelling by such famous deeds, in nobility the highest, outstanding for your Christian piety, not stained by any lust, not caught up in ambition, but solely on your merits and the

et omnium de tuis uirtutibus praedicationes ad magistratum curulem quidem illum paene tractus es, cum te profitereris indignum functionis maxime munerosae, certe periculosae. Quid igitur spe/ randum est, ni rebus fore Christianis longe melius, quando ii creantur episcopi, qui sapientes et sint pietate praestantes? Incumbe igitur, pater amplissime, in studia pietatis praecipua, Christianam capesse rempublicam non leuiter collapsam, quam tandem Carolus imperator ac rex maximus studeat erigere ac subleuare inque ueterem formam, et Christo summe gratam reducere.

G 7

Non dubium est, quin principes, si positis simultatibus, intenderint ad componendam et in pristinum statum reuocandam religionem christianam, omnibus praecipua cura sit partes suas tueri, commissaque munia sinceriter ac sancte peragere. Quid ergo restat? Carolus quidem uigilatissimus est in amplianda, producenda atque constabilienda persuasione Christiana. Vidimus ipsi, cum proxime Burgis paucos est menses commoratus, nimis anxie doluisse, quod quaedam in foro sacro minus recte fieri per uicarios collegii (erat enim uacua sedes a morte Antonii Rogii patriarchae) nuntiabantur, conuocatisque primoribus collegii /seuere quidem statim edixisse ut uicarios ea functione dignos mox legerent, qui sancte iudicarent et sibi ex alienis malis nihil omnino quaererent. Sin cunctarentur paululum, ipsum derogatis quibuscumque priuilegiis curaturum nequid detrimenti caperent ecclesiae earumque ministri. Paulo uero post, quasi consulens rebus collapsis, huius te regionis episcopum designauit. An prius non expendit bonus princeps diuque secum uolutauit, quem praefici potissimum muneri expediret, in quo profligata paene sic erat morum iudiciorumque disciplina, ut magistris, qui dicerentur morum ac religionis, unus non satis esset magister? Porro cum est auditum fore

G 7v

praises of everyone for your virtues, were virtually dragged into the curule magistracy,[61] although you declared yourself unworthy of a post highly
G 7 profitable and certainly dangerous. What, then, is left to hope for / other than great improvement in all that is Christian when such men are created bishops, men wise and outstanding in their piety? Therefore, most distinguished father, devote yourself to an eagerness for piety, apply yourself vigorously, and take in hand the Christian republic, which has fallen down in no small measure, and which the emperor and great king Carlos is so eager to build, raise up and restore to its ancient form, one highly pleasing to Christ.

There is no doubt that the rulers, if they will set aside their rivalries and give their attention to repairing and recalling to its pristine state the Christian religion, will all pay attention first to watching over their own jurisdictions and cary out the duties assigned to them in a sincere and pious way. What then remains? Carlos, for his part, is highly vigilant in expanding, leading forward and strengthening the Christian faith. When recently he stayed for a few months in Burgos, we ourselves saw how he was exceedingly anxious and distressed at the news that certain things in the ecclesiastical court were being done improperly by the vicars of the college of canons (since the bishop's chair was empty following the death of Antonio Rojas).[62] Calling together the foremost of the members of the
G 7v college, / at once he sternly decreed that they should soon appoint vicars worthy of those duties, who would make judgments in a righteous manner, seeking nothing at all for themselves from the troubles of others. But if they should delay even a little, he himself would take away some of their privileges, and would see to it that the churches not suffer harm, or their ministers. Indeed, shortly thereafter, as though seeking a solution when matters had fallen apart, he appointed you bishop of this region. Didn't the good prince weigh the possibility at first, while he was thinking over whom it would be best to appoint to a post in which the discipline of behavior and judgment had been virtually thrown to the winds, that only one teacher would not be enough for those who were said to be teachers of behavior and religion? But later, when it was heard that you were to be designated the bishop (there is no news that fame doesn't spread), immediately there was born in all those who knew you

---

[61] *Curule* described any Roman magistrate of a certain high rank, including consuls and praetors.

[62] On Rojas see note 3.

te designandum antistitem (nihil non fama diuulgat), omnibus statim, qui
te penitus norant, oborta certissima spes est, res ecclesiae melius habituras
et clericorum simul et laicorum mores reformandos. Caesari certe
felicitatem et bona cuncta precabantur, quod curam non deposuisset
G 8   Burgensium rebus consulendi, quod eum designa/re praesulem destinas-
set, cuius uita, mores atque pietas fausta omnino tempora promitterent.
Curabis ergo, si me audis, praesul amplissime, hos ut rumores de singulari tua uirtute atque pietate diligentissime re ipsa confirmes, bonum
omnibus te pastorem praebeas, quid tibi praescripserit Christus, quid
summus pontifex, quid Caesar pensiculatius animaduertas, quantum onus
sustineas semper ob oculos ponas, quam moribus praefractis, inuersis
omninoque illaudatis adhibitus sis censor et magister, penitus attendas,
quam seuere postulandus sis peculatus, si dormitaueris aut forte conni-
xeris ad errata mercenariorum et auaros insultus, mente tibi nunquam exci-
dat. Caue discedas abs te, tuum esto potius consilium, familiares et domes-
ticos, tum etiam propinquos et necessarios usque adeo quidem audies,
dum te non ad foeda lucra protrudant, si suam ita uitam ipsi instituerint,
ut luxus in eos aut auaritia non dominetur. Scimus te frugi, pium ac sin-
G 8v cerum hominem; tantum percupimus, ut quoties / aliquam praefecturam
demandas aut de procurandis uectigalibus rationem inis, tecum ante omnia
loquaris. Improbus est consultor adulator, improbus est affectus a pia
ratione deflectens, sed impius ratiocinator auarus uersipellis, quo nulla
pestis episcopis uenit acerbior. Si ueneris tamen in rem ipse praesentem
et negotiis interfueris agendis, nihil est tandem quod uereamur. Sumus nos
felices, qui bonum sortiti sumus pastorem, tu uero felicissimus, qui munus
apostolicum ex Christi regulis ac institutis pro tuis sanctissimis moribus
sis gesturus, innumeras oues recuperaturus et Christianae uere functionis
specimen tandem exhibiturus. Vale. Burgis. Nonis Decembris. Anno
uicesimo nono supra millesimum [quingentesimum].

thoroughly a very confident hope that the situation of the church would improve, and that the character of the clergy and the laity would be reformed. They certainly wished happiness and all good things for the emperor because he had not set aside his concern for remedying Burgos'
G 8 problems, because he had decided / to appoint a bishop whose life, character, and piety promised thoroughly auspicious times. Therefore, if you listen to me, mighty bishop, you will take care very diligently to confirm by your actions these reports of your singular virtue and piety, and offer yourself to all as a good shepherd. Notice very carefully what has been prescribed for you by Christ, by the supreme pontiff, and by the emperor. Always keep your gaze focused on how great a burden you bear. You will see that you have been brought in as a censor and a teacher to behavior that is crude, perverse, and praised by none. Notice carefully how strictly you may be charged with embezzlement if you should doze or maybe wink at the mistakes of the hired hands and their greedy scoffing; never let it leave your mind. Be careful not to break with yourself; let your own counsel be the best. Listen to your family and servants, even neighbors and intimate friends, only as long as they don't push you toward foul gains, and if they themselves have established their life so that luxury and avarice do not rule over them. We know that you are a
G 8v frugal, pious and pure human being; we are only anxious that as often as/ you will entrust a judgeship, or calculate the collection of tax revenue, you will, before anything else, talk it over with yourself. A flattering advisor is morally bad, as is one who turns his feelings away from pious reason, but an evil accountant is a greedy turncoat, more bitter to bishops than any plague. But if you come in person into the present situation and take part yourself in transacting the business, we will then at last have nothing to fear. We are fortunate, in that we have been assigned a good shepherd. But you are the most fortunate, since you are about to perform the apostolic office on the basis of the rules and teachings of Christ, in accordance with your very moral character. You will rescue countless sheep, and, in short, you will present to us a model of truly Christian performance of duties. Farewell. Burgos. December 5, 1529.

Gluttony and Poverty (R. Simmons)

BACCHANALIA.*

Ioannis Maldonati Geniale Iudicium siue Bacchanalia.
Interlocutores:
Accensus Minister, Ingluuies et Continentia inuicem se accusantes,
Tempus iudex, Paedor et Pudor testes.

Accensus

Pro caeleste numen! Mulierculis tantam inesse uecordiam et audaciam, ut ciuitatem audeant perturbare atque ciues in furorem et arma
ciuilia protrudere? Vix mihi spiritus prae stupore suggerit uerba, uix
anhelitum traho. Murmur tamen ex meo perturbato uultu gestuque com-
motum resideat paululum, et ego quid nuntiatum ueniam, explicabo.
Conticuistis uos? Ego promissum absoluo. Accensus ego sum, praemis-
sus a magis-[36v]tratibus, ad uos, candidi spectatores, admonendos, ne
nouitate rei, quam estis audituri, commoueamini. Ingens seditio coorta
nunc est in foro cunctisque furentibus prae studio iuuandi partes, vix a
magistratibus compressa est. Duae mulierculae cinctae ualidis copiis
ardentibus studiis se mutuo impetebant. Quas quidem si uideretis
pugnantes, alteram putaretis saeuissimam tigridem, alteram mansuetam
iuuencam. Plures tamen prosternebat huius mansuetudo, quam illius feri-
tas. Quid mussitatis admirabundi? Ingluuies et Continentia proelio
contendebant, et quamuis copiis primo et audacia praeualebat Ingluuies,
consilio et scientia militandi longe Continentia superabat. Atrox quidem
erat pugna, neque finienda uidebatur nisi cum interitione partis alterius.
Fulgebant arma, micabant tonabantque bombardae, tela saxa ligna uola-
bant; ardebant animi, clamores ingeminabantur; gemebant saucii, cade-
bant multi. Sed tandem Ingluuies uicta fugit opemque magistratuum
implorauit maxime querula quod a possessione fori sacrorumque Bac-
chanalium ui et armis fuisset depulsa. Illi non existimantes opportunum

---

* Note on orthography. Small corrections of individual words in the MS have been
entered without comment in order to standardize the spelling, e.g. *proelio* for *plaelio*, *tela*
for *tella*, *paene* for *pene*, *cena* for *coena*, *uindicat* for *uendicat*, *deliciis* for *delitiis*, *nuntiatum* for *nunciatum*, *immo* for *imo*, *litteras* for *literas*, *caritas* for *charitas*. Punctuation
has also been standardized.

BACCHANALIA.

The Delightful Judgment or Bacchanalia of Juan Maldonado
Speakers:
The minister Accensus [a name which might mean either "on fire" or "an attendant"]; Gluttony and Continence accusing one another; Time, a judge; Filth and Shame, witnesses.

Accensus

By the heavenly powers! That mere women should acquire so much folly and boldness that they dare to throw the state into turmoil, drive the citizens to madness, and bring forth civil strife! I am so astonished that I can scarcely find the breath to form words, I can hardly gasp. Still, let the muttering (which has been stirred up by my extremely agitated face and gestures) settle down a little and I will explain what I came to announce.

Have you become silent? I fulfill what I promised. I am Accensus, sent ahead [36v] by the magistrates to warn you, delightful spectators, not to be disturbed by the strangeness of the matter that you are about to hear. A massive rebellion has taken place in the marketplace. Everyone is in an uproar out of eagerness to help his own side, and it has only with difficulty been suppressed by the magistrates. Two little women, surrounded by strong forces, have attacked one another with eager enthusiasm. Why, if you should see them fighting, you would suppose that one was a very savage tigress and the other a tame heifer. Yet more were amazed by the gentleness of the one than by the savagery of the other. Why are you muttering in amazement? Gluttony and Continence were contending in battle; and, although Gluttony had the advantage at first, both in forces and in boldness, Continence was far overcoming her by good planning and knowledge of military tactics. It certainly was a fierce fight, and it did not look like it would end except by the utter destruction of one side or the other. Weapons flashed; cannons glittered and boomed; spears, rocks and wooden staffs were flying; passions grew hot, shouts were repeated; the wounded were groaning, and many were falling.

But finally Gluttony was defeated and fled; and she begged for help from the magistrates, complaining especially because she had been deprived of the marketplace and the sacred rites of Bacchus[1] by force of arms. They did not think it

---

[1] This mention of the 'rites of Bacchus' is the first indication of Maldonado's fusion of the Christian vices and the Bacchic. See Colahan-Rodríguez-Smith 1999, pp. 160-171.

tali die et lo-[37 r]-co efferatam Ingluuiem plus irritare, iudicem dede-
runt hunc senem, qui testibus adhibitis eas foro depulit et in hoc emi-
nentissimum theatrum iudicandas, cum egerit utraque causam suam,
compulit; audiantur ipsae. De iudice non est cur dubitent: bonus aequus
inexorabilis est. Caelum citius exorabitur, ut teneat cursum suum, quam
ut hic a uero discedat. Eia tu conscende suggestum, Ingluuies: tibi
priores partes forte obuenerunt. Si uicta fueris, dabis poenas, ut aequum
est; sin secus, tripudiis et choreis tuos amicos et populares laetius et
liberius exhilarabis. Euome tandem querellas tuas.

Ingluuiei oratio

Quis crederet? Quis futurum umquam putaret ut Continentia mecum
his praesertim Bacchanalibus pertinaciter auderet contendere collatisque
signis et aperto Marte pugnare? Ingluuies ego sum, Ingluuies inquam,
illa principalium domorum et fori plane regina. Cuius ab imperio uix se
montium recessus et inuia siluarum, nedum urbium loca celebria uindi-
cant, magistratus quasi du-[37v]-bii de meo iure, remittunt me ad iudicem quidem acerrimum. Non queror ad te, iudex, remitti, quem scio
numquam a ueritate deuiaturum; sed quod illi de re manifesta dubitauerint, demiror. Maiora sunt et grauiora, quae solent a iudice tanto decerni;
praesertim cum nulli non compertum sit his feriis uoracitati dicatis mihi
non obtemperare meaque non iura seruare, crimen esse piaculo luendum.
Sed quia tua grauitas, annose iudex, quid mihi nouum et lamentabile
nunc acciderit, respiciens ad maiora, forte non attendit, percurram breuiter meas aerumnas et angores attingam. Dies carniuoros tres, quibus
nunc feriamur, ab annis plus mille fuisse mihi sacros, quis quamuis au-

was opportune on such a day and in such [37r] a place to stir up Gluttony any more, wild as she was, and as judge they produced this old man. He summoned witnesses, drove the women out of the marketplace, and forced them into this very high theater, to be judged after each has personally pleaded her own case.[2] Let the women speak for themselves. There is no reason why they should have doubts about the judge. He is a good and fair man, who cannot be moved by entreaty. Heaven will more quickly be persuaded to check its course than this man to turn aside from the truth.

Come now, you, Gluttony! Mount the platform. The first speech has fallen to you by lot. If you are bested, you will pay the penalty, as is just. But if there is a different result, with leaps and dances you will delight your friends and followers more joyfully and freely. Come on, spit out your complaints.

Speech of Gluttony

Who would have believed it? Who would have thought that it would ever come about that Continence would dare stubbornly to contend with me — especially during these ecstatic rites[3] — and to fight at close quarters in public battle? I am Gluttony. I tell you that I am Gluttony, the queen of seignorial homes and certainly of the forum. From my jurisdiction, scarcely can mountain retreats and thick forests, much less regions crowded with cities, free themselves; and now the magistrates, as though [37v] doubtful about my rights, send me to a judge who is certainly very harsh.

Not that I am complaining, judge, over being sent to you, for I know that you will never turn aside from the truth. But I am amazed that they had doubts about a matter which is obvious. The issues customarily decided by so great a judge are larger and more serious, especially since no one is unaware that during this holiday (set aside for the appetites) to fail to humor me, and to follow my rules, is a crime that can only be expiated by atonement. But, oh dignified and aged judge, because of your concern with greater issues, perhaps you are unaware of the strange and regrettable thing which has recently happened to me. I will briefly run through my troubles and express my anguish.

The three meat-eating days which we are now celebrating have been sacred to me for more than a thousand years.[4] Who is so stern and strict as to think that

---

[2] This trial format reflects, as indicated in Colahan-Rodríguez-Smith 1999, its Livian source. The pitched battle between Gluttony and Continence, that has already taken place, but which is described during the trial proceedings, recalls the medieval tradition of battles between Carnival and Lent, such as that offered by Juan Ruiz's *Libro de buen amor*, in "De la pelea que ovo don Carnal con la Quaresma". Moreover Gluttony's self-defense often echoes Folly's praise of herself in Erasmus' *Praise of Folly* (1511).

[3] This refers, albeit with Bacchian terminology, to the excesses traditionally tolerated during the Christian carnival.

[4] The reference is to the three days of carnival preceding Ash Wednesday and the beginning of Lent. The reference to 'meat-eating' serves as a contrast to the abstinence from meat associated with Lent. The insistence on 'meat-eating' may also allude, in the

sterus et gravis negandum existimabit? Quis umquam meis uoluptatibus hodiernis induxit animum obstrepere aut leuiter obturbare? Ecce autem hoc ipso geniali die, cum mei ganeones et ardeliones post ientacula et ingurgitationes sollemnes ducerent choreas deque laudibus ebrietatis et ganeae carmina cantitarent, meque propitium sibi numen complecterentur et summis praeconiis celebrarent, irruit Continentia cum sua familia non admodum numero-[38r]-sa, sed uehementi, austera, pugnaci meque meosque probris incessit, agitat et contrudit. Arma latebant; uulnera tamen infligebantur, quae quo minus apparebat spiculum, tanto magis cruciabant. Ego non ferens meam familiam partim dispergi exulceratam, partim in deditionem redigi, pedem infero pugnamque capesso. Redintegratur proelium caduntque ubique multi. Ego uero ducem ipsam inuado et cum impenetrabilis ferro uideretur, in capillos inuolo; certe decaluassem, si nullae laterent insidiae. Nondum tamen digitis attigeram, cum subito perculsa procumbo, nullo apparente mucrone; moribundaque iacui, donec sum a meis sublata et uitae quasi reddita. Iamiam flagrabat uindictae rabies unguesque intendebam in hostem, cum iterum percutior nescio quo telo nec a quo, praesentemque mortem uitans, hosti cedere cogor et mea possessione deturbor. Cumque magistratus inclamassem, accurrunt illi quidem mediaeque se pugnae inferunt. Sedato tamen tumultu, quod illis erat de aliis rebus consultandum, ad tuam grauitatem, iudex, nos iudicandas reiecerunt, ut cognita causa punires, et absolueres tuo arbitatu. Itaque [38v] tria mihi potissimum in hac causa sunt agenda: de ui mihi meis feriis illata, quam sum ego solum conata repellere, de paratis insidiis, de restituenda mihi possessione saeculorum multorum, qua sum per uim fraudemque depulsa. Miseram me! Laesa sum paeneque confecta, et eo die, quo ius omne mihi multis ab annis omnisque libertas permissa est; et in dubium reuocatur, cui sit hodie uis illata et a qua sit Genii laesa maiestas. Festum ego diem agebam in meo regno, inter meos populares. Ista uelut in messem alienam irruit, praeripere conata meos honores, meam gloriam, mea gaudia plane solemnia. Repugnaui, sed uim repellens, non inferens; quis de meo iure dubitabit? Quis me non grauiter laesam et ignominia turpi quidem notatam negabit?

this can be denied? Who ever took a notion to cry out against or, lightly, to throw into confusion my pleasures of today? But just behold. On this very happy day, when my debauchees and zealous followers, after breakfasting and guzzling, were performing their festive dances and singing songs in praise of drunkenness and feasting,[5] embracing me as their presiding divinity and celebrating me with the highest proclamations, Continence rushed in with her family, who are not very [38r] numerous, but ardent and stern. She attacked me and my people, very belligerently, with insults. She harassed me and pressed hard against me. Weapons were concealed; yet wounds were inflicted that tortured us all the more because the pointed weapons could not be seen.

I did not endure my family being partly split up and wounded, partly forced to surrender. I advanced and entered the fight. The battle was renewed; many fell on all sides. Then I attacked the general herself. Since she appeared impenetrable by sword, I went for her hair. I certainly would have plucked her bald if no treachery had been lurking. But I had not yet touched her with my fingers when, being suddenly struck, I fell forward, although no blade was to be seen. I lay like a dead woman until I was picked up by my friends and, so to speak, restored to life. Now the urge for revenge was taking possession of me and I was aiming my nails at the enemy. Then I was again struck. I know not by what weapon or by how many people. I avoided death for the moment, but was forced to yield to the enemy and was deprived of my possession. When I cried out for the magistrates, they indeed ran up and rushed into the middle of the fight. Yet, when the uproar had settled down, because they had to consult about other matters, they gave us up, judge, to be tried by your eminence, so that, once the case has been investigated, you may punish or acquit at your discretion.

And so [38v] three things must be treated by me especially in this case: that which concerns the violence which was done to me during my festival, which I only tried to prevent; that which concerns the ambush which was prepared; and that which concerns the restoration to me of my possession of many centuries, from which I have been driven by violence and deceit. Poor me! I have been wounded and almost killed, and that on the very day on which for many years all power and all freedom have been permitted me.[6] And it is called into doubt against whom violence has been brought this day, and which woman has committed an offense against the sovereignty of the person. I was spending a festal day in my own kingdom, among my fellow-countrymen. She rushed in, as though invading another's harvest crop, trying to snatch away my honors, my glory, my entirely traditional joys. I fought back; but I was driving away violence, not introducing it. Who can have doubts about my rights? Who will deny that I have been gravely wounded and, indeed, branded with shameful disgrace?

Bacchian association created by Maldonado for carnival, to the Bacchic practice of devouring animals. See Dodds 1986, Introduction, pp. xvi-xvii.

[5] Dancing and singing, but especially dancing, are inseparably identified with the maenadic devotees of Dionysus/Bacchus.

[6] The day referred to is probably 'Fat Tuesday,' the culmination of carnival time.

Si testibus opus est, produxi iam decem; et alium, quem designaueram et graui morbo detentus absoluere non ualuerat, in hunc coetum, si per te, iudex, licuerit, inducam, qui de gestis ante saeculum hoc non minus quam de hodierna seditione testificabitur ex fide. Iam testes reliquos audisti, iudex, et iniquitatem aduersariae demiratus, meae calamitatis penitus deplorandae misertus es; quid cum anno-[39r]-sum audiueris? Quod autem sint mihi insidiae comparatae, tam fuit omnibus palam, ita fraus cunctis aperta, ut ea de re quisquam dubitare non possit. Corrui repente prostrataque sum; at quae me cominus impetebat, nullo ferro uidebatur armata. Innuebat illa oculis, uis aliunde manabat. Latebant certe percussores; iacula dissimulanter et clanculum contorquebantur. Sed testibus hoc comprobatum est; et qui restat adhuc interrogandus, quoniam propius aderat, plenus satisfaciet omnemque dubitationem amouebit. De sublata mihi possessione horum dierum et fori plenius agendum est, ut non solum restituatur (quod iure gentium negari non potest) sed quae per uim me depulit ab ea, grauissimas poenas det. Unde nunc exordiar? Quid potissimum querar? O mores hominum improbissi-mos! O rerum uertigines formidandas! O temporum uicissitudines admi-randas et mihi plane timendas! Regnaui semper in orbe toto, reiectis non semel, et in caelum redire coactis uirtutibus — aut si repetebant quan-doque terras, meum numen uerebantur, et abesse longe curabant. Nunc ab una Continentia iactor; diesque mihi meoque fraterculo Baccho sacros [39v] extorquet sibique uindicat? Magistratus uero (heu dolor!) conniuent ad mea damna meque censendam ad iudicem inexorabilem reiciunt, cum, si reuocassent in memoriam gesta maiorum et priscorum

If there is need of witnesses, I have already produced ten; and, if you permit, judge, I will produce in this assembly another, whom I had earlier designated but who, being detained by a serious illness, was not able to appear. He will faithfully testify about events before this age as well as about today's uprising. You have already heard the other witnesses, judge. You have marveled at the wickedness of my adversary and you have shown pity toward my plight, which is thoroughly to be deplored. What [will you feel] after you have heard this [39r] old man?[7]

However, the fact that treachery was planned against me has become obvious to all; the deceit has been cleared up for everyone, so that no one can doubt about this matter. I suddenly collapsed and was knocked down; and she who attacked me at close quarters did not seem armed with any weapon. She signaled with her eyes; the force flowed from another direction. The bandits were surely hiding. Darts were hurled, deceitfully and secretly. But this has been proved by witnesses; and he who still remains to be questioned, since he was closer at hand, will give a fuller account and remove all doubt.

Now that the possession of these days, and of the forum, has been taken from me, I must testify more thoroughly, not only so that possession may be restored to me — which could not be denied according to the law of nations[8] — but also so that she, who separated me from it by violence, may pay the most severe penalty.

Now where shall I start? What shall I complain about most? Oh, the depraved character of people! Oh, the frightening dizziness of the universe! Oh, the remarkable changes of times, which I must thoroughly fear![9] I have always been queen throughout the whole world. The virtues have been rejected more than once and forced to return to heaven,[10] or, if they eventually did come back to earth, they revered my divine power and took care to stay far away. Now I am tormented by Continence alone. She steals away from me days which are sacred to me and to my little brother [39v] Bacchus. She steals them and lays claim to them herself.

As for the magistrates — oh, the pain! —, they wink at my losses and abandon me to the judgment of an inexorable judge. Whereas, if they had called to

---

[7] The reference is to the last witness to be presented, referred to earlier in this same paragraph, who, in order to give testimony about the past, has to be, in effect, an old man.

[8] Maldonado appears to allude to the foundations of International Law fixed by Fray Francisco de Vitoria, who died in 1546. A professor of Theology at Salamanca, Vitoria had caused a great intellectual commotion in the decades before his death by questioning the legality of the Spanish conquests in the New World, a matter of interest to Maldonado (Colahan-Rodriguez 1995, pp. 296-298). See, for example, James Brown Scott 1934, I, chap. 3.

[9] These phrases spoken by Gluttony show authorial irony. Laments for the human condition and over the instability of the world are usually associated with ascetic writings.

[10] A possible allusion to Astraea, goddess of Justice, who abandoned earth in disgust at the sins of mortals. See Ovid, *Met*, 1, 150 and Juvenal, 6, 19-20.

historias meminissent, deturbanda mox erat Continentia ab indebita possessione grauiterque punienda, quod in fortunas inuasisset alienas. Non
queror, ut dixi, talem mihi iudicem datum; noui aequitatem et iuste iudi-
caturum non dubito; sed quod illi dubitauerint de meo iure, cum me
uiderint prostratam et eiectam, grauiter fero.

Possem hoc loci perfacile ad gloriam et famam meam extollendam
atque praedicandam excurrere, si pertineret ad causam, et in proprias
diuertere laudes sine insolentiae sugillatione liceret. Nam de patria et
parentibus quis uerius gloriaretur? Eua me produxit in paradiso, cum
edendi libidine percita corripuit pomum. Noas bene de me meritus est
uino uictus et soporatus. Sed non sunt, dicetis uos, ad exemplum referenda, quae accidunt in uita semel et habent nescio quid latentis mys-
terii. Neque libet etiam aut expediat iactare, quantum boni proueniat
mortalibus ex meis studiis et institutis: res ipsa [40r] plane loquitur.
Omnes discipuli et assectatores mei uigent animo, ualent corpore:
uegeti pinguiculique sunt, rubent illis malae, scintillant oculi: laetan-
tur, rident, carmina componunt, dicteria iactant, ingenium illis promp-
tum est et uiribus ualent. Itaque praetermissis his, ad possessionem
confirmandam recurrat oratio.

Quis ignorat reges olim ac principes fuisse mihi semper obnoxios, et
aetatibus paene cunctis non defuisse primates, qui non dissimulanter, sed
aperta facie mihi seruirent? Christiani fuerunt etiam pauci, nunc uero
pauciores, et his Bacchanalibus paene nulli, qui mihi refragentur. Exem-
plis ero breuis, ne uos obtundam.

Sardanapalus Assyriae rex mihi meaeque ampliandae dignitati glo-
riaeque natus, quanto me studio coluerit, quam meis uotis fuerit addictus,
testes sunt eorum temporum annales. Omnibus tamen eius praeclaris
facinoribus praetermissis, inscriptionem sepulchri, quod uiuens ipse sibi
posuit, solum memorabo, quo cetera facilius diuines:
"Sardanapalus Anaxindaxaris filius Anachialem et Tarsum una die
condidi. Ede, bibe, lude: et quando te mortalem noris,
                              praesentibus exple
deliciis animum. [40v] Post mortem nulla uoluptas.
Nanque ego sum puluis, qui nuper tanta tenebam.

memory the deeds of our ancestors, and if they had recalled the histories of earlier men, Continence would soon be deprived of the possession she does not deserve and severely punished for intruding into someone else's fortunes.

As I said, I do not complain that such a judge has been assigned to me. I know his fairness and do not doubt that his judgment will be just; but I take it very ill that they had doubts about my rights when they saw me laid low and cast out. I could at this point very easily resort to extolling and proclaiming my glory and fame, if it related to the case, and if it were permitted me to resort to my own praises without the stigma of insolence.

For who more truly could boast about her country and parents? Eve gave birth to me in Paradise when, seduced by her lust for eating, she plucked the apple. Noah did well by me when he was overcome and put to sleep by wine. But (you will say) things that happen once in life and contain some kind of lurking mystery[11] ought not to be used as examples. But it does not please me, nor is it fitting, to boast about how much good comes forth for mortals from my pursuits and customs. The matter [40r] speaks plainly for itself. All my pupils and followers are vigorous in spirit and strong in body. They are healthy and fat; their cheeks are red; their eyes sparkle; they are cheerful, they laugh, they compose songs, they toss off witty sayings; their wit is at the ready; they are full of strength.

But let us pass over them, and let my speech return to the establishment of my possession. Who is unaware that at one time kings and princes were always subject to me, and that nobles of all ages were not lacking to serve me, and in no hidden manner, but quite openly? Moreover, there were few Christians — and now there are even fewer, and during this Bacchanalian festival virtually none — who opposed me. I will be brief with my examples, so as not to tire you out.

Sardanapalus, king of Assyria,[12] was a man born to magnify me and my dignity and glory. The annals of those times are witness to the zeal with which he worshipped me, and to how he was consecrated to my vows. Nevertheless, passing over all of his very famous deeds, I will only speak of the inscription on the tomb that he built for himself while he was still alive. From this you will more easily guess everything else:

> I, Sardanapalus, son of Anaxindaxar, founded
> Anachialis and Tarsus in a single day. Eat,
> drink, play; and since you know you are mortal,
> fill up your soul with the delights of the present.
> [40v] there is no pleasure after death. for I am

---

[11] Eve: *Gen.* 3,6; Noah: *Gen.* 9,21. The finding of 'lurking mysteries' in interpreting Scripture is common to medieval and renaissance biblical exegesis. For a single example see Erasmus 1984, pp. 68-69.

[12] Legendary king of Assyria (822 B. C.), emblem of sinful weakness. Aristotle in *Nicomachean Ethics* 1, 5, 3 says the mass of mankind, who prefer the slavish life of cattle, can use the example of Sardanapalus in support of their view.

Haec habeo quae edi, quaeque exsaturata libido
hausit: at illa manent multa et praeclara relicta.

Qualis ego tum eram illo regnante, quam ab omnibus culta uenerata
dilecta? Sed nescio quid uos obmurmuratis: fauete linguis. Alexandro
Magno quis audeat derogare? Ille quidem Magnus Alexander, qui totum
orbem subegit, numquid mihi non aliquando seruiuit? Qui mero quandoque madens irruebat in amicos uirtutem praedicantes meisque repu-
gnantes studiis: quem quidem, si peruenisset ad senectutem, persuase-
ram plane mihi meis in amplexibus bellorum curas et labores,
negotiorumque molestias leuaturum mihique templa dicaturum. Quid
commemorem classicos multos philosophos et in his Epicurum, qui
parum quidem abfuit, quin mortales omnes in eam opinionem adduceret,
ut praeter unam uoluptatem, cuius ego sum filia, nihil esset in uita hominum expetendum? Quandoquidem affirmabat solam uoluptatem hominem efficere beatum atque felicem. Sed insurrexerunt postea diuersis
aetatibus argutuli quidam, qui eius sententiam improbarent et tan-[41r]-
dem efficerent, ne [non] ab omnibus reciperetur. Reiicitur tamen uerbis
magis quam re: quoniam ut uere dicam, plures habet assertores Epicurus
meus quam argutatores Stoici, quamuis contionatores nunc clamitent et
reges minentur quaestiones. Sed omittamus philosophos, quorum ego
concertationes, etiam cum uirtutem praedicant, nihil facio. Scio quid
uere sentiant, quid secum remotis arbitris probent et exsequantur.

dust who recently possessed so much. I have what I
ate; my lust has drained as much as it could hold;
but those many outstanding possessions of mine have
been left behind and remain.[13]

Oh, how I lived when he was king! How I was worshipped, revered, loved!
But you are all grumbling about something. Mind your tongues![14] Who would
dare to disparage Alexander the Great? But that very Alexander the Great who
subdued the whole world, do you suppose that he didn't serve me now and
again? Why from time to time, when he was unsteady with wine, he would
attack his friends for preaching virtue and for opposing my pursuits.[15] Certainly
if he had lived to old age, I would have persuaded him to lie in my embraces
and ease the cares and labors of war and the annoyances of his troubles, and to
dedicate temples to me.

Why dwell on the many classical philosophers, and among them Epicurus?
He came close to attracting all mortals to the opinion that beside pleasure alone
(whose daughter I am) there was nothing in human life which should be sought
after. For, indeed, he kept affirming that pleasure alone made human life happy
and blessed. But afterwards, certain clever speakers, of different epochs, rushed
in to show their disapproval of his opinion, and finally [41r] they brought it
about that he was not accepted by all.[16]

Yet he is rejected more in words than in deeds, since, to speak the truth, my
friend Epicurus has more defenders than the Stoics have clever speakers,[17]
although demagogues are now starting to shout and kings are threatening
inquiries. But let us pass over the philosophers. I have no use for their battles of
words, even when they are preaching virtue. I know what they really think, what
they approve and pursue when all witnesses are absent.[18]

---

[13] Maldonado may have found the last two lines of the inscription on Sardanapalus's
tomb in Cicero, *Tusculan Disputations*, 5, 35, 101; or Athenaeus, *The Philosophers at Dinner*, 8, 335-336. Part of Maldonado's version scans as dactylic hexameters. There are textual
variations. Cicero reads *iacent*, "lie in ruins" where Maldonado reads *manent*, "remain."
Both Latin authors read *relicta*, "left" where Athenaeus reads λέλυνται, "dissolved."

[14] Maldonado clearly indicates the public's negative reaction to Gluttony's defense of
Sardanapalus.

[15] Alexander, in a drunken rage, murdered his friend Clitus, who was himself tipsy
with wine. The antecdote was probably known by Maldonado through Plutarch's *Life of
Alexander* (50, 1-51, 11) or the biography by Quintius Curtius Rufus (*History of Alexander*, 8, 1, 22-52).

[16] The slanders against Epicurus by rival philosophers began in his own lifetime; see
Diogenes Laertius, *Lives of the Philosophers*, 10, 3-8. It was a common misconception
about Epicurus to consider him a voluptuary. See Cicero, *Tusculan Disputations*, e.g., 2,
7, 18; 3, 17, 37.

[17] The Stoics put a great emphasis on dialectic; cf. Diogenes Laertius, *Lives*, 7, 55-83.
Cicero in *Tusculan Disputations* 2, 28-29 complains that Stoics construct foolish syllo-
gisms to prove their points.

[18] This attack on philosophers parallels Erasmus, *Praise of Folly* (Erasmus 1986),
pp. 125-126. For Maldonado's Erasmian roots, see M. Bataillon 2002, and Colahan and
Rodríguez 1995, pp. 289-311.

Omnibus aetatibus usque ad Augustum Caesarem nullum habui hostem quem non facile uincerem cunctando. Nam etsi annos aliquot praeualebant nonnulli, paulatim uel eorum morte, uel aliquo stratagemate meorum uictrix ego regiones et oppida, si quae desciuerant, recuperabam.

Verum Augusto regnante ingens et horrida mihi calamitas repente suborta est. Christus Iesus Dei filius (quid manifesta negemus?) in Iudaea natus ex uirgine quidem est. Et sane antequam a diabolo meo patrono tentaretur in deserto, non eram omnino certa hostem mihi futurum, sed sapienti grauique illo responso perculsa, statim fugere decreui. Sum in Asia nata; et, quamuis soleo percurrere cunctas nationes, frequentius ibi agere [41v] consueui; tum uero praesagiens, quid sibi uellet Deum fieri hominem, abnegata patria, Romam contendi, ubi uitia libidinesque omnes rerum fastigia tenebant. Nam Catilina, uitiorum omnium receptaculum, paulo fuerat mihi ante subtractus. M. Antonius qui cum Augusto primo partitus imperium, si Cleopatra non in Actiaca pugna impedimento fuisset, solum imperium tenuisset, ad mortem compulsus. Bone Deus, qui uir mihi perit Antonius, qui uentri deditus et Veneri, diuitias ingentes uectigaliaque passim et undique continentia in dapibus exquisiti saporis perquirendis, deuehendis, et concinnandis insumebat, profundebat, dilapidabat!

Lucullus, deliciae quidem decusque meum dulce, non ante multo obierat; qui diuitias quas habebat maximas et gazam immensam, quam ex Asia uictoque Mithridate reuexerat, in extruendis domibus uillis hortisque, cum cenationibus amoenissimis, et in cenis opiparis conuiuiisque magnificis, et epulis uix credendis insumebat ac disperdebat. Ex una tamen cena raptim duobus amicis parata, reliquos eius incredibiles

In every age up to that of Caesar Augustus I had no enemy whom I did not easily conquer by delay. For even if some of them dominated for a considerable number of years, gradually, either by their death or by some strategem of my people, I prevailed and recovered whatever regions and towns had been unfaithful to me.

But when Augustus was ruling, a huge and horrible calamity suddenly rose up against me. Christ Jesus, the son of God (why should we deny what is manifest?) was indeed born in Judea of a virgin. And to be sure, before he was tempted in the wilderness by the devil, my patron, I was not completely sure that he would be an enemy to me; but stunned by that wise and serious answer of his, I at once decided to escape. I was born in Asia, and, although I am accustomed to traveling though all the nations, I used to spend [41v] time there more frequently. But then, foreseeing what it meant that God became man, I rejected my country and headed for Rome, where all the vices and lusts of the world had reached a pinnacle.[19] For Catiline, that container of all vices,[20] had a little time earlier been taken away from me. Mark Antony (who at first shared power with Augustus), who, if Cleopatra had not been a hindrance in the battle of Actium,[21] would have held power alone, was driven to his death.

Good God, what a man I lost in Antony! He was dedicated to his belly and to sex.[22] He spent, he poured out, he squandered huge fortunes and tributes — which were continually heaped on him from all sides — in seeking out, bringing together, and neatly arranging banquets of exquisite taste.

Lucullus, who was certainly my delight and my sweet glory, had died not long before. He spent and squandered the great riches which he had and the immense treasure that he had brought back from Asia after his victory over Mithridates,[23] in the construction of homes, villas and gardens, along with very pleasant dining-halls, rich dinners, magnificent parties, and banquets which can scarcely be believed. Yet you will be able to judge the rest of his incredible expenditures from a single meal prepared at the last minute for two friends.

[19] Maldonado here echoes Juvenal's lament about the vices of his age in *Satires*, 1, 149.

[20] There is a similarly hyperbolic description of the conspirator Catiline in Sallust, *Catiline*, 14, 1-4.

[21] In fact Antony himself was ineffective at the Battle of Actium, and fled even though his land army was still intact, according to Plutarch, *Life of Mark Antony*, 66, 1-68, 3.

[22] Maldonado follows Cicero's depiction of Antony as debauched, e.g. *Philippics*, 2, 25, 63.

[23] Lucullus, consul in 74 B.C., defeated Mithridates VI in the Third Mithridaic War and, after acquiring great wealth in Asia, devoted himself to his luxurious tastes; Plutarch describes some of his extravagances in *Life of Lucullus*, 39.

sumptus existimare licebit. Quodam [42r] die cum iam eum taederet reipublicae grandem natu, Cicero et Pompeius sedentem in foro otiosum uiderunt salutatoque dixerunt cenaturos eo die apud eum, modo nihil ad solitam cenam adderet. Ille cum neque impetraret ut in posterum diem cena reiceretur nec ut famulis in aurem aliquid imperaret, solum obtinuit ut uni ex seruis diceret, apud Apollinem (cenationis erat nomen) se uelle cenare. Famuli quid uellet gnari, cenam continuo apparauerunt impendio mille ducentorum et quinquaginta aureorum, quod plane Ciceronem et Pompeium stupefecit.

Fuerant etiam iam extincti multi non minus de meis studiis laudandi, quam de bellicis et ciuilibus. Sed iniquis spatiis interclusae non dabitur praescriptum tempus praeterire: proptereaque de tribus aut quattuor imperatoribus Romanis si pauca prius dixero, pergam ad reliqua.

Tiberius Caesar tenebat imperium cum Romam tum temporis ego ueni. Pro caelestia numina! qui uir erat ille, quam pius in me, quam amans uoluptatum, quam deliciis omnibus delibutus, quam edax, quam bibax, quam uorax, quam uirtutis inimicus et per-[42v]-tinacissimus hostis! Quis teneat risum tali memoria? Biberium pro Tiberio appellabant multi per iocum nec immerito quidem. Genitus uidebatur ad uina per-denda libidinesque portentosas comminiscendas et exercendas. Quis mecum tunc auderet contendere? Continentia scilicet, quae quidem cum suo grege in lucem non ausa prodire, fugiebat conspectum hominum et in cauernis totos dies et noctes latitabat. Nullus apud principem plus eo tempore ualebat, quam qui nouas excogitare uoluptates calleret et in exercendis esset ingeniosus.

Hunc imperatorem secutus est Caligula libidinibus omnibus coopertus ac contaminatus; qui si non breui fuisset e medio sublatus, mihi rerum habenas permisisset, quoniam erat in gulam (ut cetera sileam) ita pronus et affectus perdite, ut mecum uiuere maxime cuperet, mecum congredi, mecum perpetuo commorari.

De Claudio si minus dixero, iniuriam illi fecero, quandoquidem libi-dines Caligulae sic studuit superare, ut qui persuaderet sibi solum id esse

On a certain [42r] day, when he was already growing weary of the Republic, and was getting on in years, Cicero and Pompey saw him sitting in the forum at his leisure. After greeting him they said that they would have dinner at his house that day provided that he added nothing to his customary meal. They refused his requests that the meal be postponed until the next day and that he be allowed to whisper some command in the ear of his household slaves. He only obtained their permission to say to one of his slaves that he wanted to dine at Apollo, the name of a dining-hall. His household slaves knew what he wanted. At once they prepared a meal at the cost of 1, 250 gold coins. This completely astonished Cicero and Pompey.[24]

Moreover, there were many other men, already dead, who were praiseworthy as much for following my pursuits as for their civil and military exploits. But it will not be granted me, impeded by unequal intervals of time,[25] to go over the designated period. Consequently, I will say a few things first about three or four Roman emperors, then proceed to the remaining things.

Tiberius Caesar held power at the very time that I came to Rome. By the heavenly powers, what a man he was! As dutiful to me as he was a lover of pleasures, soaked in every kind of refinement, a glutton, a drunkard, an open maw, he was likewise hostile to virtue, [42v] and its most deadly enemy. Who could fail to laugh at such a memory? Many, as a joke, used to call him Biberius, drunkard, instead of Tiberius, and with good reason. He seemed to have been born for the consumption of wine and for the mingling together and practice of unnatural lusts.[26]

Who dared compete with me then? Continence did. Yet she and her herd did not dare come forth into the light. With them she used to flee from the sight of men and hide for entire days and nights in caves.[27] No one prevailed with the emperor more at that time than anyone who knew how to think up new pleasures and was ingenious in their performance.

This emperor was followed by Caligula, a man sunk in every kind of lust and contaminated by it. If he had not been removed from among us in a short time, he would have handed over to me the reins of the world. For (not to mention everything else) he was so prone and perversely inclined toward gluttony, that he wanted most of all to live with me, and meet with me, and spend all his time with me.[28]

If I spend less time talking about Claudius, I will do him an injustice. For he was actually so eager to outdo the lusts of Caligula, that he even persuaded

---

[24] Narrated by Plutarch, *Life of Lucullus*, 41.

[25] Gluttony appears to complain of being granted less time than Continence.

[26] Gluttony's slanderous portrait of Tiberius comes from Suetonius, who tells the joke about 'Biberius' at *Tiberius*, 42, 1, and describes the emperor's sexual perversions in 43-44.

[27] Probable reference to the Christian catacombs.

[28] In listing the many vices of Gaius Caligula, Suetonius does not place any emphasis on his gluttony, but does record that he would drink pearls dissolved in vinegar and serve his guests loafs and meats of gold (*C. Caligula*, 37, 1).

regnare, ganeam priorum imperatorum aemulari et ab eorum eiusmodi studiis non discedere.

Iam Nero meus amasius, mea uera uo-[43r]-luptas, quibus uerbis digne praedicabitur a me? Qui tanto studio conatus est persequi suoque regno exterminare Continentiam, ut per intemperantem furorem Senecam praeceptorem, uirtutum omnium assertorem, mori coegerit, matrem crudeliter ac inhumane occiderit, Petrum et Paulum apostolos Christi interemerit. Nam me Romae agente uenerant illi ex Asia; et eorum aduentum grauiter exhorrueram. Quippe cum audissem Christum a Iudaeis crucifixum suaque sponte carnificibus se obtulisse, percussit ilico animum meum profunda cogitatio. En Deus mori uoluit et ad hoc hominem se fecit. Altissima sunt Dei consilia, culpa primi parentis redimitur et mors morte pensatur.

Quis dubitet malum aliquod parari mihi meisque consortibus? Mutescunt idola, fugantur daemones, sanantur infirmi, mortui suscitantur, pauperculi miracula passim edunt. Quid credam, nisi interitum uitiis mihi familiaribus imminere? Sed cum uidi apostolos trucidatos, et qui uices eorum agere conati sunt, dispergi passimque necari, solabar equidem me, praesertim quod quamuis crescebat numerus Christianorum et quasi grana frumenti uno extincto, quamplurimi [43v] subcrescebant et pullulabant, frequentissima semper erat turba meorum amicorum et clientum.

Nam et imperatores amici numquam mihi per interualla defuerunt. Constantinus me sane deterruit: qui signa magna dedit, orbem ab imperio daemonis uelle uindicare. Quid commemorem terrores quibus sum affecta, cum martyres et uirgines contemnebant tyrannos, mortem appetebant et sustinebant libenti animo cruciatus? Prodigia mirandaque miracula facile sic edebant, ut corpora uiderentur habere caelestia et mentes in Deo fixas. Illo quidem tempore laborabam ego plane nimis anxia, quo tenderet tanta martyrum uirtus atque patientia, quod profundissima Dei consilia lauandum, detergendum, sanandum tanto piorum sanguine pararent. Ceterum quamuis Christiana respublica uigebat et augebatur in dies magis magisque, semper ego cum meis sororibus et matre regnabam ubique. Nulla regio neque ciuitas erat, in qua non ego primates et bonam

himself that ruling consisted entirely of matching the profligacy of previous emperors and of not departing from their pursuits.[29]

Now as for Nero — my sweetheart, my true desire! — [43r], with what words can he be worthily described by me? Why, he tried to persecute Continence and drive her out of his kingdom, with so much eagerness that in his intemperate fury he forced his teacher, Seneca, the pursuer of every virtue, to die. He killed his mother in cruel and inhuman fashion.[30] He put to death Peter and Paul, the apostles of Christ. For when I was dwelling in Rome, they had come from Asia, and I deeply trembled at their arrival. Indeed, when I had heard the news that Jesus Christ was crucified by the Jews and that he had offered himself to the executioners of his own free will, a deep thought struck my mind at once. See how God was willing to die, and not only that, but he made himself man. How deep are the plans of God: the sin of the first parent is redeemed, and death repaid by death.[31]

Who could doubt that some trouble was in store for me and my associates? Idols grew dumb; demons were routed; the sick were healed; the dead were raised; the humble poor performed miracles at every turn. What was I to believe except that destruction was threatening the vices that are customary to me? But when I saw the apostles cut down and saw those who tried to take their place scattered and killed far and wide, I found some consolation, especially since, although the number of Christians continued to rise — and like a grain of wheat, when one is snuffed out, a huge number [43v] start to grow up and increase —, the crowd of my friends and clients was always very great.

For emperors could be found from time to time, too, who were my friends. Constantine certainly discouraged me. He gave considerable indications that he wanted to win the world away from the power of the demon.[32] How can I tell you about the terrors with which I was assaulted when martyrs and virgins scorned tyrants, when they sought out death, accepting crucifixion with a pleasant disposition, when they easily performed amazing miracles, in such a way that they seemed to have heavenly bodies and minds fixed on God? Certainly at that time I was struggling, so very anxious about where this great virtue and patience of the martyrs was leading. What were the deep plans of God preparing to wash away, to wipe off and to heal by so great a flow of pious blood?

And yet, though the Christian republic thrived and increased more and more, day after day, I always kept reigning everywhere, along with my sisters and mother. There was no region and no state in which I did not have control over

---

[29] Suetonius records that Claudius was eager for food and wine at all times and in all places (*Diuus Claudius*, 33, 1).

[30] Tacitus describes the death of Seneca (*Annales,* 15, 63-64), Nero's murder of his mother Agrippina (*Annales*, 14, 8), and his persecution of Christians (presumably including Peter and Paul) after the great fire of Rome in 64 (*Annales*, 15, 38-19, 44).

[31] Death, the penalty for the first man's sin, is paid for by the death of the God-man redeemer, restoring immortality to man.

[32] Constantine adopted and legalized Christianity by the Edict of Milan, 313.

plebis partem tenerem. Nam et Magmes siue Mahumetes ut uos appella-
tis, quantum mihi populum acquisiuit, lucrifecit, subiecit, per Africam,
Asiam et partem Europae? Atque [44r] ut alios magni nominis sileam,
eius alumnus Solimanus Turca qualis est mihi nunc amicus? Quantum
pro [me] meaque gloria retinenda laborat, qui cum late regnet in Asia,
dispulit Christianos ex parte non contemnenda Europae? Equidem illi
debeo, quod Carolus Caesar non exegerit ex Europa parteque Africae
meas copias, meos amicos, et perpetuo foedere deuinctos.

De Carolo moderatius loquemur et cautius, quod agimus in suo
regno; quamuis ille nescio quid mali quotidie machinatur meis sodali-
bus et amicis. Pax, cui semper intendit belligerando, bellum mihi
meisque minatur. Sed interim plures mihi seruiunt etiam in suo regno,
quam illi. Dominatur ille quidem in corporibus, mentes et corda ego plerumque possideo. Verset fortuna suas uices, ut solet, mutationes rerum
inducat, semper mihi parent mortales plerique. Populus Christianus
numerosissimus est, qui mecum ex diametro pugnat, cum uiuit Chris-
tiane. Ceterum maior pars non ita suis legibus est astricta, quin saepe-
numero uoluptati genitrici meae prosternatur. Itaque meum regnum late
diffunditur adhuc. Nam si desciscunt alicubi quidam, ali-[44v]-bi multi
deduntur. Magmetes omnes teneo, Germanos et Anglos propemodum,
reliquos Christianos non equidem fatebor inimicos mihi. Nam etsi
concionatores multique uiri pii clamitant, minantur, deterrent non minus
ab honestis oblectationibus, quam a turpibus (ut ipsi aiunt) uoluptatibus,
tanta uis est in nobis, tantus alliciendi uigor et calliditas, ut plerosque
habeamus deuinctos. Sum familiaris iam admodum Christianis (ut hoc
te, iudex, non fugiat) et eorum festos dies maxime probo, quod sacris
peractis, statim omnes me complectuntur, arrident, sauiant mecumque
ludere gaudent.

the leading citizens and a good part of the common people. For even Magmes[33] — or Mahumet, as you call him — how great a population did he not acquire to enrich me and subject to me throughout Africa, Asia and part of Europe?

And [44r] not to mention other men of great reputation, his pupil Soliman, the Turk, what a friend he is of mine now! And how he works to maintain me and my glory! He has a large kingdom in Asia and he has driven the Christians out of a considerable part of Europe. In fact, I owe to him that Emperor Carlos has not driven my forces, my friends, who are bound to me by perpetual treaty, out of Europe and part of Africa.[34]

Concerning Carlos we shall speak more moderately and cautiously, as we are in his kingdom. Even so, every day he plots some sort of trouble against my companions and friends. The peace toward which he always aims in his war-making threatens me and my people with war. But in the meantime, more people serve me, even in his kingdom, than do him. He certainly dominates over bodies; I, for the most part, possess minds and hearts.[35]

Let Fortune make her changes as she usually does, let her introduce every kind of variation in the world; but most mortals always obey me. The Christian population is very numerous, and they fight on the opposite side, against me, when they live as Christians. But most of them are not so tightly bound to their own laws that they fail to bow, time and again, before Pleasure, my mother. And so my kingdom continues to be very widespread. For even if some do abdicate, now and again, many [44v] others surrender to me. I possess all the Muslims and almost all the Germans and English.[36] As for the remaining Christians, I will not indeed admit that they are hostile to me. For even if public speakers and many pious men keep shouting, threatening and scaring people as much away from honest diversions as from (to use their expression) shameful plea-sures, there is so much strength in us, so great a power of seduction, and such shrewdness, that we have most people under our sway. I am already extremely familiar with Christians (make sure that this doesn't escape you, judge), and, for the most part, I approve very heartily of their festive days, when, having per-formed their holy ceremonies, they all at once embrace me, smile at me, kiss me. They rejoice at playing with me.[37]

---

[33] Maldonado's allusion to Muhammed as 'Magmes" and (below) his followers as 'Magmetes" may be a conscious fusion of Mohammed, founder of Islam, and Manes (or Mani; Latinized as Manichaeus), the legendary founder of Manicheism, a sect that com-peted with early Christianity. Alternatively, he may allude to the Greek word μάγοι, which became *madjus* in Arabic, referring to the Zoroastrians.

[34] For Carlos V's constant wars against Soliman, the Turkish sultan, in Europe, and against Barbarossa, the Berber pirate, in Africa, see P. de Sandoval 1955-1956, II-III. Erasmus was councillor to the future Carlos V and dedicated his *Education of a Christian Prince* to him (1516).

[35] Maldonado is critical of his own Spain.

[36] Maldonado refers to Protestant Europe.

[37] Maldonado is critical of the gluttonous aspects of Christian feasts. The gluttony of the clergy was ridiculed by Erasmus, e.g. *Praise of Folly* (Erasmus 1986, pp. 131-132).

Quare grauis est mihi hodie impacta contumelia quod inter quos iam dudum amicos agnosco, et diebus mihi sacris sum bello petita meoque foro depulsa. Frustra quidem laborassem, iudex, commemorando, quae sunt a me tuo in conspectu relata, si docere aut monere te constituissem. Nosti quae sunt dicta, facta, cogitata non minus ab orbe condito quam, ut Christianorum est sermo, ab orbe redempto; et ita quidem nosti, ut habeas apud te iam damnata quae sunt iniusta, probata uero aequa. Ceterum non mihi consilium fuit monere te, sed hos [45r] quidem docere, qui me forte non uiderunt prostratam, et ad iudicium spectandum conuenerunt, ut simul et ipsi causam intelligant, et cum te uiderint iudicantem, et causam meam aequam pronuntiantem, sciant, quibus rationibus ductus iuste sancteque iudicaueris. Dixi.

Chorus bacchantium

Sint procul hinc graues, discedant longe seueri, Bacchanalibus concedant morosi: sua sunt tempora rebus. Orgia nunc facimus Maenades, Bacchae, Mimallones, Chiae simul cum Satyris, Tityris et Silenis. De Libero male sentiunt, qui nos obturbant. Io Bacche, Liber, io tua canimus praeconia. Tu nobis Morychus et Adoneus, tu Lyaeus, Lenaeus et Erebinthius: cur non etiam eris nobis Sabazius, Scythites et Milichius? Nomina tua nobis lingua quacumque placent. Tu nobis adsis uinumque propines merum, purum, taurinum, uel potius hoc anno uinis infausto, uetus Samartinum. Dabis tuis, si uis orgia esse laeta, mera meracissima,

Consequently, the insult that has been forced on me today is hard to bear; for while among those whom I have known as friends for a long time and in a period that is sacred to me, I was attacked bellicosely and driven away from my own forum. I would have certainly labored in vain, judge, in reporting all the things that have been related by me in your presence if I had intended to teach or advise you. You know what has been said, done and thought about since the creation of the world as well as (to use a Christian term) since the redemption of it; and you know it well enough to bear in mind things already condemned, which are unjust, and things approved, which are just.[38] But it was not my plan to advise you, but rather [45r] to teach these, who perhaps did not see me laid low and have come together to view the trial, so that they too may understand the case, so that when they have seen you standing in judgment and delivering a verdict in my just case, they may know by what considerations you have been influenced when you deliver a judgment in a righteous and holy manner. I have spoken.

Chorus of Revellers

Let the stern stay far from here. Let the strict go far away. Let the gloomy give way to the revellers. Everything has its own season. We are now holding Bacchic orgies, we Maenads, Bacchae, Bacchantes, Chians,[39] together with Satyrs, Tityrians,[40] and Sileni.[41] Those who disturb us have a wrong opinion of Liber.[42]

Io Bacchus! Io Liber! It is your proclamation that we sing. You for us are Morychus and Adoneus;[43] you are Lyaeus, Lenaeus and Erebinthius.[44] Why shouldn't you also be to us Sabazius, Scythites and Milichius?[45] Your names are pleasing to us in any language. Be present with us; serve us wine, unmixed, pure, from Toro! Or rather, in this year not propitious for wines, some old San Martín.[46] Grant to your people, if you are willing, that your orgies be happy and

---

[38] Gluttony's plea that established, accepted, norms (such as carnival itself) be respected may well reflect Maldonado's Erasmian wish to re-spiritualize certain traditional aspects of Catholicism.

[39] Chians: inhabitants of Isle of Chios, famous for their licentious lifestyle.

[40] Tityrians: generic name for shepherds, from Virgil, *Eclogues*, 8.55.

[41] Sileni: creatures that were part human and part horse.

[42] Liber: Roman equivalent of Bacchus. The name is evidently used here partly for the sake of playing on the meaning of "free." Compare also the praise of Bacchus (who can "free the mind from care") in Erasmus' *Praise of Folly* (Erasmus 1986, p.119).

[43] Morychus and Adoneus: epithets used for Dionysus/Bacchus.

[44] Lyaeus, Lenaeus and Erebinthius: synonyms for Dionysus/Bacchus.

[45] Sabazius, Scythites and Milichius: Sabazius, an Eastern Dionysus-like god, later fused with Dionysus/Bacchus (see Dodds 1986, Introduction, p. xxiii); Scythites, northern barbarians to the Greeks, famous for heavy drinking (see Dodds 1986, Introduction, p. xxi); Milichius, legendary Iberian king.

[46] The wines from the areas of Toro and San Martín were apparently those preferred in Burgos, because Maldonado makes reference to them in other writings. See, for example, his *Ludus Chartarum Triumphus* (this volume, pp. 50-51).

quae praecordia calfaciant, mentes exhilarent. Quid sibi uult Continentia? A-[45v]-beat malum in profundum tenebrarum. Baccho Genioque litamus. Maleuoli discedant. Quid opus iudicio? Taceat iudex, dissimulet, coniueat, uel nobiscum ludos ludat, et Bacchanalia, cantitans «Euoe, Liber, Euoe, Bacche, tua facimus orgia, tibi litamus, tibi nos deuouemus et consecramus».

Accensus

Conticeant omnes iam tandem; cessent bacchantes. Ingluuies egit causam suam satis cum silentio. Mimallones et Satyri debacchati sunt omnino libere; Continentia nunc audiatur et ei silentium idem praestetur, quo Iudex utriusque cognita causa ferat ex aequo sententiam.

Continentiae oratio

Si tua singularis aequitas, uenerande iudex, et in dignoscendis hominibus perspicax iudicium iam olim omnibus notum non esset, uerecundius mihi sane cederet cum hac bestia uel potius immani fera contendisse. [46r] Non enim mulier iudicanda est, quae sepulta ratione bonos omnes abiurauit affectus et in gulae uentrisque sentinam sese praecipitauit. Sed quia cognita tibi satis haec est, et quibus artibus irretiat mortales intelligis, breuissime quae perperam exaggerauit in me confutabo.

Tu iam pridem nosti me et quem in finem mei tendant conatus haud ignoras. Solummodo restat ut haec cristas ponere cogatur, et commentum, quo usa est in dicendo, fuisse uanum et ad praedicandas et extollendas suas sordes foedasque cogitationes effictum, luce clarius appareat. Dixit irruisse me cum satellitibus in suos populares et familiam solitis uoluptatibus indulgentem. O saecula, o mores, o socordiam magistratuum! Iactor nunc, deturbor, propellor cum bonis omnibus a perditissima turba ganeonum; et dux eorum haec uiuit? Et non modo uiuit, sed in lucem prodire audet atque in conspectum tanti iudicis uenire? Quid dixi uenire? Immo cum fiducia uerba facere suasque turpitudines et foeda flagitia praedicare! Sed omittamus querellas: rem ipsam, quando te non esse deceptum certo scio, tractemus.

Venisse me in forum Bacchanalibus et ipsam uulnerauisse fami-[46v]-liamque fugasse conqueritur et lamentatur. O pestis hominum acerba,

that the wine be purer than pure. Let it heat up everyone's breast and bring joy to their minds. What is Continence up to? [45v] Let her get the hell out of here, to the lowest depths of the infernal regions. We make our offerings to Bacchus and Genius. Let ill-wishers begone. Why is there need for a trial? Let the judge keep silent; let him conceal the truth or connive; or rather, let him sport with us, join the orgies, singing over and over: "Evoe, Liber, evoe, Bacchus!, it is your orgy that we celebrate. To you we pay homage, to you we devote and consecrate ourselves."

Accensus

Quiet, everyone! Be quiet at last! Let the revelers settle down. When Gluttony pleaded her case there was silence enough. The Bacchantes and Satyrs have finished their wild revel with complete freedom. Let Continence now be heard, and let us grant her the same silence, so that when both sides have presented their case, the judge may reach a fair decision.

Speech of Continence

Oh, venerable judge!, if your unique fairness and your keen perception in judging men had not already been well known to all, this task imposed on me would have surely caused me greater shame. I mean, competing with this animal, or should I say this monstrous wild beast. [46r] For how can she be judged a woman when she lulls reason to sleep, renounces all good emotions, and hurls herself into the cesspool of the maw and the belly?

But since she is already well known to you, and you understand the tricks by which she snares the human race, I will very briefly refute her false exaggerations against me. You have known me for a long time, and you are well aware of the goal toward which my efforts aim. This only remains: that she be forced to lower her crest and that it appear brighter than day that the lie that she used in her speech was in vain and was invented to advance and extol her own foul and filthy schemes.

She claimed that I rushed forward with my retinue against her followers and family when they were indulging in their customary pleasures. Oh, what an age, what customs! Oh, the laziness of the magistrates! I am tossed about, battered, thrown out along with all good people by this depraved gang of gluttons; and she, their leader, lives? Not only lives, but dares to come forward into the light and in view of so great a judge?[47] Why did I say 'to come forward'? No, rather to cheat good faith and preach her own foul and shameful practices. But let us leave aside our complaints. We will deal with reality itself, since I know for certain that you have not been deceived.

She laments and complains that I came into the forum during the festival, wounded her, [46v] and chased away her family. Oh, bitter plague of the human

---

[47] The last sentences echo the opening of Cicero's *First Catilinian Oration* (1, 2).

non uereris hoc dicere iudicisque ueracis aures mendacio tam impudenti diuerberare? Veni quidem in forum hodierna die, sicuti quotidie soleo non in forum modo, sed in omnes urbis uicos et plateas, et comitata paucis sum forum ingressa. Ratio, ueritas et prudentia me praecedebant; fides et caritas dextrum latus claudebant; sinistrum metus et spes; pone sequebantur integritas et constantia. Irruisse me dicit. Suspenso quidem, ut soleo, gradu processi; cumque me prospectaret huius acies postrema, poenitentia plerique ducti, quod barbare despicientem et ignauam fuissent secuti, concurrerunt ad me, uerecundantur et tacent; cupiunt et assentatione tacita prorsus efflagitant ab huius contubernio, in quod inciderant imprudentes, uindicari; quare blandiuntur et operam suam pollicentur. Socors Ingluuies uidens me turba cinctam, cum adipe maderet et uino, putauit, qui mihi ex suis adhaeserant, meos esse commilitones, atque clamoribus urbem commouet, ciues concitat et ipsa praecedens aggreditur in me. Cum uero in rationem et ueritatem prius incurrisset [47r] imprudens, stimulis conscientiae perculsa uinoque supplantata corruit amens; et paulo post erecta clamitat a me fuisse uulneratam, quam solam prae stupore mentisque caligine uidebat, quippe quae mecum graues gerat simultates, et propterea meas germanas neque satis uidit neque pili quidem fecit. Contrudit in me perditos omnes et ni magistratus commodum interuenissent, pessimum fuisset facinus patratum.

Ad confirmationem huiusce rei testibus non erat opus apud iudicem rerum scientem. Produxi tamen locupletissimos iam aliquot praesentaboque alium, si per te, iudex, licuerit; et quando petit Ingluuies suum quendam annosum audiri in hoc coetu, non quem morbus solum detinuit et quem ipsa denuo struxit ad mendacia confingenda, meus item non minus annosus in hoc solum adesse testimonio permittatur, ut refellat quae fuerint ei comperta mera esse mendacia. Haec ipsa fatetur me sine telo fuisse percussamque nullo apparente mucrone. Quod est ualidissimum argumentum delirasse prius et nunc penitus insanire, cum fateatur quod maxime facit contra se measque partes fulcit atque confirmat. Ratio, ueritas scelerumque [47u] conscientia perturbauerunt ipsam. Nam et magistratus idipsum animaduertentes, ad te nos, iudex integerrime, miserunt, ut dum illi urbem percurrunt, et a seditionibus, quas excitat huius diei libertas, perditos ciues auocant, tu tua sententia huius audaciam et temeritatem comprimeres ac suffocares.

Quod ut tu faceres libentius et spectatoribus ego causam meam facilius probarem, possem in laudes et praeconia mea longe discurrere multaque

race! Do you not fear to say this? Are you not afraid to pound on the ears of a truth-telling judge with such an impudent lie? I did indeed come into the forum, as I am accustomed to doing every day, and not only into the forum, but into every district and square of the city. And I entered the forum in the company of a few. Reason, Truth and Prudence walked ahead of me. Faith and Charity protected my right side; Fear and Hope, my left side. Behind there followed Integrity and Constancy. She says that I 'rushed in'. Actually, I moved at a modest pace, as I usually do. When her rearguard had a look at me, most were moved by repentance because, in a barbarous manner, they had followed a lazy fool. They ran toward me, were ashamed and were silent. They desired — and virtually begged in silent agreement — to be set free from the association with her into which they had carelessly fallen. Consequently, they flattered me and promised their help.

Lazy Gluttony, stinking of lard and wine, seeing me surrounded by a crowd, thought that those people of hers who clung to me must be my fellow-soldiers. And so, with shouts, she stirred up the city; she aroused the citizens; and, she herself leading the way, attacked me. But after she had imprudently clashed with Reason and Truth [47r], she was goaded by conscience and, unsteady with wine, she fell down in a fit. A little later, when raised up, she kept shouting that she had been wounded by me, since I was the only one that she could see due to her confusion and mental fog. Moreover, she carries on a serious feud with me, and for that reason she neither saw my sisters nor gave a straw for them. She caused all depraved people to push forward against me, and if the magistrates had not intervened just in time, a terrible crime would have been committed.

To verify this matter, there was no need of witnesses before a judge who is knowledgeable about things. Yet I have already brought with me certain very trustworthy men, and I will present another one, if that is permitted by you, judge, so that, whenever Gluttony wants, her own elderly witness can be heard before this gathering, not only someone who was seized by illness, but someone whom she has prepared well to make up lies. Just the same, my own elderly witness should be permitted to provide testimony for this purpose alone: to show that the things dreamed up by her are nothing but pure lies.

She admits herself that I was without a weapon, and that she was struck although no sword was visible. This is the most compelling proof that she was hallucinating before and that she is now downright mad, when she admits a fact that tells greatly against her and supports and strengthens my side. Reason, Truth [47v] and an awareness of her crimes have confused her. For the magistrates, noticing this very thing, too, sent us to you, oh most upright judge!, so that, while they roam through the city and call depraved citizens away from the quarrels that the freedom of this day encourages, you, by pronouncing your judgment, might check and submit her boldness and rashness.

In order that you might do this more willingly, and that I more easily gain the approval of the spectators for my case, I could discourse at length in praise and celebration of myself. There is certainly a very wide field in which to maneuver,

de me uere praedicare. Spatiosissimus est plane campus ad euagandum, cum innumerabilia fuerint a me generi humano bona profecta malaque simul immensa detracta. Continentes quippe fuerunt, qui pietatem induxerunt, qui de uirtute bonisque moribus praeceperunt, qui bonas artes inuenerunt, qui mortales ad concordiam pellexerunt, qui respublicas instituerunt, qui sancte simul dixerunt et uixerunt. Incontinentes uero impii flagitiosique omnes per quos mala cuncta mundo ingruerunt, uirtutes exulauerunt, sectae penitus detestandae disseminatae longeque propagatae fuerunt, ciuitates et regna penitus interierunt.

Sed haec sunt omnia praetermittenda, cum haec ipsa nega-[48r]-re non possit, me esse bonorum omnium fontem, se uero malorum seminarium. Impudentissimi etiam uidetur oris frontisque perfrictae, multa de se dicere, quae magis iactari putantur ad uelanda, quae non probantur, quam ad explicanda, quae uere si bona sunt, quo magis dissimules, eo magis digna praeconio censentur. Itaque de me, iudex, nihil utique praedicabo; huius de se praedicationes et iactantiam de principibus olim et nunc sibi obnoxiis, ita confutabo, ut tibi perspicuum sit, me non ignorare quanta manauerint mala semper ab hac furia, ipsaque fateatur se iuste fuisse damnatam. Sardanapalum dixit sibi fuisse obsequentem et fidelissimum amicum seque tum temporis diffusissime quidem regnasse. Hoc exemplum sufficere deberet ad hanc perdendam et ex orbe penitus amandandam, quandoquidem inficit mortales omnes, quos semel pellexit, et non modo improbos reddit peiores, sed et bona mente praeditos nonnumquam conturbat et a recto sensu penitus alienat.

O intolerandam procacitatem! Virum ausa est nominare, quo regnante uirtutes omnes in Syria grauiter aegrotarunt interissentque omnino, si non mature fuisset ad mor-[48v]-tem compulsus. Tales enim plerumque sunt homines quales sunt imperantes. Quid pestilentius contingere potuit illi saeculo, quam regem ab hac fuisse penitus eneruatum et omnino corruptum? Iam illa quam iactat inscriptio sepulchri iudicio cunctorum et eius ipsius, si ponat aliquando belluinos affectus, magis bouis sepulchro quam hominis quadrare uidetur. Quod autem praedicat Alexandrum Magnum nonnumquam sibi litasse mero madentem et ebrium, magis in dedecus et

since there have been innumerable benefits to the human race which have emanated from me, and also innumerable evils which I have removed. There have surely been temperate people who have introduced piety, taught about virtue and good character and discovered the good arts, who enticed mortals to reach a state of harmony, who established governments, who not only spoke in a holy manner but also lived so.

But as for intemperate people, they are all sinners and troublemakers. Through them all sorts of evils invaded the world, and virtues went into exile, and cults which were completely detestable were spread abroad and multiplied far and wide.[48] Whole states and kingdoms went down to their doom.

But we can pass all this by, for she herself [48r] cannot deny that I am the source of all good things, whereas she is the seed-bed of evils. Moreover, she appears to put up a very bold front, and has wiped away her blushes; she says a lot about herself, but what she says is intended more as a boast to cover up what is not commonly approved than to explain it. But when it comes to things which are really good, the more you cover them up, the more they are considered worthy of public proclamation.

And so, judge, concerning myself I shall, in any case, assert nothing. But as for her assertions about herself and her boasts about princes who were, then and now, subject to her, I will refute them in such a way that it will be clear to you how aware I am of the enormity of the evils which have always flowed from this Fury; and she herself will be forced to confess that she was justly condemned.

She said that Sardanapalus was her fawning and most faithful friend, and that at that time her rule was at its widest extent. This example ought to be enough to destroy her and banish her completely from the world, since, in fact, she puts her stain on all mortals, once she has seduced them; and not only does she take bad men and make them worse, but sometimes she even confuses those endowed with good minds and completely turns them aside from good opinion. Oh, the unbearable shamelessness! She dared to mention a man under whose rule all the virtues in Assyria came down with a deadly illness and would have completely died off if he had not been driven to death, [48v] and just in time. For most people are pretty much the same as their rulers. What more deadly could have befallen that age than a king to be rendered completely spineless and thoroughly corrupted by her? As for the inscription on his tomb that she brags about, in the opinion of all (and in her own opinion, too, if she would ever put aside her bestial appetites), it appears more suited for the tomb of a cow than of a human being.

As for her claim that Alexander the Great sometimes offered sacrifices to her when drunk and soused with wine, that claim redounds more to her shame and

---

[48] This passage perhaps best exemplifies how Maldonado — like religious thinkers of all ages — uses Gluttony, the most widespread and ostensible of the sins of incontinence, as primary source and representation of sinfulness in general. Dante, one may recall, fixed incontinence, represented by Gluttony in Maldonado, as one of the three major categories of sin (cf. *Inferno*, 5, 38-40).

ignominiam suam conuertitur, quam in gloriam, quandoquidem praedicat suum, quod in Alexandro fuit turpissimum ac detestandum. Nam uirtutes illius hominis numquam mortalis quisquam adaequasset, si bis aut ter in conuiuiis modum non excessisset et in amicos nimio potu furens desaeuisset.

Haec ipsa de se dicit fateturque flagitia, quorum ob causam erat mundo exterminanda et in barathrum Plutonis detrudenda; quoniam uiri bene nati summaque dexteritate praediti et propterea sua natura ad uirtutem compositi denigrantur ab ea turpiaque facere coguntur. Sed ait impia cum Alexandro regnasse, quia semel aut iterum in uita possederit eum; [49r] et non uidet uirtutis amantem Alexandrum fuisse et bonis omnibus studiis praestantem, eiusque praeceptorem fuisse Aristotelem, qui praeclare quidem de uirtutibus bonisque omnibus disciplinis scripsit; atque paulo ante uixisse Platonem et Socratem, qui tam arcte coluerunt uirtutem, ut pro stercore conculcassent Ingluuiem, si sub oculos aliquando uenisset.

Neque est cur iactet M. Antonium et Lucullum uoluptatibus solum natos fuisse: certis horis tenuit ipsos, et non totos, quod erant natura compositi ad magnanimitatem. Lucullus cenas apparabat magni sumptus ad captandam magis auram popularem et inanem quandam gloriam, quam ut uoracitati penitus inseruiret. Antonius aspirabat ad magnos conatus et culmen honorum; ita tamen capiebatur uino dapibusque selectis, ut interdum deturparet uirtutes eximias, quibus merito posset gloriari. Itaque non minus uiri boni quam illustres ambo censerentur, si penitus hanc, ut decuit, abnegassent et eius pestilentissimas cenas effugissent.

Potuisset tamen Ingluuies etiam inter suos sat uere nominare M. Apicium, altissimum, ut ait quidam, nepotum gurgitem. Sed uerita est ne [49v] supploderetur, quoniam Apicius praeterquam quod libros de gula composuit, auiditate nimia cuiusdam pisculi nauigauit in Africam et cum se deceptum intellexit, de suspendio cogitauit.

Ait tamen habere se uiros et habuisse Christianos sibi non minus deditos quam priores illos ethnicos. Credo equidem maximeque doleo Christianos, quibus ueritas omnis reuelata est, contra leges quandoque diuinas

disgrace than to her glory, since, in fact, she claims as her own the thing that was most shameful and detestable in Alexander. For no one on earth would ever have matched the virtues of that man, were it not for the fact that two or three times he went too far in banquets and made a violent attack on his friends while out of his head with too much drink.[49]

She makes the confession herself, and admits to outrages which are reason for her to be removed from the earth and thrust into the pit of Pluto. For, indeed, men of good birth, men endowed with the highest skills and consequently predisposed to virtue by their nature, are debased by her and forced to do shameful deeds.

But she shared the throne with Alexander, says the evil woman, because she had possession of him once or twice in his life; [49r] and she fails to see that Alexander was a lover of virtue and outstanding in all good pursuits, that his teacher was Aristotle, who wrote in a very commendable manner about virtues and all good disciplines, and that before him lived Plato and Socrates, who so avidly worshipped virtue that they would have stepped on Gluttony as though she were excrement if she had ever come within their sight.

Nor does she have reason to boast that Mark Antony and Lucullus were born for pleasure alone. She possessed them at certain hours, but not their whole beings, because they were predisposed to generosity by nature. Lucullus prepared banquets at great expense more to strive after popular favor and a kind of empty glory than totally to give himself over to his appetite. Antony strove after great accomplishments and the highest honors, yet he was so enticed by wine and exquisite foods that he sometimes debased the outstanding virtues of which he could rightly boast. And so they both would be considered good men, as well as famous, if they had completely rejected this woman, as they should have, and had fled from her most abominable banquets.

Even so, Gluttony would have still been able to truly name among her own people Marcus Apicius, the deepest whirlpool, as someone said, of all her descendants. But she was afraid [49v] that she would be whistled at,[50] since Apicius, aside from the fact that he wrote books about appetite,[51] was moved by his inordinate appetite for some little fish to sail to Africa, and when he realized that he had been deceived, he thought of hanging himself.[52] Nevertheless, she says she has men, and Christians, not less dedicated to her than those earlier pagans. I actually believe, and it grieves me very much, that Christians, to whom all truth has been revealed, sometimes act against divine law and commit

---

[49] On the death of Clitus see above note 15.

[50] In the Hispanic world this is the equivalent of booing.

[51] Marcus Apicius was a gourmet who lived under Tiberius. To him is attributed the cookbook, *De re Coquinaria, Cooking and Dining in Imperial Rome*. Athenaeus, *The Philosophers at Dinner*, 1, 7, relates the anecdote referred to by Maldonado. For the formula "altissimus nepotum gurges", see Pliny, *Natural History*, 10, 133.

[52] According to Seneca, *To Helvia on Consolation*, 10, 8, Apicius committed suicide, by poisoning, when his wealth was reduced to twelve million sestercies.

agere et illa committere, pro quibus mors illis aeterna denuntiata est. Quis enim Christianorum ignorat uoracitati poenam esse perpetuam constitutam a Deo? Et uidemus heu multos primates ab hac ita deceptos, ut gulae cenisque magnificis audaciter indulgeant, posthabito timore poenae, quam deliciis capti saneque oppressi, grauiter ferunt admoneri, tanto fore grauiorem, quanto tardior illis acciderit.

Sed o pernicies hominum Ingluuies, qua tua improbitate, socordia somnoque profundo Christum es ausa nominare, cum eius tu famulos et amicos fallas, inficias omninoque perdas? Fateris Deum, quia negare non potes, et mortem eius intelligis ad eluendam culpam primi parentis obitam et ad redemptionem generis humani diuinitus [50r] superatam; et ita curas pellicere libertos eius ac libertinos, quasi facias nihil, Christiani sint quos perdas, an ethnici, cum ii perditi sint etiam si tu cesses, et illis sola tu sis interdum pereundi causa praecipua? Profecto omnibus in orbe degentibus commodissimum et ualde necessarium est te pestilentissi-mam Hydram impunitam non abire, sed grauiter caesam in terras omni-bus hominibus inaccessas relegari, unde nullus tibi pateat reditus. Et si cunctis mortalibus necessarium, Christianis maxime, quibus maiora peri-cula instant abs te.

Tu etiam, teterrima belua, feras aequo animo damnationem tuam. Nosti quae facinora perpetraueris, quos homines perdideris. Praestabilius multo tibi est fateri culpam et in exilium uoluntarium ire, quam resti-tando committere ut digna censearis, in cuius perniciem et internicionem mundus uniuersus conspiret. Ethnicos multos per omnes aetates tua causa decoxisse penitus ac conturbasse, bene meministi. Nam Christia-nos non queror per te decoxisse tantum, quamuis inde malorum multo-rum principia ducuntur, quam quod alii corpus, alii animam, multi cor-pus et animam per te tuasque [50v] sorores perdiderunt. Quod maxime dolendum est neque amplius tolerandum. Tuam igitur, iudex integer-rime, diuturnitatem, perpetuamque constantiam obtestor, ut causam communem doleas populique Christiani miserearis. Et quando pestis haec contagiosissima conata est hodierna die ciuitatem primo ciuilibus armis, deinde, cum male cederent arma, mendaciis et falsis testimoniis perturbare omniumque animis perpetuam miseramque caliginem offun-dere, tum ipsa de se fateatur scelera damnaque Christianis illata, nullis cruciatibus nullaque morte satis pensanda, saltem ea poena coerceas,

acts for which they have been threatened with eternal death. For what Christian does not know that an eternal punishment for gluttony has been established by God? And we see — alas! — many high churchmen so deceived by her that they boldly indulge in their appetites and magnificent banquets, disregarding the fear of punishment, a punishment that, captivated by pleasure and virtually overwhelmed by it, they resist being sternly warned about, though it will be the more severe the longer it delays happening to them.[53]

But — Oh, Bane of Mankind! — with what wickedness and sloth, and out of what deep sleep, have you dared, Gluttony, to speak the name of Christ, when you yourself are deceiving his servants and friends, corrupting them and completely ruining them? You confess he is God, because you cannot deny him; and you realize that his death was undertaken to wash away the sin of the first parent and also that he overcame death by a miracle [50r] to redeem the human race. And yet do you take pains to entice his redeemed, as well as the unredeemed,[54] as though you don't care whether those whom you destroy are Christian or pagan, on the grounds that they were already ruined even if you did nothing? But you alone are sometimes the main reason for their ruin! Surely for all who dwell on earth it is most convenient, and indeed necessary, that you — you disease-bearing Hydra — that you should not go away unpunished, but be seriously wounded and banished to lands that are inaccessible to all men, from which no return will lie open to you. And if this is necessary for all men, it is especially so for Christians, threatened by you with greater dangers.

You, you most foul beast, actually would calmly endure your own damnation. You know what crimes you have committed and what people you have ruined. It would be much better for you to confess your guilt and go into voluntary exile, rather than to resist, and bring it about that you be deemed worthy of having the entire world plot your destruction and massacre. You well remember that heathens, in every age, have suffered losses and gone bankrupt for your sake. As for the Christians, I am not so much complaining that they have suffered losses through you — although the origins of many evils can be traced to that — as I complain that some have lost their bodies, some their souls, many, both [50v] body and soul, through you. This is much to be lamented and can be endured no longer. Therefore, oh, most honest judge, I plead by your long life and perpetual constancy that you grieve over our common cause and take pity on Christian people. And since this most virulent plague has on this very day made an assault on the state — at first with weapons; then, when weapons did not succeed, tried to cause trouble with lies and false testimony, casting an eternal and wretched dust on the minds of all —, then make her admit, herself, to the crimes and losses perpetrated against Christians, crimes that no crucifixion and no death would be enough to offset. Thus, check her at least with a penalty which

[53] See note 37 above.
[54] Maldonado's contrasted terms, 'libertos'/ 'libertinos,' may play on the Castilian sense of 'libertino' as a defier of Christian ethics: 'libertos'/liberated-redeemed/Christian; 'libertinos'/viceful/pagan.

quae illam perpetuo luce priuet et conspectu mortalium per saecula cuncta releget. Erit enim eiusmodi poena si non par eius consonaque sceleribus ac improbitati, tuae certe sapientiae benignitatique censebitur apta. Dixi.

Chorus prudentium

Procul hinc, procul sint ganeones: uirtutes adsumus, nostrae consulturae, prospecturae, fauturae sorori. Quis umquam uidit? Quis audiuit nec somniauit quidem iudicium [51r] admirandum et inauditum? Ingluuies accusat Continentiam: uirtus agitur rea, uirtuti dicitur dies. Euentus tamen tollet admirationem. Iudex cuncta uidet et cogitat alte. Talis erit sententia, qualis iudicis fides ac integritas. Fugabuntur ignaui, exterminabuntur socordes, perditi ganeones aqua et igni interdicentur, Ingluuies in caecum carcerem contrudetur et ad perpetuas tenebras damnabitur. Plaudite, concinite ciues, ueritas ualeat, iustitia uigeat, impietas relegetur. Ingluuies cum suo paedore praeceps abeat malam in rem.

Tempus iudex; paedor et pudor testes.
Tempus

Quoniam non solum hic agitur de hodierna seditione, quae facilis erat iudicatu multorum testimonio, sed priorum etiam aetatum intenduntur et refelluntur crimina, quae nullis mortalium testimoniis ualent comprobari, propterea me iudicem constituerunt magistratus; qui noui quod gestum est ab orbe con-[51v]-dito et falli nullo modo possum. Sed antequam pronuntiem, ne querantur partes iudicium fuisse non aequum, testes audiamus grandaeuos, qui praesentia feruntur uidisse et praeterita multorum saeculorum meminisse. Prodeant tandem in medium.

Paedor

Ego sum testis in causam Ingluuiei iuratus.

will deprive her constantly of light, keeping her away from the sight of mortals for all time. For a punishment of this sort, even if it is not equal to and on a parity with her crimes and wickedness, will surely be considered appropriate to your wisdom and kindness. I have spoken.

Chorus of the Wise

Depart from here, depart, all you gluttons. We, the Virtues, are present, ready to give advice to, look after, and show support to our sister. Who ever saw such a thing? Who ever heard, or even dreamed, of a court case [51r] so amazing and unprecedented? Gluttony accuses Continence; virtue is on trial as a defendant, a court date is set for virtue. But the outcome will remove all surprise. The judge sees all and his opinions are lofty. The judgment will be suited to the faithfulness and integrity of the judge. The lazy shall be chased out. The sluggish will be killed off. The depraved gluttons will be deprived of fire and water. Gluttony will be thrust into a dark prison and condemned to perpetual shadows. Applaud and sing together, citizens. Long live truth! Let righteousness reign and impiety be checked. Let Gluttony, with her Filth, go straight to hell!

Time, the judge; Filth and Shame, witnesses.
Time

Since it is not only a question here of today's uprising, which was easy to judge due to the testimony of many, but of crimes, also, of many previous ages that are presented and refuted — crimes that could be assented to by the testimony of no mortals —, the magistrates have appointed me as judge, I, who know what has been done [51v] since the beginning of the world and can by no means be deceived. But before I pronounce judgment, lest the parties complain that it is not fair, let us listen to witnesses of great age who are reported to have seen the present and to remember the actions of many past centuries. Let them, finally, come forward.

Filth

I am a witness sworn to testify for the cause of Gluttony.

Tempus

Ergo si probas eius causam, suspectus eris testis.

Paedor

Mittamus proprietatem uerborum: argutiae grammaticorum non sunt huius loci.

Tempus

Nisi proprie fueris locutus, testimonium tuum erit ambiguum nec usque faciet fidem.

Paedor

Dico me iurasse uera dicturum in hac causa.

Tempus

Satis: qui uocaris?

Paedor

De nomine quaeris? Non mihi nomen simplex nec uelim prolatum.

Tempus

Profer inquam.

Paedor

Nutritores suillum appellarunt, quod e partu mortua matre, sus me lac-tauerit. Postea cum essem aetate integra, hirudinem me compellarunt sodales et illud nomen per aliquot saecula retinui.

Time

Then, if you approve of her cause,[55] you will be a suspect witness.

Filth

Let us not consider the propriety of words. The subtleties of grammarians are not appropriate to this place.

Time

Unless you speak precisely, your testimony will be unclear and will convince no one.

Filth

I tell you that I have sworn to speak the truth in this case.

Time

Enough. How are you called?

Filth

Are you asking about my name? My name is not a simple one. I would rather not state it.

Time

State it, I tell you.

Filth

Those who raised me called me a swine. My mother died in bearing me and a sow nursed me. Afterwards, when I had grown up, my companions called me a blood-sucker and I kept that name for some generations.

---

[55] Filth appears to use *causa* in the sense of "legal proceeding" or "case," but Time understands the word in the sense of "justificatory principle," "claim."

Tempus

Exugebas tu forte pampinorum sanguinem?

Paedor

Non mihi male quadrabat nomen.

Tempus

Nunc uero quod tibi nomen est?

Paedor

Bibacchus.

Pudor

Non tergiuerseris; alio nunc compel-[52r]-laris nomine, quo solo cognitus es ubique.

Paedor

Quid tua refert? Age quod agis et mitte mea cognomina.

Tempus

Bene quidem facit. Nam et hic iurauit, quae falsa tu dixeris confutaturum.

Time

Did you, perhaps, suck out the blood of young vines?[56]

Filth

The name was not ill-suited to me.

Time

But what is your name now?

Filth

Bibacchus.[57]

Shame

You must not be evasive. You are now [52v] addressed by a different name, the only one by which you have been known everywhere.

Filth

What is it to you? Mind your own business and don't talk about my names.

Time

He is acting correctly, for he has also sworn to refute whatever lies you may tell.

---

[56] Time ties Filth, via wine, the Dionysian representation par excellence (see Dodds 1986, Commentary, p. 105), to Bacchus.

[57] Possible word-play by Maldonado. The word could be read as derived from 'bibax,' given to drink; but could also be read as 'Twice-Bacchus,' possibly recalling the Dionysian legend, in which Zeus makes a 'second' or 'simulacrum' of young Dionysus in order to deceive his wife Hera. See Dodds 1986, p. 108.

Pudor

Tacet nomen quasi turpe, cum sint quae fatetur turpiora et sane si causas suorum nominum recenseret, oblectaret spectatores et nihil sui honoris deperiret.

Paedor

Non facit ad causam; rem nostram agamus.

Tempus

Dic tu Pudor, quando cessat hic et contra naturam erubescit.

Pudor

Dicam nominis causam, quod uitat; reliqua nunc sileantur. Cum Nero Romam incendit, in culina cuiusdam senatoris abdomine plenus et uino hic oscitabat neque flammas intellexit, donec omnibus fuga dilapsis, ignis circum tempora crepitabat; tum repente perterritus et amens, cum reliqua teneret ignis, in latrinam se praecipitauit, atque inde uix tandem extractus olensque oletum, uitabatur ab omnibus acclamantibus et se mutuo cohortantibus «Paedorem, Paedorem fugite», unde illi nomen adhaesit, quod numquam ualuit eradere.

Paedor

O pessimos hominum mores, nouerunt displicere mihi nomenclaturam et propterea libentius [52v] iterant; et cum mecum nihil habeant, nominant tamen, quo mordeant et infestent.

Tempus

Non mireris: naturale quidem est. Esto tuum nomen nunc Paedor et illuc da os scribae. Sed quo patre genitus?

Shame

He omits mention of his name as though it were shameful, whereas what he confesses to is more shameful. And surely, if he were to recount the reasons for his names, he would amuse the spectators and lose nothing of his honor.

Filth

This is not helping the case. Let us handle our own business.

Time

You speak, Shame, since he is hesitating, and blushing against his nature.[58]

Shame

I will state the reason for the name that he is avoiding. Let us pass over the rest for the present. When Nero burned Rome, this man, stuffed with fat and wine, was dozing in the kitchen of a certain senator. He was unaware of the flames until, when all had escaped by flight, the fire was crackling around his very forehead. Then, suddenly maddened by fright, since everything else was in flames, he jumped into the privy. From there he was finally dragged out later, stinking of filth. Everyone avoided him while shouting and urging one another: "Filth! Run from Filth!" Thus, that name stuck to him, which he has never been able to erase.

Filth

Oh, wretched character of men! They know that I don't like that name, and so they repeat it all the more. And although they have no quarrel with me, they still use the name in order to hurt me and cause me trouble.

Time

Don't be surprised. It is perfectly natural. Let your name now be Filth and so give it there as a bone to the clerk. But who was your father?

---

[58] Because, as Filth, shame is not in his nature.

Paedor

Nullo quidem.

Tempus

Ergo tu nihil: quandoquidem, ut garriunt philosophi, ex nihilo nihil fit.

Paedor

Patrem non noui. Nam in extructione turris Babylonicae cum perturbarentur linguae, meus pater, qui bitumen conficiebat ad coagmentandos lapides, abiit in longinquas regiones, et salsamentorum conficiendorum et concinnandorum artem inuenit, docuit et exercuit; neque mihi uisus amplius.

Tempus

Nomen quaero, non ubi sit gentium.

Paedor

Nomen fugit a me.

Pudor

Quamuis ingurgitationes somnique profundi memoriam suffocent neque sinant quandoque etiam hesterna meminisse, tu tamen nunc mera mendacia fingis. Gestas insignia parentis et imaginem tamquam egregia

Filth

I had none.

Time

Then you are nothing, inasmuch as, so the philosophers babble,[59] nothing can come from nothing.

Filth

I do not know my father. For at the construction of the Tower of Babel, when the languages were being mixed up, my father, who was making pitch to make stones adhere, went away into distant parts and discovered the art of making and preparing pickled fish.[60] He taught and practiced this art and was never seen by me again.

Time

I want to know his name, not his whereabouts.

Filth

His name escapes me.

Shame

Gorging yourself and sleeping deeply have dulled your memory and some- times do not even allow you to remember what happened yesterday. Even so, what you are doing now is making up pure lies. You are wearing the insignia of your father, and his image,[61] as though they were excellent decorations, and his

---

[59] Christians, believers in God's 'creation,' see the classical philosophical maxim, *Nihil ex nihilo fit*, as unacceptable. Maldonado may have noted the maxim, for example, in the Epicurean thinker Lucretius, *De Rerum Natura*, 1, 150.

[60] Filth's father's identity is made purposely obscure, and, in this case, he is laughably demeaned. Maldonado may be alluding to Erasmus's colloquy "Ichthyophagia," 'Con- cerning the Eating of Fish' (1526). Erasmus despised fish and his colloquy is a debate on religious issues between a butcher and a fishmonger. See Erasmus 1965, pp. 312-357.

[61] *Insignia* could refer to medals or coins, which is what is suggested by their having an image and having to be pulled out. There were, in effect, coins with the image of Dionysus (See Dodds 1986, p. 81).

decora, et excidit tibi nomen? Profer insignia eorumque redde rationem, et iudici satis erit.

Tempus

Volo, iubeo.

Paedor

Risistis ante quam noritis causam. Pudor explicet; ego iam uestro sum derisu praepeditus.

Tempus

Dic [53r] tu tandem, quando haesitat hic.

Pudor

Libenter. Fuit huius pater et est (opinor), si uiuit, in ganeam propensus; et ita laetitia perfundebatur, cum dici se audiebat uini pinguiumque capacem, ut duceret strenuum in conuiuiis deglutiendo bibendoque superare. Cum autem Aeneas duxit Creusam, studuit Venus, neruis omnibus intentis, ut conuiuium nuptiale lautum mirum in modum esset ac opiparum. Huius autem pater secum reputans non semper opportunitatem dari nominis illustrandi, corripere constituit occasionem, et omnibus nectari ambrosiaeque intentis, uidens in parte mensae diuersa botellum pinguiculum, inuolat et correptum uno haustu deuorare festinat. Sed partem postremam, quae crassior erat, non ualens transmittere, spiritu compresso prosternitur et sub mensam resupinus, parte botelli propendente, ore diducto, insternitur. Concurrunt omnes ad subleuandum et, cum botellum ore uidere pendentem ipsumque mortuum credidere, alii miserebantur, alii dolebant inopinatum casum; plerique ridebant et cachinnis excipiebant aduentantes. Ille autem reuixit tandem atque uno uehementi screatu botellum et quod [53v] erat in stomacho congestum expulit circumstantemque turbam uino iureque indigesto respersit.

name has escaped you? Bring out the insignia and give an account of them, and that will be enough for the judge.

Time

I so wish and order it.

Filth

You laugh before knowing the reason. Let Shame explain it. I am restrained by your mockery.

Time

Then [53r] you answer, since he is hesitating.

Shame

Gladly. His father was — and is, I suppose, if he is alive — a frequenter of public houses and was so overjoyed when he heard it said that he had an exceptional capacity for wine and fat, that he considered it a sign of strength at banquets to win out at drinking and gorging himself. However, when Aeneas married Creusa, Venus strove with all her might so that the wedding banquet be fine and elegant to a remarkable degree.[62] But his father, thinking to himself that such an opportunity would not always present itself to glorify his name, decided to seize the occasion, and when everyone was intent on nectar and ambrosia, seeing in a different part of the table a rather fat sausage, he rushed in, grabbed it, and hastened to devour it in one bite. But not being able to swallow the last part of it, because it was very thick, his breath was cut off and he was laid low. Because he lay flat under the table — with part of the sausage sticking out, with his mouth wide open — he was covered up. Everyone ran forward to carry him out; and when they saw the sausage hanging out of his mouth and believed he was dead, some showed pity, others grieved at the sudden disaster, many laughed and greeted him with guffaws as they came forward. He, however, finally came back to life, and, after loudly hawking and spitting, [53v] he expelled the sausage and what had congealed in his stomach and showered those who were standing around with wine and undigested soup.

[62] There is no description of Creusa's wedding to Aeneas anywhere that we know of. Venus, Aeneas' mother, took him under her protection. Maldonado, because he is offering a description patently his own, perhaps avoided—while giving a semblance of realism, that is, mentioning Creusa/Aeneas—any wedding of which there was a classical description, which he would have had to distort.

Paedor

Narras tu facinora mei parentis tamquam magis ridenda quam praedicanda; nos aliter sentimus. Perinde sunt res ut existimantur. Ferro uel globulis plumbeis confossi et transuerberati laudantur a uobis, ut qui putetis egregium uulnera pati ferroque mori; nos impendio magis stultum putamus in acie mori quam in caupona. Immo cautius uidetur uino perturbatum occumbere nihil sentientem, quam plagis discerptum perhorrendos cruciatus oppetere. Conualuit tunc meus pater; non tamen existimaremus deflendum, si mortem tam dulcem obiisset.

Pudor

Scio non periisse, nomenque fortuitum [an *sortitum*?] ex eo casu botellum et botiuoram, quod tu fugis nominare, cum antea farcimiuoram quidam, alii uinipotam appellarent.

Paedor

Maledicus es; nolim tecum contendere. Iudex quaerat, tu tace, nisi rogatus.

Tempus

Omittamus nomen parentis. Dic quod magis necessarium est. Nosti Continentiam?

Paedor

Noui quidem de facie aliorumque commemoratione; apud eam numquam sum diuersatus nec in [54r] colloquium ueni, quod eius studia mihi displicent et ieiunia deterrent.

Tempus

Aderas hodie prope, cum est proelium commissum?

Filth

You are talking about my father's deeds as though they were to be laughed at rather than praised. We have a different opinion. Things are pretty much as they are thought to be. Those who have been pierced or pounded by the sword or by lead balls are praised by you, since you think it is excellent to suffer wounds and to die by the sword. But we think that it is very much more stupid to die in battle than in a whorehouse. Indeed, it appears more prudent for someone to die when he feels nothing because he is befuddled with wine than to undergo horrible torture and be torn apart by blows. My father regained his health that time, but we would not have considered it cause for weeping if he had died such a sweet death.

Shame

I know he didn't die, and that from that accident he got his name "Sausage" or "Sausage-gobbler," which you are failing to mention. While before that some people called him "Sausage-Bolter" or "Winebibber".[63]

Filth

You are a slanderer. I will not argue with you. Let the judge ask questions, and you be quiet unless you have been asked.

Time

Let's leave out your father's name. Tell us what is more to the point: do you know Continence?

Filth

I know her by sight and from the remarks of others. I have never spent time with her nor have I talked with her, because her interests displease me and her fasts drive me away.

Time

Were you close at hand today when a fight broke out?

---

[63] Wine, of course, and sausage (both as meat and as a phallic representation) are associated with Dionysus/Bacchus. See Colahan-Rodríguez-Smith 1999, pp. 168-169.

Paedor

Aderam et omnia diligenter sum contemplatus.

Tempus

Quae prior inuasit alteram?

Paedor

In uasa pronior erat Ingluuies.

Tempus

Mitte nunc uasa; quae prior incurrit in alteram? Dic tandem.

Paedor

Curru non uehitur Ingluuies, et Continentia nihilominus pedibus incedebat.

Tempus

Parum percipis tu Latinam grammaticam. Verba communia passimque obuia non intelligis?

Paedor

Grammaticam aliquando didici neque culinariam artem Latine quisquam explicabat proprius nec elegantius. Vina tamen suffocant ingenium memoriamque perturbant.

Tempus

Dic tandem quae prior adorta.

Filth

I was, and I observed everything very carefully.

Time

Which woman attacked the other first?

Filth

Gluttony was faster in her cups.[64]

Time

Forget about cups. Which was the first to assault the other? Come now, speak!

Filth

Gluttony does not ride in a chariot.[65] Both she and Continence were on foot.

Time

You inadequately grasp Latin grammar. Don't you understand common words, words used every day?

Filth

I learned grammar once, and no one was has ever more correctly or more elegantly set forth the art of cooking in Latin. And yet wine impedes clear thinking and disturbs the memory.

Time

Tell us, finally, which woman attacked first.

---

[64] Maldonado has Filth's prevaricative word confusion be based on *invasit* versus *in vasa*.
[65] The word-play, this time, is between *incurrit* and *in curru*.

Paedor

Pares uidebantur aetate neque diuinauerim facile quae sit annosior.

Tempus

Aut ignorantia teneris Romani sermonis profundissima, aut tergiuersa-
ris quae scire dissimules.

Paedor

Remoue nunc compositiones ac praepositiones, quas neque ualui dis-
cere neque libet meminisse, quoniam odi maxime ex eo tempore, quo
me seuere caedebat Didascalus, earum nomina et usum [54v] requirens;
atque grammatici transfugam appellarunt, quod ex eorum arte transfuge-
rim ad popinariam et artocreariam; quod utinam fecissem maturius!

Pudor

Vere commemora quid te disturbauerit a grammaticis et schola. Quid
te pudere simulas?

Paedor

Non libet.

Tempus

Dic tu. Sine paedorem aliquando pudere tecumque uiuere uel simu-
late.

Pudor

Nihil equidem mentiar. Grammaticus qui hunc instituebat adeo
ferox, asper et inhumanus erat, ut praeter ferulas duri corticis, etiam
ferreas haberet litteras et syllabas surculo sculptas, quas igni candentes

Filth

They seemed equal in age. I would not be able to guess easily which one is the older.[66]

Time

Either you are handicapped by profound ignorance of the Roman tongue or you are evading me and pretending not to understand.

Filth

Don't give me compound verbs and prepositions, that I never could learn and that it doesn't please me to remember, since my hatred starts especially from the time when Didascalus (my teacher) used to beat me severely, asking me [54v] their names and uses, and the grammarians used the word 'deserter' because I deserted from their art to kitchens and meat-shops. I wish I had done it sooner.

Shame

Give a true report of what drove you away from the grammarians and from school. What do you pretend to be ashamed of?

Filth

I don't want to.

Time

You must speak. Let Filth be ashamed, finally, and at least pretend that he lives with you.[67]

Shame

I will tell no lies. The grammarian who taught him was so fierce, harsh and inhuman that in addition to his rods of hard wood, he even had iron letters and syllables formed out of twigs which were as hot as fire and with which he

---

[66] Filth understand *adorta*, 'attack,' in its secondary sense, 'start out,' 'be born'.
[67] Another reference to Filth's natural shamelessness.

pulpamentis displicentium sibi discipulorum inurebat. Atque die certo, cum is uino dapibusque repletus socorditer responderet ad interrogata, coniunctiones ipsas et praepositiones sinistre redditas ac denominatas inussit flagrantes postico pulpamento. Quo dolore percitus fugit, grammaticae grammaticisque maledicens, ustori praesertim perpetuas inimicitias et uindictam denuntians. Nam Latine scit, cum sobrius est minimeque furens ut nunc, recordatione cicatricum. Utere tu, iudex, simplicibus, ne refrices eius ulcera.

Paedor

Potuisses tu hoc dissimulare, si bo-[55r]-nam in hanc causam mentem induisses.

Tempus

Feras aequo animo; non utar compositis deinceps, ne tibi ebulliant cicatrices. Dic tandem a qua parte orta primum est seditio.

Paedor

Ingluuies tenebat forum iure suo geniali die. Ludebant, saltabant, cantitabant, potabant, seque ingurgitabant omnes et laetitia perfundebantur, cum ecce Continentia instat ex parte diuersa propellere postremos, donec uia quasi ferro facta, peruasit ad Ingluuiem. Illa commota, uidens suos plerosque uertisse faciem, ruit et asserere suas partes liberali causa manu contendit. Cumque committi satagit cum Continentia, repente corruit grauiter uulnerata.

Tempus

Quo telo percussa est?

branded the flesh of the pupils he didn't like. And on a certain day, when he was filled up with wine and feasting and answered the questions in a sluggish manner, giving the wrong names for the conjunctions themselves and the prepositions, the teacher branded him on the flesh of his buttocks. Struck by the pain of this, he fled, cursing both grammar and the grammarians. He in particular vowed eternal hostility and revenge toward the one who had burned him. For he knows Latin when he is sober and is not raging as much as he is now, remembering the scars. You, as judge, must use simples[68] so as not to reopen his wounds.

Filth

You could have covered this up, if you [55r] had adopted a good attitude in this case.

Time

Endure it calmly. I shall not use compounds after this;[69] so your scars need not flare up again. Tell us, finally, which of the parties first instigated this quarrel.

Filth

Gluttony was holding sway in the forum, as is her right on her birthday.[70] They were playing, dancing, singing, drinking, eating like pigs and enveloped in happiness. Then, behold, Continence started, obliquely, to drive out the people in the back, until, having cleared a path as though with a sword, she pushed her way forward toward Gluttony. Gluttony was stirred up when she saw that most of her people had turned their faces away. She rushed up and strove to exert her rights by force in a cause involving her freedom.

While she was all in a rush to clash with Continence, suddenly she fell back, having been seriously wounded.

Time

By what weapon was she wounded?

---

[68] Maldonado plays on the medical/grammatical context by using 'simples,' which could both refer to verbs and to medicines concocted from only one ingredient.

[69] The use of 'compounds' here rounds out the word-play indicated in the previous note.

[70] Gluttony, quite logically, celebrates her birthday on Fat Tuesday.

Paedor

Telum non apparebat, sed illa prostrata iacebat.

Pudor

Viden', ut fatetur nullum fuisse telum et illam iacuisse? Iacuit quidem, sed praeter uini supplantationem reminiscentia scelerum, uisa
ratione conscientiaeque stimulis agitata, corruit, ueritate perspecta. Sentire deberes tu Ingluuiesque tua, uos uobis nocere uestraque uobis crimina uestros tortores esse. Male quippe conscia sibi mens graues sentit
cruciatus; nulli tamen debet imputare, cum ipsa sibi sit causa doloris.
[55v]

Paedor

Miseram illam! Palpitabat moribunda, percussoresque sentiebantur, si
non uidebantur, et imputabitur ipsi, quod patiebatur immerito.

Tempus

De hodierna seditione sit satis. De regno quod iactat saeculorum multorum et possessione continua quid habes exploratum? Sed ante omnia
dicas oportet quod primo fueras interrogandus: quot annos agis?

Paedor

Quid ais? Asini aguntur et muli, non anni.

Filth

No weapon could be seen, but she lay there, stretched out.[71]

Shame

Do you see how he admits that there was no weapon but that she lay flat? She did indeed lie flat, but, in addition to being befuddled by wine, it was from remembering her crimes, from having seen Light[72] and Truth and being pricked by goads of conscience, that she fell down. You and your Gluttony ought to realize that you do harm to yourselves and that your crimes are what cause you torture. Surely a guilty mind is aware of heavy pains. Yet it ought to blame them on no one, since it is the cause of pain to itself.

Filth

The poor woman! She was throbbing with pain and near death. Assassins could be sensed, even if they could not be seen. And will she herself be charged for something that she suffered without deserving it?

Time

Let that be enough about today's disturbance. Concerning the kingdom of many centuries' duration that she boasts about, and her continuous possession of it, what have you proved? But before anything else, you should answer the question that you should have been asked to begin with. How old are you?

Filth

What are you saying? Donkeys and mules are driven, not years.[73]

---

[71] Gluttony's unexplained fall, especially as described in this passage (after 'dancing') may well be an allusion to the description of the frenzied/unconscious falls which normally occurred in consequence of the wild dancing indulged in by the maenadic followers of Dionysus. See Dodds 1986, p. 87.

[72] Light is used synonimically for Reason, who, along with Truth, preceded Continence in the forum and would be the first encountered by Gluttony in her charge.

[73] Filth avails himself of the confusion possible in the idiomatic Latin use of 'to drive' for 'spending of time' and, thus, for telling age.

Tempus

Quando libet asinari, dum tu agis asinum, asinus te praecedit et cum interrogaris quot annos agas, intellige sciscitari quot anni te praecedant. Nam et agere asinum, etiam significat asinum referre et esse pecus Arcadicum.

Paedor

Perdat Deus grammaticos et eorum sophismata. Nam quod subterfugeram dicere, nominis mei tam turpis ipsi causa fuerunt, quod synonymum putaui, proptereaque non respui statim ut est inditum. Quis non crederet idem esse paedorem quod pudorem? Una litterula tantum ualebit, ut uirtutem uertat in uitium? Multos equidem annos credidi me bene nominatum, donec in macello Romae grammaticus quidam Paedianus forte praeteriens uidit me nominatum libenter respondere: ri-[56r]-sitque maxime. Ego non intelligens causam, "Qui cachinnaris", inquam? "Non rideam", inquit, "qui te uideam nomini turpissimo adlubescere?" "Hem", inquam, "non idem est quod pudor?" "Heu bone Deus" inquit, "disdiapason distant". Tum ego miser parum abfuit, quin ex aegritudine perirem.

Tempus

Tu quidem male sentis de grammaticis. Sed dic tandem annos.

Paedor

Annos quaeris? Saecula potius saeculorum: ante diluuium natus sum et post diluuium renatus.

Time

Since it pleases you to act like an ass, while you drive an ass an ass walks ahead of you. So that when you are asked how many years you 'drive,' you must understand that you are being asked how many years 'go ahead of you'. For to drive an ass also means 'to act like an ass' and to be a 'herd from Arcadia'.[74]

Filth

May God destroy the grammarians and their sophistries. For — something I was avoiding to mention — they were the reason for my very disgraceful name. I thought it was a synonym, and for that reason I did not reject it as it was given to me. Who would not believe that 'paedor,' [filth], was the same as 'pudor,' [shame]? Will one little letter have so much power that it can turn virtue into vice? For many years I certainly believed that I had been well named, until in the meat-market at Rome a certain grammarian named Paedianus,[75] by chance walking past, saw that when I had been named I answered freely, [56r] and he laughed loudly. I, not understanding the reason, said "Why are you laughing?" "Why shouldn't I laugh," he said, "when I see you take pleasure in such a shameful name?" "Huh!," I answered. "Isn't it the same as 'pudor,' [shame]?" "Oh, good God!," he cried, "it is different by a double octave!"[76] Poor me! Then I came close to dying of sickness.

Time

You certainly have a bad opinion of grammarians. But, finally, tell me your age.

Filth

You want to know my age? You should speak, rather, of ages upon ages. I was born before the Flood and born again after the Flood.

---

[74] Arcadia was supposed to contain herds of donkeys, and its inhabitants were reputed to be asinine. See Varro, *De Re Rustica*, 2, 1, 14.

[75] The name Paedianus is itself reflective of his profession, educator.

[76] The musical reference is appropriate because of the phonetic phenomenon being discussed.

Tempus

Annorum tibi satis. Vidistine regnantem semper Ingluuiem saeculis prioribus?

Paedor

Vidi quidem; nam et in nuptiis Hippodamiae reges et multi principes illi parebant, ut taceam cenam Thyestis et bellum Troianum in quo ualuit plurimum. Philosophos etiam atque poetas fidos habuit plurimos, quorum grandiloquentia ciuitates et regna continuit in officio.

Pudor

Ita perfricta fronte audes dicere regnasse, cum tyrannidem exercuerit ad tempus, et, cognito damno, iugum eius excusserint, et in libertatem se uindicauerint bene sani et quos impietas non reddiderat insanabiles? Nam de Christianis improbe mentita est Ingluuies, eorum sibi uindicans studia.

Paedor

[56v] An tu negabis pluris fieri cocos selectos apud Christianos quam apud ethnicos et Turcas, esseque maiores culinarum apparatus et instrumenta?

Pudor

Sunt quidem splendida Christianis quae memoras, et concinnandi cibos peritia inter liberales artes censetur; non tamen ea gulae causa tantum adhibetur, quantum ad ostentationem iactatur. Nam multi sunt in ea re diligentes et solliciti, quo uitent auaritiae suspicionem et cognatorum amicorumque obsequantur studiis. Soli tamen cum sunt, respuunt lautitias modestiaeque seruiunt.

Time

You are old enough. Did you behold Gluttony always reigning in previous centuries?

Filth

I did indeed. For even at the wedding of Hippodamia,[77] kings and many princes obeyed her, not to mention the banquet of Thyestes,[78] and the Trojan War, in which she had much power.[79] She also had very many faithful philosophers and poets, whose grandiloquence sustained cities and kingdoms.

Shame

Do you brazenly dare to say that she reigned, when she held sway only for a time? And when they recognized their loss, being in their right minds, they shook off her yoke and went over to the side of liberty, at least those whom impiety had not rendered incurable. For Gluttony told a wicked lie about Christians, claiming their interests for herself.

Filth

[56v] Will you deny, then, that master cooks are held in higher esteem among the Christians than among the heathens and the Turks? And they have more elaborate equipment and cookware?

Shame

The Christians do, indeed, have those elaborations that you mention, and skill in preparing foods is counted among the liberal arts. But that skill is not used so much for the sake of gluttony, as it is flaunted for boasting. For many are anxious and careful in this art to avoid any suspicion of avarice and only humor the interests of their relatives and friends. But when they are all alone, they reject extravagance and are servants of modesty.

---

[77] The reference is to the wedding of Hippodamia and Pirithous, Hercules' great friend, at which the Centaurs, wishing to rape the women, occasioned a great battle with the Lapiths.

[78] The reference is to the banquet in which Atreus tricked Thyestes into eating his own children.

[79] The Trojan War was instigated, of course, to recover Menelaus' adulterous wife.

Paedor

Nescio quid dicas; omnes aberramus et alii in alios culpam conferimus. Scio nullam esse domum per orbem, in qua non Ingluuies excipiatur benigne osculoque libato ceu domina suscipiatur. Sed tamen ut uere dicam quod sentio: percurri semper terras omnes et nunc quotannis saepe recurro; testor tamen tuum meumque caput, iudex, quod terrarum ubiuis, et in Europa maxime, quam iactat Continentia suam, semper ostendisse mensas dapibus refertas et cibis exquisitissimis uariatas, nisi sicubi deerant forte pecuniae. Vide quid possit Ingluuies et quam late pateat eius imperium. [57r]

Pudor

Nondum perorasti, mane parumper. Iube illum, iudex, causam cessationis expromere, si uis penitus nosse.

Tempus

Iubeo ac impero.

Paedor

Non equidem erubescam; humanum est et fieri solet; nausea sum repente correptus tantumque farciminis euomui, ut paene simul animam exspuerim.

Pudor

Nondum satisfacis: profundior est causa.

Paedor

Molestus es in re nihili. Corripueram peracto prandio nimis auide frustum porcinum semicrudum et in barathrum recondideram; cumque pararem postea testimonium dicere, illa mole cocta caro porcina minusque mansa, repente sua cruditate perturbat omnia uiscera; et tamquam sul-

Filth

I don't know what you are saying. We are all committing faults, and each of us places blame on the other. I know that there is no home throughout the world in which Gluttony is not kindly received, given a kiss, and taken in as mistress. But if I may truly tell you what I feel, I have always traveled through every land, and now, every year, I return again. I swear by your head and mine, judge, that everywhere on earth, and especially in Europe, which Continence boasts of as her own, tables are crowded for feast, varied with the most exquisite foods, unless it is a place where money is lacking. Note what power Gluttony has and how widely her empire extends.

Shame [57r]

You have not yet finished your testimony. Wait a moment. Order him, judge, to state the reason for the pause in the trial, if you want to know everything.[80]

Time

I order and command it.

Filth

I won't be ashamed. It is human and often happens. I was suddenly seized with nausea and threw up so much sausage that I almost vomited out my soul.

Shame

That is not good enough. The reason is deeper.

Filth

You are causing trouble over a thing of no importance. After lunch was over I too eagerly snatched up some half-cooked pork and jammed it down into my gullet. Afterward, when I was getting ready to give my testimony, that pork, cooked in a lump and poorly digested, suddenly, by its rawness, upset all my

---

[80] The reference is to the interruption of the giving of testimony alluded to earlier, but that does not form part of the recorded trial.

phureus puluis succensus, quaeritans uiam ad erumpendum, ni duplicem inuenisset, rupto uentriculo disectisque uisceribus ego perissem.

Tempus

Satis est. Digna est Ingluuies sua reste. Noui quid tu sentias, et quid me uelis sentire. Personam retines nutricis tuae et a maioribus et patre non degeneras. Sententia crastina die medio foro pronuntiabitur, ut qui pugnae interfuerunt, aequum esse iudicium intelligant. Ingluuies damnabitur et Continentia absoluetur dignaque iudicabitur, quam [57v] omnes suspiciant et complectantur. Ite felices et plaudite Temporique uos iudicandos permittite. FINIS

insides. Like a pile of ignited sulphur, it sought a path to burst out. If it had not found a double path, either my stomach would have burst or my intestines would have been torn apart, and I would have died.

Time

That is enough. Gluttony deserves her punishment. I know what you feel and what you want me to feel. You retain the character of your nurse, and you are no worse than your ancestors or your father. Sentence will be pronounced tomorrow in the center of the forum, in such a way that those who were present at the fight will perceive that the judgment is just. Gluttony will be condemned and Continence will be set free and judged worthy of [57v] being taken up and embraced by all. Go happily and applaud, and allow yourselves to be judged by Time.

WORKS CITED

1. *Works by or about Juan Maldonado*

Ayala Picón 1972 = Isaac Ayala Picón, *Juan Maldonado, historiador de la espiritualidad burgalesa, a principios del siglo XVI* (M.A. thesis, U. de Burgos, 1972, unpublished).

Colahan-Rodríguez 1995 = Clark Colahan – Alfred Rodríguez, 'Juan Maldonado and *Lazarillo de Tormes*', *Bulletin of Hispanic Studies*, 72 (1995), 289-311.

Colahan-Rodríguez-Smith 1999 = Clark Colahan – Alfred Rodríguez – Warren Smith, 'Juan Maldonado's *Bacchanalia* and the Young Lazarillo', *Humanistica Lovaniensia*, 48 (1999),160-241.

García García 1983 = Heliodoro García García, *El pensamiento comunero y erasmista de Juan Maldonado* (Madrid: H. García García, 1983).

Maldonado 1529 = Juan Maldonado, *Vitae Sanctorum brevi elegantique stylo compositae…* (Burgos: Juan de Junta, 1529).

Maldonado 1541 = Juan Maldonado, *Ioannis Maldonati quaedam opuscula nunc primum in lucem edita. De Felicitate Christiana, Praxis sive de lectione Erasmi, Somnium, Ludus Chartarum, Desponsa Cauta* (Burgos: Ioannes Giunta, 1541).

Maldonado 1549 = Juan Maldonado, *Opuscula quaedam docta simul et elegantia. De senectute Christiana, Paradoxa, Pastor bonus, Ludus chartarum, Tridunus et alii quidam, Geniale iudicium sive Baccanalia* (Burgos: Ioannes Giunta, 1549).

Maldonado 1975a = Juan Maldonado, *De motu Hispaniae* = *El levantamiento de España,* trans. and ed. M.A. Durán Ramas (Madrid: Centro de Estudios Constitucionales, 1975).

Maldonado 1975b = Juan Maldonado, *La Revolución Comunera: El movimiento de España, o sea, Historia de la revolución conocida con el nombre de las Comunidades de Castilla,* trans. José Quevedo, ed. Valentina Fernández Vargas (Madrid: Ediciones del Centro, 1975 [= 1840]).

Maldonado 1975c = Juan Maldonado, *La Revolución Comunera,* trans. Valentina Fernández Vargas (Madrid: Ediciones del Centro, 1975).

Maldonado 1980 = Juan Maldonado, *Paraenesis ad Litteras: Juan Maldonado y el humanismo español en tiempos de Carlos V,* eds. E. Asensio-J. Alcina Rovira (Madrid: Fundación Universitaria Española, 1980).

Maldonado 1981 = Juan Maldonado, *Somnium,* trans. and intro., in Avilés Fernández 1981, pp. 149-178.

Maldonado 1983 = Juan Maldonado, *Hispaniola = La Española,* ed. M. Durán Ramas (Barcelona: Bosch, 1983).

Peinador Marín 1991 = Luis Jesús Peinador Marín, 'Un diálogo del siglo XVI español: *Eremitae* de Juan Maldonado', *Criticón,* 52 (1991), 41-90.

Rhodes 1988 = Dennis Rhodes, 'Juan Maldonado and the Press in Burgos', *Gutenberg-Jahrbuch,* 63 (1988), 141-145.

Smith 1987 = Paul Stephen Smith, *A humanist history of the "Comunidades" of Castile: Juan Maldonado's De motu Hispaniae* (Ottawa: Canadian theses on microfiche 419903, 1987).

2. Other Works

Avilés Fernández 1981 = Miguel Avilés Fernández, *Sueños ficticios y lucha ideológica en el Siglo de Oro* (Madrid: Editora Nacional, 1981).

Azcona 1980 = Tarsicio de Azcona, ' La Elección y reforma del espiscopado español en tiempo de los Reyes Católicos', in *Historia de la Iglesia en España,* III-1: *La Iglesia en la España de los siglos XV y XVI,* ed. J. L. González Novalín (Madrid: Editorial Católica, 1980), pp. 115-210.

Bataillon 1937 = Marcel Bataillon, *Erasme et l'Espagne: recherches sur l'histoire spirituelle du XVIe siècle* (Paris: Droz, 1937).

Bataillon 1968 = Marcel Bataillon, *Novedad y Fecundidad del Lazarillo de Tormes,* trans. L. Cortéz Vásquez (New York: Las Americas, 1968).

Bataillon-Devoto-Amiel 1991 = Marcel Bataillon – Daniel Devoto – Charles Amiel, *Erasme et l'Espagne: recherches sur l'histoire spirituelle du XVIe siècle* (Geneva: Droz, 1991).

Bataillon-Margolin 1998 = Marcel Bataillon – Jean-Claude Margolin, *Erasme et l'Espagne: recherches sur l'histoire spirituelle du XVIe siècle* (Geneva: Droz, 1998).

Bataillon 2002 = Marcel Bataillon, *Erasmo y España: estudios sobre la historia espiritual del siglo XVI* (Mexico City: Fondo de Cultura Económica 2002 [= 1950]).

Bernal Díaz de Luco 1530 = Juan Bernal Díaz de Luco, *Libro de instrucción para los perlados, o memorial breue de algunas cosas que deuen hazer para el descargo de sus conciencias y buena gouernacion de sus Obispados y dioceses* (Alcalá de Henares: Casa de Joã de Brocar, 1530).

Bietenholz-Deutscher 1985-1987 = Peter Bietenholz -Thomas Deutscher, *Contemporaries of Erasmus: A Biographical Register of the Renaissance and Reformation*, 3 vols (Toronto-Buffalo: University of Toronto Press, 1985-1987).

Brown 1998 = Jonathan Brown, *Painting in Spain 1500-1700* (New Haven: Yale University Press, 1998).

Cañizares Llovera 1973 = A.Cañizares Llovera, *Santo Tomás de Villanueva* (Madrid: Instituto Superior de Pastoral, 1973).

Cardano 2006 = Girolamo Cardano, *Liber de Ludo Aleae*, ed. Massimo Tamborini (Milan: FrancoAngeli, 2006).

Castillo 1528 = Diego del Castillo, *Tratado muy útil y provechoso en reprobación de los juegos y no menos provechoso para la vida y estado de los hombres* (Valladolid: Nicolaus Tyerii, 1528).

Castillo 1557 = Diego del Castillo, *Sátyra e invectiva contra los tahures, en que se declaran los daños que al cuerpo y al alma y a la hazienda se siguen del juego de los naipes*, [corrected edition, under a new title, of the book from the preceding entry] (Seville: Martín Montesdoca, 1557).

Catholic Encyclopedia (www.newadvent.org/cathen) Jan 2008.

Colahan 1991-1992 = Clark Colahan, 'El asturiano renacentista, rey del juego', *Archivum,* 41-42 (1991-1992), 65-75.

Colahan 1999 = Clark Colahan, 'Imágenes hagiográficas de cabeza en el Lazarillo', *Hispanic Journal,* 20 (1999), 49-56.

Colahan 2001 = Clark Colahan, 'Epicurean vs. Stoic Debate and Lazarillo's Character', *Neophilologus,* 85 (2001), 555-564.

Colahan-Masferrer 2007 = Clark Colahan – Roberto Masferrer III. *Díaz de Luco's Guide for Bishops: Spanish Reform and the Lazarillo* (Tempe: Arizona Center for Medieval and Renaissance Studies, 2007).

Colahan-Rodríguez 2000 = Clark Colahan – Alfred Rodríguez. '¿Por qué se llaman 'tratados' los capítulos del *Lazarillo*?', *Hispanófila,* 130 (2000), 21-25.

Colahan-Rodríguez 1995 = Clark Colahan – Alfred Rodríguez, 'Juan Maldonado and *Lazarillo de Tormes*', *Bulletin of Hispanic Studies,* 72 (1995), 289-311.

Cruz 1999 = Anne Cruz, *Discourses of Poverty: social reform and the picaresque novel in early modern Spain* (Toronto, Buffalo: University of Toronto Press, 1999).

Diccionario de Historia = *Diccionario de Historia Eclesiástica de España,* eds. Quintín Aldea Vaquero-Tomás Marín Martínez -José Vives Gatell, 4 vols (Madrid: Instituto Enrique Flórez, 1972-1975).

Diccionario de uso = *Diccionario de uso del Español,* ed. Maria Moliner (Madrid: Editorial Gredos, 1997).

Dictionary of the Royal Spanish Academy = *El Diccionario de la Real Academia Española: ayer y hoy,* eds. Mar Campos Souto-José Ignacio Pérez Pascual (Coruña: Universidade da Coruña, 2006).

Dodds 1986 = E.R. Dodds, ed., *Euripides' Bacchae,* 2nd edition (Oxford: Oxford University Press, 1986).

Dunn 1988 = P. Dunn, 'The Case of the Purloined Letter', *Revista de Estudios Hispánicos,* 22 (1988), 1-14.

Erasmus 1906-1958 = Erasmus, *Desiderii Erasmi Roterodami Opus epistolarum,* ed. P.S. Allen- H. M. Allen, 12 vols. (Oxford: Oxford University Press, 1906-1958).

Erasmus 1965 = Erasmus, *The Colloquies of Erasmus,* trans. Craig Thompson (Chicago: University of Chicago Press, 1965).

Erasmus 1980 = Des. Erasmi Rot. *Moriae Encomium* ed. Gerardus Listrius (Oxford: W. Hall 1980 [= 1633]).

Erasmus 1982 = Erasmus, *Collected Works of Erasmus,* 31: *Adages Ii.1 to Iv.100,* trans. Margaret Mann Phillips; annotated by R.A.B. Mynors (Toronto: University of Toronto Press, 1982).

Erasmus 1984 = Erasmus, *Collected Works of Erasmus, 42: New Testament Scholarship: Paraphrases on Romans and Galatians*, ed. J. Payne- A. Rabil-R. Sider- W. Smith (Toronto: University of Toronto Press, 1984).

Erasmus 1986 = Erasmus, *Collected Works of Erasmus, 27: Literary and Educational Writings: Panegyricus (Panegyric), Moria (Praise of Folly), Julius Exclusus (Julius Excluded from Heaven), Institutio Principis Christiani (Education of a Christian Prince), Querella Pacis (The Complaint of Peace)*, ed. A.H.T. Levi (Toronto: University of Toronto Press, 1986).

Erasmus 1989 = Erasmus, *The Praise of Folly and other writings: a new translation with critical commentary*, ed. and trans. Robert Martin Adams (New York: Norton, 1987).

Erasmus 1991 = Erasmus, *Collected Works of Erasmus, 46: Paraphrase on John*, trans. Jane Phillips, ed. R. Sider (Toronto: University of Toronto Press, 1991).

Erasmus 1992 = Erasmus, *Collected Works of Erasmus, 34: Adages IIviiI to IIIiii100*, trans R.A.B. Mynors (Toronto: University of Toronto Press 1992).

Erasmus 1995 = Erasmus, *Collected Works of Erasmus, 56: Annotations on Romans*, ed. J. Payne – A. Rabil – R. Sider – W. Smith (Toronto: University of Toronto Press, 1995).

Erasmus 1997 = Erasmus, *Collected Works of Erasmus, 39-40: Colloquies*, trans., ed. by Craig R. Thompson (Toronto/Buffalo/ London: University of Toronto Press 1997).

Etienvre 1982 = J.P. Etienvre, 'Le symbolisme de la carte à jouer dans l'Espagne des XVIe et XVIIe siècles' in *Les Jeux à la Renaissance, Actes du XXIIIe colloque international d'études humanistes, Tours, Juillet 1980* ed. Philippe Ariès and Jean-Claude Margolin (Paris: Libr. philosophique J. Vrin, 1982), pp. 421-444.

Etienvre 1987 = J.P. Etienvre, *Figures du Jeu: études lexico-sémantiques sur le jeu de cartes en Espagne (XVIe-XVIIIe siècle)* (Madrid: Casa de Velásquez, 1987).

Frazer 1940 = J.G. Frazer, *The Golden Bough: The Roots of Religion and Folklore* (New York: Macmillan, 1940).

García Sainz de Baranda 1967 = Julián García Sainz de Baranda, *La ciudad de Burgos y su concejo en la Edad Media*, 2 vols (Burgos: Tip. de la Editorial El Monte Carmelo, 1967).

Gitlitz 1989 = David Gitlitz, 'The Political Implications of a Sixteenth-Century Spanish Morality Play', in *Everyman and Company: Essays on the Theme and Structure of the European Moral Play*, ed. Donald Gilman (New York: AMS Press, 1989), pp. 111-128.

Gitlitz 2000 = David Gitlitz, 'Inquisition Confessions and Lazarillo de Tormes', *Hispanic Review*, 68.1 (2000), 53-74.

Gutiérrez Alonso-Méndez Sáez 1997 = Adriano Gutiérrez Alonso – Pablo Méndez Sáez, 'La hacienda municipal de Burgos en la época moderna. Los bienes de propios (1500-1750)', *Boletín de la institución Fernán González*, 1997, no. 2, 327-354.

Herrero 1976 = J. Herrero, 'The Great Icons of the *Lazarillo*: The Bull, the Wine, the Sausage, and the Turnip', *Ideologies and Literature*, 1 (1976), 10-12.

Herrero 1978 = J. Herrero, 'The Ending of Lazarillo: The Wine Against the Water', *Modern Language Notes*, 93 (1978), 313.

The Holy Bible = *The Holy Bible, containing the Old and New Testaments. Revised Standard Version. Catholic Edition*, ed. Bernard Orchard and Reginald Cuthbert Fuller (Toronto: Thomas Nelson and Sons, 1966).

Hurtado de Toledo 1964 = Luis Hurtado de Toledo [and Micael Caravajal], *Cortes de casto amor y cortes de la muerte* (Valencia: Libreria Bonaire 1964 [= Toledo 1557]).

Isidore of Seville 1962 = Isidore of Seville, *Isidori Hispalensis episcopi Etymologiarum sive Originum libri XX*, ed. W. M. Lindsay (Oxford: Clarendon Press, 1962).

Lázaro Carreter 1972 = Fernando Lázaro Carreter, *Lazarillo de Tormes en la Picaresca* (Ariel: Espluges de Llobregat, 1972).

León 1955 = Fray Luis de León, *Poesías*, ed. Angel Custodio Vega (Madrid: Sociedad Española de Traductores y Autores, 1955).

Lexipedia = *Lexipedia*, 2 vols. (Mexico: Encyclopaedia Britannica de Mexico, 1995).

López Estrada 1974 = F. López Estrada, *Los libros de pastores en la literatura española* (Madrid: Gredos, 1974).

Luque Fajardo 1603 = Francisco Luque Fajardo, *Fiel desengaño contra la ociosidad, y los juegos: utilissimo a los confessores, y penitentes, justicias, y los demas, a cuyo cargo està limpiar vagabundos, tahures, y fulleros de la republica Christiana: en dialogo* (Madrid: Casa de Miguel Serrano de Vargas, 1603).

Márquez Villanueva 1968 = F. Márquez Villanueva, *Espiritualidad y literatura en el siglo XVI* (Madrid: Alfaguara, 1968).

Metzger-Ehrman 2005 = Bruce Metzger-Bart Ehrman, *The Text of the New Testament. Its Transmission, Corruption, and Restoration*, 4th edition (Oxford: Oxford University Press, 2005).

Moakley 1966 = Moakley, Gertrude, *The tarot cards painted by Bonifacio Bembo for the Visconti-Sforza family; an iconographic and historical study* (New York: NY Public Library, 1966).

Nowak, Jr., 1990 = S.J. Nowak, Jr., 'The Blindman's New Function: An *Exemplum* of the Capital Sin of Anger in *Lazarillo de Tormes*', *Hispania*, 73 (1990), 901-905.

Ore 1953 = Oystein Ore, *Cardano, the Gambling Scholar* (Princeton: Princeton University Press, 1953).

O'Reilly 1984 = O'Reilly, T, 'The Erasmianism of Lazarillo de Tormes', in *Essays in Honour of Robert Brian Tate*, ed. Richard A. Cardwell (Nottingham: University of Nottingham, 1984), pp. 91-100.

Ortega Martín 1973 = Joaquín Ortega Martín, *Un reformador pretridentino: Don Pascual de Ampudia, obispo de Burgos (1496-1512)* (Rome: Iglesia Nacional Española, 1973).

Otto 1988 = Otto, A. *Sprichwörter und Sprichwörtliche Redensarten der Römer* (New York: Georg Olms Verlag, 1988 [= Leipzig, 1890]).

Otto 1965 = W.F. Otto, *Dionysus: Myth and Cult*, trans. R.B. Palmer (Bloomington: Indiana University Press, 1965).

Oxford Companion to Classical Literature = *The Oxford Companion to Classical Literature*, 2nd edition, ed. M.C. Howatson – Paul Harvey (Oxford/New York: Oxford University Press, 1997 [= 1989]).

The Oxford Latin Dictionary, ed. P.G.W. Glare (Oxford: Oxford University Press, 1982).

Rey Hazas 1984 = Antonio Rey Hazas, ed., *La vida de Lazarillo de Tormes* (Madrid: Editorial Castalia, 1984).

Ricapito 1973 = J. Ricapito, ' "Cara de Dios": Ensayo de rectificación', *Bulletin of Hispanic Studies,* 50 (1973), 142-46.

Ricapito 1976 = J. Ricapito, ed. with introd., *La Vida de Lazarillo de Tormes* (Madrid: Ediciones Cátedra, 1976).

Ricapito 1997 = J. Ricapito, 'Commonality of Thought: Juan Luis Vives and Lazarillo de Tormes', *Crítica Hispánica,* 19 (1997), 24-40.

Rico 1980 = Francisco Rico, ed., *Lazarillo de Tormes* (Barcelona: Planeta, 1980).

Rico 1988 = Francisco Rico, *Problemas del Lazarillo* (Madrid: Cátedra, 1988).

Rodríguez-Aleixandre 1994 = Alfred Rodríguez -E. Aleixandre, 'Sobre la intensidad irónica del comienzo del *Lazarillo*', *Quaderni Ibero-Americani,* 75 (1994), 65-69.

Ruiz 1972 = Juan Ruiz, *Libro de buen amor* ed. Raymond S. Willis (Princeton: Princeton University Press, 1972).

Ryan 1995 = William G. Ryan, ed., *The Golden Legend: Readings on the Saints/* Jacobus de Voragine (Princeton: Princeton University Press, 1995).

Sandoval 1955-1956 = P. de Sandoval, *Historia de la vida y hechos del emperador Carlos V,* ed. C. Seco Serrano (Madrid: Atlas, 1955-1956).

Scott 1934 = James Brown Scott, *The Spanish Origin of International Law: Francisco de Vitoria and His Law of Nations* (Oxford: Clarendon Press- London: H. Milford, 1934).

Sieber 1978 = Harry Sieber, *Language and Society in La vida de Lazarillo de Tormes* (Baltimore: Johns Hopkins Press, 1978).

Smith 1984 = Warren Smith, 'Horace Directs a Carouse', *Transactions of the American Philological Association,* 114 (1984), 255-271.

Tellechea Idigoras 1963 = J. Tellechea Idigoras, *El obispo ideal en el siglo de la reforma* (Rome: Iglesia Nacional Española, 1963).

Torre 1907 = Fernando de la Torre, 'De unos naypes por coplas que fizo mossen Fernando a la señora Condessa de Castañeda', in *Cancionero y obras en prosa de Fernando de la Torre* ed. A. Paz y Mélia (Dresden: Gedruckt für die Gesellschaft für romanische Literatur, 1907), pp. 128-136.

Truman 1975 = R.W.Truman, 'Lazarillo de Tormes, Petrarch's De Remediis Adversae Fortunae, and Erasmus's Praise of Folly', *Bulletin of Hispanic Studies,* 52 (1975), 33-53.

Valdés 1986 = Alfonso de Valdés, *Dialogue of Mercury and Charon,* trans. with intro. and notes Joseph Ricapito (Bloomington: Indiana University Press, 1986).

Valdés 1993 = Alfonso de Valdés, *Diálogo de Mercurio y Carón,* ed. Joseph V. Ricapito (Madrid: Editorial Castalia, 1993).

Vitoria 1932-1952 = Francisco de Vitoria, *Comentarios a la Secunda secundae de santo Tomás,* ed. V. Beltrán de Heredia, Salamanca: Biblioteca de Teólogos españoles; 1-5 (1932-1935), 6 (1952), 328-350.

Vives 1782 = Juan Luis Vives, 'Ludus Chartarum, Seu Foliorium', *Joannis Ludovici Vivis Valentini Opera Omnia.* 8 vols. (Montfort: Valentinae Edetanorum 1782), 1, 378-385.

Vives 1940 = Juan Luis Vives, *Diálogos,* intro. J.J.M. (Buenos Aires: Espasa-Calpe Argentina, 1940).

Vives 1959 = Juan Luis Vives, *Diálogos,* 4th ed. trans. C. Coret y Peris (Madrid: Espasa-Calpe 1959 [= Mexico: Imprenta de Galvan á cargo de Mariano Arévalo, 1827]).

Vives 1992 = Juan Luis Vives. *Opera Omnia,* ed. Antonio Mestre e.a. (Universitat de València 1992-), five vols published.

Vives 2005 = Juan Luis Vives, *Los diálogos: linguae latinae exercitatio,* ed. García Ruiz (Pamplona: Ediciones Universidad de Navarra, 2005).

Vox diccionario = Vox diccionario actual de la lengua Española (Lincolnwood: NTC Pub. Group, 1996).

Wardropper 1977 = B. Wardropper, 'The Strange Case of Lázaro Gonzáles Pérez', *Modern Language Notes,* 92 (1977), 202-212.